GENDERED
GENRES

GENDERED GENRES

Female Experiences
and Narrative Patterns
in the Works of Matilde Serao

Laura A. Salsini

Fairleigh Dickinson

Madison • Teaneck
Fairleigh Dickinson University Press
London: Associated University Presses

Associated University Presses
440 Forsgate Drive
Cranbury, NJ 08512

Associated University Presses
16 Barter Street
London WC1A 2AH, England

Associated University Presses
P.O. Box 338, Port Credit
Mississauga, Ontario
Canada L5G 4L8

The paper used in this publication meets the requirements
of the American National Standard for Permanence of Paper
for Printed Library Materials Z39.48-1984.

Library of Congress Cataloging-in-Publication Data

Salsini, Laura A. (Laura Anne)
    Gendered genres : female experiences and narrative patterns in the
works of Matilde Serao / Laura A. Salsini.
      p. cm.
    Includes bibliographical references and index.
    ISBN 0-8386-3801-5 (alk. paper)
    1. Serao, Matilde, 1856–1927—Criticism and interpretation.
2. Women in literature. I. Title.
PQ4841.E7Z89   1999
853'.8—dc21   98-54788
                                                  CIP

PRINTED IN THE UNITED STATES OF AMERICA

To Douglas,
with all my love

Contents

Acknowledgments

I am grateful to the following periodicals for permission to cite previously published portions of this book:

Italian Quarterly

Italiana

Romance Languages Annual

I am also indebted to Liguori Editore for permission to cite from *Il romanzo della fanciulla.*

I also have some personal acknowledgments to make:

For those whose comments and suggestions helped shape this book into its present form—Laurel Cummins, Margaret Flynn, and Francesca Parmeggiani—I am deeply indebted.

To Lawrence Baldassaro for his guidance, and to Anthony Tamburri, for his helpful suggestions and advice.

To Edoardo Lèbano, for his support and enthusiasm—not just for this particular project, but over the past ten years.

To Robin Pickering-Iazzi, who has helped me more than she knows as mentor, role model, and friend.

My heartfelt gratitude goes to Virginia Pichietti, "mia sorella dal cuore," whose unstinting encouragement and insight have proven so valuable on both a professional and a personal level.

I would also like to thank my parents, Paul and Barbara Salsini, who taught me to appreciate the written word; and thanks to Avis, for making me laugh and to my husband, Douglas Tobias, for his love and his faith in me.

GENDERED GENRES

Introduction: Matilde Serao's City of Women

Matilde Serao's richly detailed narratives metaphorically create a city of women who must negotiate the social and cultural conventions of turn-of-the-century Italy. With each text, Serao adds another stratum to her imaginary metropolis, grounding her narratives in realistic detail and acute social observation. I borrow this image of the metaphoric city from Serao herself, whose 1884 work *Il ventre di Napoli* (The Belly of Naples) depicts both the vitality and the despair of her beloved Naples.[1] This text, which will be examined in the following chapter, focuses to a large degree on the women of Naples, underlining Serao's lifelong interest in interpreting female experiences. Although hers is not an exclusively female domain—Serao's city is also populated by husbands, lovers, and fathers—the author's attention remains clearly fixed on her female protagonists and the world in which they live. Over the course of almost thirty novels, more than one hundred short stories, and innumerable newspaper articles and columns, Serao articulates her own vision of female destiny in a society governed by traditional, often restrictive paradigms of feminine behavior. This vision cuts across class and social lines, for Serao's city is inhabited by scullery maids, ballerinas, schoolgirls, seamstresses, housewives, and Neapolitan nobility.[2] By exploring such issues as the construction of female identity, female sexuality, friendships among women, the role of women in the workforce, and motherhood, Serao uncovers a subterranean, woman-centered world seldom examined by earlier or even contemporary authors.

The geography of Serao's landscape is more clearly illuminated by a consideration of both generic and thematic concerns. This approach allows a multilayered interpretation of the author's work, yielding a more critical appreciation of its legacy. This study draws on several methodologies, examining Serao's work primarily through the intersection of genre and feminist criticism. The

13

category of genre studies has lately been viewed suspiciously by scholars reluctant to classify texts under a seemingly inflexible set of literary tenets. Carol Lazzaro-Weis, for example, describes the misgivings shared by many feminists about employing a methodology that emphasizes such literary divisions: "[G]enre theory is often perceived as a facile means to construct and maintain unequal social and literary hierarchies. . . ."[3] Indeed, female-authored texts have often been considered weak facsimiles of standard, male-authored paradigms. But although the limitations of genre criticism must be acknowledged, its principles still prove useful, for an author's employment of specific genres constitutes a choice based on his or her fictional designs. In Serao's case, these choices are fundamental tools in her depictions of female experiences. I use as my starting point Ralph Cohen's more flexible strategy in evaluating texts by genres, a model that allows each author the freedom to change or even challenge the genre in question.[4] Cohen adds an interesting point that becomes particularly significant for an exploration of Serao's work: "My assumption is that an author in making a generic choice involves himself in an ideological choice. . . ."[5] This definition of choice, subversion, and creative license propels an examination of why and how Serao employed different genres, including realism, the romance narrative, and Gothic fiction, throughout her literary career. An investigation of such issues leads to an understanding of how Serao challenges the hegemonic discourses of literary tenets by manipulating generic conventions. This approach also permits a less orthodox categorization of Serao's works, as an examination of some texts reveals innovations that call into question traditional classifications.

Feminist criticism, too, with its focus on women's struggle with restrictive ideologies, offers an illuminating and often provocative way to consider Serao's texts. Certainly Serao's emphasis on female protagonists and plots warrants such an approach. By female plots, I mean those narrative patterns that specifically treat the (limited) life choices available to her protagonists.[6] The depiction of a heroine's negotiation of prevailing social expectations underlies many of Serao's narratives and cuts across the boundaries of genre. A feminist approach results in an insightful rereading of Serao's works, one that gives voice to the author's provocative and innovative stylistic and thematic choices.

Feminist critics concerned specifically with Serao or with Italian

women writers in general offer the most penetrating and pertinent insights into the works of this particular author, but studies
of other scholars play an important role in this inquiry as well.
Critical works that deal primarily with English or American
women writers are also considered, taking into account, however,
the differences in social, cultural, and historical conditions. By
borrowing from scholars concerned with literary production in
other countries, I underline the communality of Serao's female-
centered project. Her literary texts possess many of the same
themes evident in other authors working in Europe and the
United States. I will also have occasion to refer to the work of
scholars in other fields, most notably cultural studies, history, and
anthropology. These particular fields of study further situate both
Serao and her works in turn-of-the-century Italy. This interdisci-
plinary approach broadens the knowledge and appreciation of
the complexity of Serao's narratives.

In order to understand this subtext and Serao's significant literary innovations, both the author and her work must be contextual-
ized within the Italian literary tradition, a tradition notably
different from that of other national literatures. The country's
relatively late unification meant it lagged behind other European
nations in creating a national language and in exploring the many
variations of a burgeoning new genre, the novel. Italy also lacked
a Jane Austen, George Eliot, or George Sand to break the ground
for this genre and to inspire future generations of (female) authors. As Umberto Eco points out, the first novels were often
written by, and for, women: "When the snobs of various epochs
wrote that novels of love were for women or servants, they were
gloriously right. The novel was born as merchandise for women
and maids."[7] Although the female poetic tradition in Italy, beginning in the 1200s with La Compiuta Donzella, has been docu-
mented, the sister tradition in prose still calls for more archival
research and critical analysis. Recent anthologies of female-
authored texts, however, begin to trace the trajectory of women's
literature in Italy, revealing a strong, unbroken genealogy of female writers.[8] These anthologies and inquiries by other scholars
have uncovered a number of heretofore unknown women artists
who deserve study for their contributions to the creation of a
national literature.[9] More probing analyses, incorporating various
critical approaches, are now being undertaken of the handful of

women writers who did achieve critical and popular success in nineteenth- and early-twentieth-century Italy.[10] Along with Serao (1856–1927), these women include Neera (Anna Radius Zuccari, 1846–1918), Ada Negri (1870–1945), Grazia Deledda (1871–1936), and Sibilla Aleramo (1876–1960). Although these authors, like Serao, were either self-taught or had only a limited exposure to formal education, they left a legacy of work that today interests scholars concerned not only with literary analysis but also with feminist and cultural studies for their depictions of female experiences.[11]

Many of these authors legitimized their entry into mainstream literary circles by taking advantage of a new forum for their work, the woman's magazine. These periodicals, many founded by women, were devoted primarily to "women's issues." For example, *Cordelia,* founded in 1881, published poetry, serial novels, information, and editorials on the nascent feminist movement, as well as columns on fashion, cuisine, and hygiene.[12] Through the forum of these periodicals and other publications, women writers, poets, educators, and journalists forged a role in the intellectual life of the country. Antonia Arslan writes that these women came to be seen as a "'social category' unto itself, with well-defined peculiarities and characteristics."[13] Their voices became heard with increasing intensity in the traditionally male-dominated social, cultural, and literary spheres.

These authors produced a body of work diverse in both style and content, ranging from the harsh realism of Deledda to the intensely intimate and autobiographical narratives of Aleramo; however, some modern critics have found several points of similarity. Elisabetta Rasy believes late-nineteenth-century female writers often drew on their own experiences as women to craft their narratives: "Woman's writing is . . . private writing, that is, writing from the internal, writing of that figure whose presence is not recognized."[14] It is precisely this intimacy, this reconstruction of a woman's interior life, that becomes so central to Serao's own works and that merits exploration in her texts. Her sociological rendition of female experiences, expressed in a variety of forums, is unique in its inclusivity and depth.

Serao's approach creates a special affinity with her public, as this depiction of the "hidden world" so often found in women's writing creates a singular relationship between writer and reader.[15] Both Arslan and Paola Blelloch have called attention to a mutually supportive bond between female authors and their (female) public. "The story lives only as an exchange, as the desire to transmit a fundamental subjective experience so that it lives again in the reader," writes Blelloch.[16] Arslan goes on to suggest that the women writing at the turn of the century, conscious of their status as transmitters of female experience, felt a certain responsibility toward their readers. In her reading of the realistic portraits of female protagonists and the social worlds created by these authors, "One intuits a sort of psychological deviation, a form of fear, almost of their own audacity and of the influence that they could exercise on the reading public."[17] These authors may have been relegated to a minor role by male critics, but they were forging a special bond with their public, articulating for their female readers a woman's interior life.

The popularity of this emerging cohort of female authors did not go unremarked by the literary establishment. Some male writers and critics resented what they considered an encroachment on their intellectual turf and subjected women authors to merciless, and often misogynist, scrutiny. The philosopher Camillo De Meis, in a conversation recorded by the author Luigi Capuana in 1907, claimed women were able to enter literary and artistic fields only because their way had been paved by male writers: "No woman in the world has ever done what they [male authors] have done: the imaginative intellect is masculine." He goes on to note that women artists would only add "an element all their own, femininity, but nothing else" to their literary production.[18] Unfortunately, De Meis neglected to define just what he meant by "femininity" or to explain the increasing number of women novelists who managed to ignore their alleged lack of "imaginative intellect" to write bestselling novels.[19]

Even Enrico Nencioni, one of Serao's most ardent champions and the author of several long articles on her work, reveals a telling contradiction in his analysis regarding women and writing. He first dismisses critics who judge female authors by different standards: "I have said frankly and publicly what seems to me to be the truth about Matilde Serao, without fear of being accused of indelicacy toward a woman. In art there is no distinction between the sexes: there are only artists."[20] Later in that same essay, however, Nencioni falls back on the gendered split between intellect and emotion, relegating Serao's talent and work to more sentimental concerns. Thus, he theorizes that her artistry would benefit if she would only abandon herself "more often to the voice and instinctive and infallible impulse of her female heart. . . ."[21]

This traditionalist categorization of female writers informs much of the critical reception of women's literary production in conservative, turn-of-the-century Italy. Indeed, when women writers such as Serao succeeded in capturing public acclaim, both male and female critics responded by attributing their talents to an appropriation of allegedly masculine characteristics, such as virility and intellect. The journalist and contemporary Federigo Verdinois ascribed Serao's talent to what he considered the male attributes of "solidity, purpose, seriousness."[22] In 1927, on the occasion of Serao's death, Giuseppe A. Borgese echoed this sentiment: "But even today one can say that this woman . . . has brought female literature to a virile force and fullness; in fact, she never gave any sign of being female, . . . weak or distracted. . . ."[23] And ten years later, Pietro Pancrazi wrote that Serao "has the intelligence of men, a very clear opinion of life. She never abandons the sense of the concrete, of the real."[24] A tribute written by Lola Bocchi just after Serao's death reiterates these sentiments in no uncertain terms: "[O]ne can say of Matilde Serao that she was a 'would-be man' for the virility of her talent, for her pugnacity, for the indomitable energy with which she knew how to face up to life and its events."[25] I have emphasized this point about the gender-oriented critical reception awarded Serao, and by extension other female authors, to illustrate the patronizing attitudes of the intellectual world in which she worked.[26]

Interestingly, the very critics who attributed Serao's success to an assimilation of male intellectual ability also emphasized what was considered an exclusively female trait—the maternal instinct. By explicitly linking Serao's work to her gender and reproductive capabilities, these critics devalued her literary output. Pancrazi, in an article describing Serao's life-long love for Naples,[27] wrote, "Her fundamental feeling toward life was maternal: in her lively, searching eye, one always feels present concern . . . and pity."[28] Ugo Ojetti, a journalist and critic, concluded his account of an 1894 interview with Serao by painting a sentimental scene of the author surrounded by her young children. Clearly, the author's gender and the literary establishment's standards for female writers influenced her critical reception as an artist. The female author was caught in a peculiar double bind; although her intellectual abilities were attributed to masculine characteristics, her talents were also reduced and associated with an essential genderism.

Early in her life Serao was exposed to this masculine intellectual domain, for she first began her literary career within the traditionally male-dominated world of journalism in the 1870s.[29] She was one of the first full-time female journalists in Italy, publishing her work in such newspapers and magazines as *La Farfalla, Il Piccolo, Capitan Fracassa, La gazzetta letteraria piemontese, Il giornale di Napoli,* and *Roma capitale.* Despite a growing acceptance of Serao's journalistic skills, the initial reaction among her male colleagues was based on considerations of gender and was, therefore, negative: "At first the masculine pride of the readers was offended. They considered this initiative on the part of a woman almost the violation of an unspoken privilege."[30] Serao, however, ignored the resistance, as she explained in an 1878 letter to her friend Gaetano Bonavenia:

> I am in good physical health. As for morale, I am in a period of such feverish production that it is alarming: I am writing everywhere and about everything, with a singular audacity, I am winning my place by dint of pushing and shoving, with the absolute burning desire to get there without anyone helping me, or hardly anyone. But you know that I don't listen to the weaknesses of my sex and I keep going as if I were a young man.[31]

This illuminating letter reveals Serao's professional ambitions and her awareness that succeeding in the male world of literature meant fighting the debilitating stereotype of the intellectually limited female.

Throughout her life, Serao consistently confounded this nineteenth-century notion, excelling in the fields of journalism and literature. As many writers of this time were involved in both of these disciplines, their literary and journalistic work often shared a symbiotic relationship, rather than an oppositional one. Serao was especially adept at moving easily between the occasionally antithetical demands of journalism and literature, although in her hands the two media shared a common goal, according to R. Ceserani and E. Salibra: "Her narrative writing alternates with that of engaged journalism; she almost always tried to address a varied public by dealing with social problems which were the concern of even the highest levels of society."[32]

Serao found herself in a particularly fruitful period of Italian journalism, for newspapers flourished in the years following the unification of the country, entering into the cultural and political debates arising from the creation of the new nation. Serao and her husband, the journalist Edoardo Scarfoglio, became part of an esteemed group of writers refashioning the features of Italian journalism. In 1884 the two founded the newspaper *Corriere di Roma* and, when that folded, moved on to Naples, where they launched two other newspapers, the *Corriere di Napoli* and later *Il Mattino.* In 1902 Serao helped establish a weekly literary magazine called *La Settimana.* Before it ceased publication two years later, its contributors had included some of the leading intellectual and literary names of late nineteenth-century Italy—Pascoli, Verga, Pirandello, Capuana, D'Annunzio, Fogazzaro, Croce, and Neera. In 1904, now legally separated from her perpetually unfaithful spouse, Serao founded her own newspaper, a remarkable achievement for a woman in conservative southern Italy. *Il Giorno* thrived until just after Serao's death in 1927. For years Serao not only oversaw the general management of the paper, but also wrote a daily column discussing social, cultural, literary, and political issues.[33]

Because I examine several of Serao's journalistic pieces in this study, this is an opportune place to discuss the relationship between Serao as journalist and Serao as novelist. Even with the success of her fictive work, she remained involved with journalism during her entire adult life, reveling in the immediacy and impact provided by publishing a daily newspaper. The connection between the spheres of literature and journalism is certainly evident on a strictly stylistic basis. Serao's realist works, in particular, resonate with the direct style, clear prose, and attention to detail that is the hallmark of her journalistic endeavors. Turning to a thematic discussion of these two disciplines, one could even take the title of a collection of her short stories, *Dal vero,* as a metaphor for her output in general. "From the real," as this title translates, underscores the element of factuality in Serao's fiction, for she often transcribed events and characters (disguised with different names) from her own world and from her own journalism articles, into her novels and short stories. Perhaps more important for the purposes of this study is the indication that both her newspaper essays and her fiction were directed toward the same reading public: women. Wanda De Nunzio Schilardi, in her comprehensive study of Serao's journalism career, articulates the affinity the author felt toward her female readers. Serao, in effect, "speaks their language, expresses their feelings, foresees their expectations, she acts, in a word, as interpreter."[34] In both her novels and her newspaper articles, Serao explicates and shares the experiences of women from all walks of life.

There is, however, a fundamental difference between Serao's journalism and her literary production that points to the inconsistencies inherent in her work in general. As a journalist, Serao typically espouses fundamentally conservative positions—supporting the Italian monarchy, for example, or opposing the political and social agenda of the nascent feminist movement.[35] This is not to imply that her fictive works are instead models of radical ideology, for they, too, reflect the author's traditional mores. But even in her most pessimistic literary works, Serao occasionally succeeds in moving away from this innate conservatism, creating for her heroines a "partial but ambiguous empowerment within the 'safe' world of fiction."[36] These feminine figures are allowed brief moments of flight and fantasy, even if their stories ultimately end in shattered dreams.

It is Serao's depiction of the role of women in contemporary society, a topic addressed throughout her life in both fiction and journalism, that must be taken up here. I will briefly discuss one piece in particular, for it addresses Serao's own assessment of the position of the woman writer in late-nineteenth-century Italy. In this article, which appeared in *Il Giornale di Napoli* November 15, 1876, Serao reviews several recently published novels, including *Un romanzo* (A Novel) by Neera. While praising Neera's literary talent, Serao takes the opportunity to examine the attributes of woman writers in general, singling out the gifts of observance and perception. But she stops short of championing the cause of all female authors, arguing that women are inherently incapable of creating masterpieces of poetry, no matter to what sublime heights their prose may reach. Serao joins many other critics in conferring poetry with the long-standing valuation as the more exalted of literary art forms. Even more telling, however, is her desire to carve out literary territory that resonates in particular with woman authors; that is, the novel.[37] Serao's attitude toward her own writing, then, was colored by her view of women authors in general. As a journalist, she made no distinction between her male colleagues and herself; as the creator of novels and short stories, she measured herself (and by extension, other female authors) by more conventional standards. Surely these standards, founded after all by a male literary establishment, were a potential source of anxiety for a female author with her own ideas about the construction of literary genres. Occasionally this anxiety encroaches upon her work itself, revealing a portrait of an inconsistent, sometimes frustrated, but always human author.

Serao's literary legacy is certainly as impressive as her journalistic achievements. Along with novels and short stories, she wrote etiquette manuals, religious works, travel books, and short monographs on the leading luminaries of Italian theater and intellectual life, many of whom were her friends. Immensely popular, her reading public included not only the humble Neapolitans who greeted her on her daily afternoon drive to her newspaper offices, but members of the royal family as well. Indeed, Queen Margherita professed to be an ardent admirer of Serao (confessing, however, that she preferred the author's later romance novels to her earlier realist texts). Serao's works were widely translated, and her admirers in other countries included the French author Paul Bourget and the American writers Henry James and Edith Wharton.[38] Serao was even proposed as a candidate for the 1926 Nobel Prize for literature but, according to literary legend, Benito Mussolini, apparently angered by the antiwar sentiments expressed in her newspaper and in a recent book, allegedly blocked the nomination. The prize was subsequently awarded to Grazia Deledda.

Despite Serao's prominent place in intellectual and literary circles and her well-situated position as journalist and editor, she played no part in Italy's nascent women's movement. In fact, in newspaper articles, public statements, and correspondence with Anna Maria Mozzoni, one of Italy's leading feminists, Serao voiced her opposition to women's suffrage, advanced education for girls, and the legalization of divorce.[39] In recent scholarship exploring the many facets of Serao's work, much attention has been paid to her apparent antifeminism.[40] The debate has led to widely disparate conclusions about the author's convictions, with I. T. Olken going so far as to declare Serao the "literary spiritual godmother of Italian feminism."[41] Nancy Harrowitz, however, takes a more moderate view, pointing out the dilemma in affirming the political and personal philosophy of a writer whose narratives so often spell doom for their heroines.[42]

Serao's attitudes toward women and her apparent antifeminism will be explored more thoroughly in the conclusion of this book, after an extensive examination of her portrayal of her female protagonists. But because the issue permeates this study, a few brief comments should be made at the outset. Serao's preoccupation with gender, both stylistically and thematically, is reflected in her narratives. Most of her protagonists are female, and their worlds revolve around the traditional female space, the domestic sphere. But along with an exploration of the institutions of marriage and family, Serao examines other, more troubling issues that depict the problematic position of women in turn-of-the-century Italy. These include social restrictions on female behavior and the lack of alternative life choices in a cultural matrix privileging the marriage bond. Each chapter will explore these issues and offer various interpretations of Serao's representations of her heroines' worlds. This approach reveals how Serao's articulation of female experiences occasionally undermines her repeated repudiation of feminist objectives and endeavors. It also emphasizes the difficulty of situating this author in the spectrum of feminist ideology.

Although Serao has long been considered part of the Italian literary canon, critical reception of her work has been inconsistent at best. Contemporary critics, such as Nencioni, Ojetti, Benedetto Croce, and Joseph Spencer Kennard, typically engaged with Serao's narratives through a generic approach, generally praising her early realist texts but ignoring or criticizing her later sentimental works, despite (or perhaps because of) their immense success with the general public.[43] Part of this criticism may stem from the literary establishment's refusal or inability to validate any work that focused on a domestic narrative rather than on the traditional "quest" plot of male-authored texts. This critical blindness had a significant effect on the reception of women's writing, especially in Italy, where turn-of-the-century critics tended to be both male and conservative. Interestingly, Serao was rarely compared to other female authors. But it is difficult to judge whether that was because her work was deemed superior to that of these other writers or whether it was merely a reflection of the scant attention paid women artists in nineteenth-century Italy.

After Serao's death in 1927, discussion of her works was absent entirely from critical literary discourse or, on rare occasions, was relegated to brief notations in anthologies and literary histories. In the 1960s and 1970s, however, several monographs were published that resurrected Serao's reputation as a significant and innovative author. These works, which provide varied critical interpretations rather than a strictly generic approach, include Anna Banti's affectionate biography, *Matilde Serao,* Anthony Gisolfi's *The Essential Matilde Serao,* which shares Banti's approach of reading the author's fiction in part through an examination of her personal life, and Marie-Gracieuse Martin-Gistucci's thematic approach in her monograph, *L'Oeuvre romanesque de Matilde Serao.* Only with the 1981 collection of essays entitled *Matilde Serao tra giornalismo e letteratura,* edited by Gianni Infusino, did analysis of Serao move significantly beyond earlier scholarship and treat the author as a significant artist in her own right, without constant (and often belittling) comparisons to other writers.[44] The importance of this slim collection of essays cannot be overemphasized, for it firmly and unequivocally situates Serao within the canon of nineteenth- and twentieth-century Italian literature while examining the many different aspects of her literary production.

The advent of feminist and cultural studies has had a dramatic impact on Serao's critical reception, as scholars have investigated the correlations between the author and other women authors and have analyzed her focus on female protagonists and their concerns. In a series of illuminating articles, Ursula Fanning examines such issues as friendship between women and the female double in Serao. Lucienne Kroha, whose work focuses on nineteenth-century women writers, situates Serao within the novelistic tradition in Italian literature. Nancy Harrowitz takes a broader approach, examining in several long essays how Serao's textual misogyny and antisemitism were rooted in her own marginalization as a female writer in turn-of-the-century Italy. Sharon Wood, in her thoughtful survey of women writing in postunification Italy, is one of the few critics to explore how Serao's vast literary production confounds attempts to classify the author and her work by conventional periodization or generic standards. By focusing on specific thematic concerns such as the author's treatment of female characters and their domestic spaces, these critics uncover the multiple readings and subtexts often overlooked by earlier scholars. These critics also focus attention on texts that have long been neglected or ignored. Whereas critics of the early 1900s evaluated Serao's narratives on a purely aesthetic level, these later scholars trace the connections among all of Serao's texts, from her masterpieces to those works long considered of secondary importance. As a result, they offer richer, more conclusive evidence of the significant role Serao plays in world literature.

Until now, however, students of Serao and of Italian literature in general have lacked a comprehensive, thorough examination of the author's female-centered works. This study fills a lacuna in such analysis, for it addresses Serao's stated purpose of examining female experiences in a patriarchal society. When appropriate, this study also investigates the intersection of gender and class, a topic often given short shift in criticism of the author. Serao's focus on these two elements creates a more integrated vision of a community, or city, of women, while allowing the reader a multi-leveled interpretation of her works.

Because of the parameters set by this topic and by Serao's substantial literary legacy, all of her works are not studied here, although a selection of lesser-known but relevant writings are examined. Several of her novels that focus on male protagonists and their worlds, such as *La conquista di Roma* (The Conquest of Rome) and *Vita e avventure di Riccardo Joanna* (The Life and Adventures of Riccardo Joanna) fall beyond the scope of this study, although they certainly merit examination. Because of the vast number of Serao's journalistic writings, only those especially pertinent or illuminating will be included.

The structure of this study reflects the various genres employed by Serao—realism, romance, and Gothic narratives. Chapter 1 examines and situates Serao within the tradition of literary realism in Italy. Her critical statements on *verismo* are examined in relation to the precepts and traditions established by Luigi Capuana and Giovanni Verga, Italy's foremost realist authors. Serao's realist texts are also examined in light of the growing body of scholarship on the female *Bildungsroman,* or novels of development. Susan Fraiman, in her discussion of such texts, writes, "I would like to imagine the way to womanhood not as a single path to a clear destination but as the endless negotiation of a crossroads."[45] How do Serao's heroines, hovering on the brink of maturity and trapped in a sometimes repressive world, attempt to negotiate this crossroads to achieve a sense of integrated personhood? In her realist texts, Serao often challenges the conventional social roles open to her heroines, questioning the very cultural matrix that gives rise to models of feminine behavior. This chapter also examines Serao's depiction of the institution of marriage, the importance of female friendship, and the role of work in the lives of her protagonists. Texts include the short stories "La virtù di Checchina," "Per monaca," "Telegrafi dello stato," "Scuola normale feminile" *(sic)*, "Non più," "La moglie di un grand'uomo," "Nicoletta," the novel *Suor Giovanna della croce*, and the investigative report "Il ventre di Napoli."

Chapter 2 moves into the realm of popular literature to examine Serao's romance narratives. Several scholars working specifically in the field of cultural studies, including Fredric Jameson, have challenged earlier critical standards that devalued works grouped under the rubric "popular literature." Jameson decries the opposition between high and mass culture, calling for a strategy that integrates all forms of literary production. This approach, he writes, "demands that we read high and mass culture as objectively related and dialectically interdependent phenomena, as twin and inseparable forms of the fission of aesthetic production under late capitalism."[46] Works of popular fiction, many critics note, often provide a means of entering into the cultural consciousness of a particular time and place. By treating the romance narrative in part as a sociological document, Serao's "city of women" becomes especially important in the reader's understanding of turn-of-the-century Italy. For example, the second chapter looks at the relationship between female sexuality and female destiny. Serao's depiction of the *femme fatale*, a stock literary figure, broadens the boundaries of acceptable female behavior and implicitly criticizes the cultural discourse shaping this construct. Works considered in this chapter include the short stories "O Giovannino o la morte," "La grande fiamma," "Livia Speri," and "Paolo Spada," and the novels *Addio, amore!, La ballerina, Cuore infermo, Fantasia*, and *Tre donne*.

The final chapter turns to the Gothic text, a genre traditionally considered a vehicle to express female anguish and rebellion. The structure of the Gothic text, with its emphasis on the domestic sphere, offers a particularly fitting forum in which to investigate the dynamics found within the family, specifically the relationship between mother and daughter, but also these roles as they are played out in the patriarchal family structure. The maternal figure, rarely seen in Serao's *oeuvre*, often substitutes in these texts for the romantic hero, a significant and intriguing vision of female power and the relationships between women. The domestic space, then, becomes a metaphor for the social world at large, while the

dynamics of family bonds reproduce the male-female relationships of a patriarchal culture. Texts examined in this chapter include the short stories "Un inventore," and "La donna dell'abito
nero e del ramo di corallo rosso," and the novels *Castigo, Il delitto
di via Chiatamone, La mano tagliata,* and *Il paese di cuccagna.*

The conclusion of this study examines in greater depth the
debate surrounding Serao's apparent antifeminism. Despite the
author's many newspaper articles condemning the feminist movement, the depiction of female experiences in her fictive works
and her own active role in the intellectual life of turn-of-the-
century Italy contradict her public statements. The conclusion
also discusses the legacy of Serao's literary production, specifically,
her influence on twentieth-century Italian women writers.

1
Realist Revisions

Matilde Serao's realist texts have often been judged in relation to the works and precepts of other authors working within the *movimento verista*.[1] Although Serao was highly praised for narratives that embodied the tenets established by the realist authors Capuana and Verga, she was quickly criticized for texts that incorporated her own articulation of realism. Limiting a critical analysis to a cursory hunt for similarities and differences between her narrative practices and those elaborated by the *veristi,* however, neglects Serao's own contribution to the realist movement. Her emphasis on women-centered narratives creates a realistic portrait of the social, emotional, and physical accommodations women make as they reconcile their own needs and ambitions with a patriarchal social structure. No other realist author so thoughtfully and consistently addressed pivotal aspects of female experiences. Despite a growing interest by modern critics in Serao's work, few have systematically examined the significance of her dedication to chronicling female experiences and the influence of this project on the realist movement in general. To continue the metaphor begun in the Introduction, Serao's realist texts can be viewed as the literary construction of a city of women. This fictive metropolis encompasses a spectrum of woman-centered experiences, explicitly tied in these texts to the social and cultural expectations of turn-of-the-century Italy.

This study proposes to reread Serao's texts in light of her own articulations of realism, writings that reveal the strikingly different critical frameworks used by Serao and other realist authors. Moreover, through the lenses of feminist theory, these works reveal essential issues that Serao confronted in her works, including such topics as societal expectations of female behavior, the importance of ties between women, and the emotionally crippling effects of the narrowly prescribed roles for women. Exploring

Serao's works from this critical viewpoint leads naturally to an examination of how she broadens, both thematically and stylistically, the conventional interpretation of the realist movement.

Italian *verismo,* a literary school of the late 1800s, arose in reaction to the sentimentality of romanticism and was encouraged by the ideals of social reform stemming from the *Risorgimento,* the period leading up to the unification of Italy. The realist movement came late to Italy which, unlike France, lacked a national language and the scientific innovations needed to foster the type of novel that later evolved into the realist text.[2] Fundamental tenets of *verismo* included the ideal of the objective author and a concern with the economic and social plight of the lower classes. Classic realist narratives include Verga's *I Malavoglia* (The House by the Medlar Tree) (1881) and the short stories collected in *Vita dei Campi* (Life in the Fields) (1880) and *Novelle Rusticane* (Little Novels of Sicily) (1883), and Capuana's novels *Giacinta* (Giacinta) (1879) and *Il marchese di Roccaverdina* (The Marquis of Roccaverdina) (1901).

That Serao played an influential role in the promulgation of *verismo* has never been questioned. Indeed, two prominent literary critics view Serao's work as estimable and original examples of literature produced during this movement. Anna Banti, noting that Serao wrote in one of the most significant moments in Italian literary history, believes she was one of the earliest realist authors in Italy. Serao, Banti continues, must be considered "among the first experimenters of a moral and artistic perspective that, by that time, one breathed along with the air."[3] Many of Serao's realist narratives, including the short story "La virtù di Checchina" (Checchina's Virtue) (1884)[4] and those stories collected in *Il romanzo della fanciulla* (A Young Girl's Story) (1885), were written during these early days of *verismo* and because of their focus on realist elements must be considered pivotal texts in this literary movement. Indeed, Michele Prisco sees Serao occupying a central position in the *movimento verista,* believing that she not only helped to pioneer it, but also modified its original principles to reflect her own interests.[5] In his assessment, Prisco recognizes Serao's ability to refashion the realist tradition to suit her own thematic concerns.

Not all critics have been as insightful in locating Serao's works within the cultural context in which they belong, and it is their evaluations that must be addressed. The most frequent criticism

leveled at Serao is precisely her unwillingness to adhere to realist
tenets. Rather than considering her narrative choices as a conscious manipulation of literary forms, these critiques interpreted
her reluctance—which some critics labeled simple ineptitude—as
sentimentality and intellectual shallowness. This outright dis-
missal of Serao's intentions leads one to ask if perhaps it is rather
her position within a male literary domain that is questioned
and criticized. Indeed, these critiques seem founded in part on
gender-oriented expectations and assumptions. For example, one
of the most widely cited analyses of Serao's work came from
Benedetto Croce, who claimed that although Serao had the "ready
perception" necessary for describing people, customs, and places,
she lacked "reflection" and "culture." In what has since become
the definitive verdict, he characterized Serao's approach as "observation moved by sentiment."[6] Other early critics also seemed determined to negate Serao's literary skills by disparaging her
alleged lack of culture or sophisticated linguistic skills. Francesco
Bruno, continuing the established Crocean line of criticism even
into the 1960s, praises Serao's indifference to rhetorical analysis
but goes on to say that this very absence makes her particular
expression of realism incompatible with that of Verga's, which
revealed an innate profundity.[7]

I would argue that this critical reception was blind to the gendered revisions of genre demonstrated by Serao. Instead, it insisted on the existing tenets of realism that had been established
and championed by male authors and intellectuals. Serao's realist
texts do, in fact, share many attributes of the precepts established
in the theoretical writings of Verga and Capuana. She was clearly
influenced by them, and even classified herself with these authors.[8] But, significantly, her manipulation of the established
principles created a type of *verismo* uniquely suited to Serao's engagement with female-centered narratives, an argument she
makes clear in her brief writings on realism. If this examination
is expanded to include not just an analysis of stylistic similarities
to and differences from other *veristi* writers, but also a study of
the thematic concerns and ideological underpinnings of these issues, a rich and provocative reworking of the traditional realist
text unfolds.

It is useful here to look directly at critical statements made by
Verga and Capuana. Capuana was *verismo's* most articulate and
perceptive theoretician, writing critical essays on Zola, Balzac, and

French naturalism as well as on Italian authors. He emphasized the ideal of *"impersonalità,"* calling a work of art "perfect" when "the hand of the artist remains absolutely invisible. . . ."[9] This "cult of impersonality" was one of the cardinal concepts of *verismo,* stemming in part from the scientific influence of positivism. The author was charged with recording, rather than interpreting, reality. Other fundamental tenets, many of which are evident in Capuana's novels *Giacinta* and *Il marchese di Roccaverdina,* include the use of antiliterary language and dialect, an interest in the experiences of the lower socioeconomic classes, a preference for an ensemble cast rather than a single protagonist, and a concern with the psychology and passions of the fictional characters. *Verismo* has also been considered a regional phenomenon, linked primarily with the literature of Sicily and other parts of southern Italy.

Perhaps the most widely cited articulation of the principles of *verismo* is found in Verga's letter to his friend Salvatore Farina, which was used as an introduction to the 1880 short story "L'amante di Gramigna" (Gramigna's Lover). In this document, Verga defined the ideal of the impersonality of a literary text. He wrote that "the work of art must seem to have been made by itself, to have matured and to have arisen spontaneously as a natural fact, without maintaining any point of contact with its author, any stain of original sin."[10] Many of Verga's works, including his masterpiece *I Malavoglia,* are tinged with a sense of pessimism as he describes the economic misery and feudal conditions of his native Sicily.[11]

Like Verga, Serao was considered a regional writer concerned with the lower classes and was highly praised for her faithful depictions of life among the common people of Naples. Often forsaking a pure and grammatically correct literary style, she preferred to render her dialogues and descriptions in a prose that not only better reflected the spoken word, but also enlivened her texts.[12] This sense of life, of movement, also stemmed from her use of a choral structure, "where," as she wrote, "the movement comes completely from the masses, where the soul is in the multitude. . . ."[13] Serao also was concerned with psychological depictions of the passions and emotions driving her characters, a key principle of *verismo.*

How, then, did Serao transfigure the existing axioms of *verismo* to fashion a genre suitable for her concerns? Unlike Verga and Capuana, she apparently did not write extensively about the characteristics and objectives of her own version of realism. But her writings on the subject, found primarily in the short introduction to *Il romanzo della fanciulla* and in her letters, offer a concise and penetrating glimpse of her vision of this literary movement. Perhaps the most striking element of these writings is her vehement rejection of the notion of authorial objectivity. Her texts are not detached observations but, perhaps more important for the modern reader, chronicles of lived experiences and, above all, memories. "[M]y psychology is made of memory," Serao writes, adding that she never wanted to be more than a "faithful, humble chronicler of my memory" (4–5). The "fanciulle," or young girls of these short stories originate from the images of all the young girls Serao has known. "All those young girls have passed near me: they passed by, they went away, they disappeared . . . but their image has remained in me, vibrant" (4). She continues her discussion of her own, unique muse: "Instead of fabricating a young girl, I evoked all the companions of my childhood; instead of constructing a heroine, I lived again with my friends from long ago" (6). This reliance on memory and relived experiences colors Serao's works with a more personal, female-centered hue, two important characteristics of the author's approach to *verismo*.

Serao's rejection of the fundamental principle of a disinterested author, then, reiterates the symbiotic relationship she has with her protagonists. She explicitly merges her identity with that of her subjects, writing, "*Together* we lived the life of this book. I have written it, and I give it to you" (6; emphasis added). Instead of authorial detachment, Serao enjoys an affectionate intimacy with her heroines. Perhaps Serao deliberately fostered this empathetic bond between author and heroine in order to create similar, equally intimate relationships between both reader and heroine and reader and author. Her rejection of certain tenets of realism allowed her to build a bridge to her readers, permitting them to relive the very real experiences of the heroines. Serao's portrayals are invaluable to the modern reader's understanding of women's experiences in turn-of-the-century Italy, for she never becomes detached from the subject. She purposely offers a multifaceted picture of women and their position within the larger social world.

Serao moves from the world outside to that within in her desire to reveal the "internal drama, imposed on the young girl. . . ." by traditional society (4), a second fundamental component of Serao's realism. To understand Serao's position, it is worth quoting at length her description of the double existence a young girl is compelled to live:

> She must live in contact with men, without a current of communication opening between them and her; she must guess everything, after having suspected all, and she must seem ignorant; she must have a burning and consuming ambition, a gigantic desire, an unstoppable will to catch hold of a man, and she must seem cold and must be indifferent. (3)

Here, Serao clearly articulates her vision of a female existence shaped and restricted by social norms, a theme underlying many of her works, regardless of genre. Indeed, in several of the subsequent texts, the heroine becomes almost eliminated from the text itself as she slowly ceases to participate actively in the expectations of the world around her. Serao's depiction of the limitations faced by women is also apparent in works dealing with various social classes, for although wealth and social status might lighten the chains of female oppression, they do not dismantle them completely. As Serao notes so emphatically, "Hard is the battle in a woman's life, but the discouraging motto of Job was made for the young girl" (4). With this statement, Serao clearly indicates the futility of resisting the hegemonic social order.

Serao knew she would be censured for rejecting the tenets of realism.[14] In the opening paragraph of the aforementioned introduction to *Il romanzo della fanciulla,* she anticipates this criticism and asks that the "first word" go to her, so that she is not misunderstood (3). Her only wish, she claims, is to make several "simple and humble explanations." By taking this deferential approach, Serao cleverly disarms critics who might otherwise feel threatened by an impertinent woman writer. She addresses her audience directly, bypassing the literary experts to solicit those readers most sympathetic to her work. To her male readers, Serao will present "material unfamiliar to them"—topics, however, that will be "very dear" to her female readers (3). Serao assumes that a female-centered text will be foreign to male readers more accustomed, perhaps, to narratives featuring vigorous heroes and exotic adventures, rather than the domestic fictions often employed by nineteenth-century women authors. Her preface serves, therefore, not only to state her case before the ultimate judge of her

fiction—the public—but also to alert her readers to her own gendered vision of the realist text.

Serao's unique approach to *verismo* serves as a point of departure for an examination of her realist texts. Because I am concerned primarily with Serao's interpretation of female
experiences, I have organized her works according to their portrayal of various life situations, such as marriage and work. Other,
broader themes found in Serao, such as the bonds of love and
friendship among women and the professional and social limitations confronting young girls will also be examined. That Serao
intended to focus attention on her female protagonists is evident
merely by a brief examination of her titles; of the eight fictive
texts analyzed in this chapter, six bear titles containing the name,
role, or profession of the heroine.

Many of Serao's works are framed by the institution of marriage, the standard narrative structure of eighteenth- and
nineteenth-century texts by women.[15] Most of these female-
authored novels close with the depiction of a matrimony, signifying the heroine's successful integration into the approved family
and social dynamic. The traditional ideal of matrimony, however,
was often subtly challenged by female authors who questioned
the mythology of a "happily-ever-after." These authors instead
examine the often grievous effects of marriage on women, such
as the loss of independence and autonomy. Serao, in both her
realist and romance texts, explicitly examines the traditionally idealized images of female marital bliss. By doing so, she not only
challenges conventional literary endings (a subject addressed
more thoroughly in the following chapter), but also interrogates
the traditional image and role of wife.

In "La virtù di Checchina," perhaps Serao's most probing and
sensitive examination of the female psyche, the title character is—
significantly—unhappily married. The 1884 short story recounts
Checchina's failed attempts to realize a tryst with a handsome and
rich marquis. But this story is more than the description of an
aborted liaison; Serao calls into question the institution of marriage itself while masterfully depicting how the stifling bonds of
wedlock can extinguish a woman's spirit.[16] The reader must look
beneath the conventional plot, as it were, to discover its subtext of
female despair and destiny. In her own work on women-authored
plots, Anna Nozzoli has commented that female writers were best

suited to create these subtle subtexts, hidden under narratives
that often featured humble and simple protagonists:

> It is a given, moreover, that the most authentic testimony on the "femi-
> nine" condition comes in fact from that area of feminine narrative in
> which . . . the silent dramas of women, frustrated by the autonomy of
> their feelings and brutalized by the mechanical, imperceptible, pitiless
> flow of daily reality, are relived.[17]

Nozzoli is discussing the poetry of Serao's contemporary, the
author Contessa Lara, but her analysis can clearly be applied to
Serao's short story, and to her work in general. Checchina's "silent
drama" is depicted through the monotonous rhythms of her daily
life as a middle-class Roman housewife. The story, considered one
of Serao's most compelling and stylistically sophisticated pieces,
deserves to be dealt with at length, for it is a powerful example
of Serao's ability to capture the hopes and the anguish of her
heroines. "La virtù," which delineates many of the themes Serao
would elaborate upon throughout her literary career and in a
variety of formats, portrays the internal drama of a young female
protagonist, a central component of Serao's realism.

The story begins with the opening of a door, instantly drawing
the reader into Checchina's world, a world rendered in the sort
of realistic detail that mirrors the protagonist's own interior life.
Isolina, the protagonist's sophisticated and beautiful friend, has
come to call on Checchina.[18] She waits in the cold and unwelcom-
ing sitting room, which Serao describes in painstaking detail, from
the cheaply upholstered chairs covered with antimacassars, to the
empty candy dishes, to the pathetic plate of artificial fruit. Anna
Banti, among others, has discussed the importance of detail in
Serao's work, attributing it in part to her training as a journalist.
"[Serao's] eye catches in a flash . . . the smallest of objects, the
imperceptible movements," she notes.[19] Carlo Madrignani, who
points to this particular passage as an example of Serao's interpretation of realism, dismisses it as an "auction list" of furniture.[20]
Although both critics have called attention to this stylistic technique, neither has recognized its importance in "La virtù di Checchina." When Serao describes Checchina's sitting room with such
exactitude, she is, in effect, portraying her heroine's entire world,
the "closure of the female life."[21] This cramped and modest house
represents the entire sphere of Checchina's activity. She is re-

stricted by both physical and social parameters, boundaries that not only limit her movements but also demarcate her expectations and subsequent comportment. Her friend Isolina, on the other hand, is never seen within her own home. She enjoys a significant degree of movement, and that, combined with her slightly elevated social class, allows her certain liberties in her behavior.

The differences between the two women are immediately apparent when Checchina joins her friend in the sitting room. Checchina appears almost immobile next to the flighty Isolina, who has come to borrow money so she can buy the necessary accoutrements for her next liaison. The protagonist reacts "with the serious and calm air of the non-temperamental, without a quiver," to Isolina's description of the passion she feels for her latest lover.[22] Serao's repeated use of the word "without" (*senza* in Italian) in this passage underscores Checchina's passivity. Again, the reader is struck by the contrast between the two women. Isolina appears confident and assertive, while Checchina seems trapped in a submissive and limited existence. After Isolina sweeps out, off to prepare for her rendezvous, Checchina quietly returns to her cleaning.

If Isolina represents carefree independence, Checchina's husband, Toto Primicerio, epitomizes the stolid, repressive bourgeoisie. Toto has just informed his wife that the Marchese Ugo d'Aragona will be dining with them the following Sunday. Toto, a doctor, had treated the marquis for a slight injury earlier that summer while the two vacationed in the same area. Oblivious to the financial and social complications created by his invitation, Toto will remain equally blind to Checchina's growing sense of physical and emotional constriction. This fundamental lack of insight into the female psyche (by male characters) was to become an important theme in Serao's works. This motif serves to challenge the idealized portrait of marriage while depicting the isolation and despondency of a woman attempting to project herself beyond the domestic sphere.

Checchina's first attempt to enlarge this constricting world follows an afternoon devoted to the preparation of the upcoming supper. Her preoccupation with the meal ties her definitively to that most ubiquitous symbol of domestic duty, the hearth. Once again Checchina's physical and psychic space has been demarcated. To those limitations the author adds another, that of pecuniary impediments. Serao, who was able to support herself and her family through her journalism and literary activities, was keenly aware of the importance of financial independence for women. In many of her texts she links the acquisition of money with a certain freedom within the marriage bond (although not, apparently, in the social world beyond). In "La virtù," Checchina is terrified of asking her parsimonious husband to increase her housekeeping allowance in order to pay for this elaborate supper. Unable to change her financial status, Checchina attempts a physical makeover, an alteration in keeping with her limited means. She asks her maid if she can fashion her hair in curls "like those of Isolina" (218). This seemingly insignificant passage represents Checchina's first attempt to create a more assertive, active persona. She models herself after the independent and confident Isolina, her only link with the world beyond her doorstep.

Serao's depiction of the dinner party plays on the difference in social class between the marquis and his lower-middle-class hosts. The self-assured marquis apparently has no compunction about abusing their hospitality, for as soon as Toto succumbs to his postprandial nap, the marquis attempts to seduce Checchina.[23] Recognizing that Checchina would be moved more by tangible symbols of his social class than by idle expressions of love, the marquis woos her with words, describing the silk curtains, thick carpeting, and heady scent of Oriental incense in his apartment. The marquis also paints a picture of the ideal woman with whom he could share his elegant quarters, "a dream, a phantom, a beautiful woman, simple and good ..." (222); in short, an abstract ideal of womanhood, not an individual in her own right. In his eyes, Checchina becomes just that, this "phantom" of the marquis, who marks her as his possession by kissing her on the neck. The marquis even "baptizes" her with an exotic nickname, whispering seductively, "Come Wednesday, from four to six o'clock, come, Fanny," (222). Not persuaded by the kiss, Checchina is "won over by that name," perhaps envisioning in this renaming a new, more assertive self (222). She concedes, unable to assert her own will when confronted with a forceful personality.

Nor can she resist the directives of her own maid, who is suspicious of the marquis's subsequent gift of white roses. Susanna, who prizes conformity with religious and socially acceptable morals and norms, sees the flowers as a symbol of sensuality and temptation. She first warns Checchina not to take in the heady scent: "Be careful because the stench of flowers can hurt your head. I'm warning you because a lady I worked for once had such a headache, an affliction to die from" (224). Susanna, as representative of the lower social classes, is clearly tied to the physical; for her, illicit desires become manifested through corporeal, rather than emotional, reactions. She tells Checchina to send the blossoms to a church, which would, in effect, negate the forbidden message they imply. Checchina, helpless before her domineering maid, complies. Her immediate capitulation to both the marquis *and* her maid points to Checchina's uneasy position in regard to these two representatives of social class. Interestingly, it is Checchina's gender, manifested by her sexuality, that has placed her in this ambiguous situation. Both the marquis and Susanna expect the compliant Checchina to act out the role of unfaithful wife, little realizing the psychic significance of such an act to the story's heroine. They imitate Toto's blind inability (or unwillingness) to read the subtext of Checchina's behavior, to link an emotional metamorphosis to the changes in her outward demeanor.

Checchina's reaction to the demands of these two powerful figures is a telling one, as her physical condition mirrors the confusion and uneasiness of her mind. Overcome by a strange and dissipating lassitude, she neglects her household chores, refusing, perhaps, to fulfill if only for a few hours her role as housewife. She does pick up some sewing and works in a sort of dream state, but eventually the sewing slips from her hands, leaving a trail of bright red thread across her black dress. This striking image of blood and passion reflects the turbulent state of Checchina's subconscious, while the conventional feminine activity of sewing, here associated with blood, marks the protagonist's body with a sign of her femaleness.

Serao traces Checchina's quest to create a new self-image through a more prosaic transformation, that of the protagonist's preoccupation with her wardrobe. According to Maryse Jeuland-Meynaud, who has studied physicality in Serao's work, the act of changing clothing represents a change in identity. Donning new attire, "the character changes at the same time as her psychic perspective. . . ."[24] Checchina searches through her closet for something suitable to wear to a romantic assignation, but finds only worn and shabby dresses. She is determined, however, to fashion her own identity, although it is still modeled after that of Isolina.[25] Pulling an old hat from her closet, Checchina sets about remaking it. The remodeled hat stands as a metonymic symbol of her own refashioning. Tellingly, her husband, perhaps only dimly aware of the hat's significance, scolds her for fussing with one of her "womanly whims" instead of preparing his lunch (229). He criticizes her millinery skills, brutally declaring, "It looks bad on you, bad, that's all, since you want the truth. The other one was better" (229). Toto implicitly warns his wife against changing her passive identity to a more assertive one. He serves as the conventional agent repressing Checchina's figurative and literal attempts to transform herself.

Only during the stillness of the night, as she lies awake next to her snoring husband, is Checchina able to figuratively throw off the chains tying her to her home. She feels a great well of determination surging up inside of her, one capable of defeating "her two enemies," Toto and Susanna (236). As Checchina mentally traces the route to the marquis's apartment, the author includes for the first time an image of the protagonist outside the walls of her house. Throughout this story, the physical limitations of Checchina's world have reflected her mental and emotional condition. Just as she is trapped inside her house, she feels imprisoned within her subservient and passive role. Isolina's freedom of movement symbolizes, on the other hand, an unwillingness to remain chained to the domestic sphere and the psychic limitations it represents. Sandra Gilbert and Susan Gubar, who have examined physical and psychic spatiality in various nineteenth-century narratives, conclude that a woman author's concern with physical space often reflects her sense of spiritual imprisonment, an emotional confinement caused by a perception of being "duty bound."[26] Checchina's mental meanderings represent a movement away from the bonds confining her to the hearth and toward a newly found sense of freedom:

> It seemed as though she had a new strength that she had never felt before, a great courage, an audacity that easily overcame any obstacle, a will so steady that nothing could defeat it or break it. She laughed with pride, in the night, raising her shoulders as if she wanted to try and lift an immense weight, as a game, to test her own strength. ("La virtù di Checchina," 237)

This "immense weight" that oppresses her so heavily is the burden of conforming to the spiritually debilitating behavior prescribed by a patriarchal world.

Checchina's efforts to enlarge the spatial confines of her world are accompanied by a more acute consciousness of her own physicality. This awareness takes the form of a deliberate self-scrutiny in front of her mirror, an event occasioned by her decision to meet the marquis. As she combs her hair, she notices for the first time "three spots of freckles under her left eye . . ." (242). Another glance in the mirror discloses "a very shabby figure, very miserable . . ." (242). Jeuland-Meynaud believes that these brief moments in front of the mirror reveal Checchina's self-loathing and disgust.[27] However, Jenijoy La Belle's work with the literature of the mirror documents that female characters often use the looking glass as a form of self-scrutiny and even psychic survival: "For some women, their consciousness that they exist at all is dependent on seeing themselves in the glass."[28] I believe Checchina's exploration before the mirror illustrates a desire to see herself through her own eyes. An alteration in her physical appearance, in this case the newly discovered freckles, symbolizes the emotional transformation Checchina is undergoing as she attempts to rebel against the forces crushing her spirit.

The ending of this beautifully crafted story is both prosaic and tragic. After being thwarted by a series of domestic intrusions, Checchina succeeds in defying her suspicious maid in order to slip outside and make her way to the marquis. Terrified of meeting an acquaintance, Checchina is horrified when she encounters Isolina. She has joined Isolina on her turf, as it were, both physically and spiritually. In fact, when Isolina discovers Checchina's objective, she is overjoyed, even saying, "Give me a kiss, dear, we're more than friends, now we're sisters" (255–256). This kiss, mimicking that swift kiss bestowed by the marquis on Checchina's neck, signals Checchina's initiation into Isolina's sorority. But Checchina fails the test; she is not Isolina's sisterly counterpart. She will not follow her friend's example and consummate her affair as a symbol of her liberty and freedom. Breaking free from Isolina's insinuations, Checchina makes her way to the marquis's building but is unable to muster the courage to enter. "Then Checchina lowered her head and went home, giving up" (256).

The story ends with this sentence and with it, Checchina's rebellion. Her attempt to create her own individuality has failed. Unable to throw off the weight of years of social conditioning, Checchina must return to the confines of a loveless marriage and a spiritually limited existence. Is this, then, the "virtù" of the title?

Carlo Madrignani, in his analysis, believes that the enigmatic title is the clue to its interpretation: "Is the renunciation of Checchina in the end the victory of her 'better part'? [O]r does it derive only from an obstacle, and is not at all virtuous?"[29] Certainly, the title can be construed either way, and Madrignani suggests that the interpretation depends on the individual reader. I would go farther and suggest that this ambiguity is intentional, as Serao deliberately undermines the moral implications of a tale involving female adultery. A careful reading of the subtext indicates that Checchina's virtue stems, perhaps, more from the socialized values and physical obstacles impeding an affair than from her own principled convictions. As I. T. Olken points out, Checchina is virtuous by default. If she does not act, it is because "she has no well-defined self-identity, but that she cannot act is in turn determined to a crucial extent by the fact that she is not allowed choices in determining her identity or her destiny."[30] Serao does not overtly challenge the effects of the marriage bond on a woman struggling to create her identity, or, in a wider sense, the traditional values isolating her at home. But in this superbly crafted story, she does implicitly raise these issues.[31] Serao's text embodies the subtle criticism of the institution of marriage found in many texts by women, who often depict "matrimony as one of the primary tools for dulling a [female] hero's initiative and restraining her maturation."[32] In "La virtù di Checchina," Serao emulates this narrative model, her sensitive probing of the ideal of marital bliss questioning its effect on the female psyche.

Serao tackles the issue of women's confinement in matrimony again in the little-known story "La moglie di un grand'uomo" (The Wife of a Great Man). This wickedly comic story mocks the fairy-tale tradition that depicts a fair maiden, a Prince Charming, and a happily-ever-after.[33] Although Serao employs a fairy-tale framework in this narrative, the text is firmly grounded in realist techniques, including a contemporary setting, lively, direct language, and, more important for the purposes of this study, the author's own unique perspective on the bonds of matrimony. Serao sets up her parody with the opening sentence: "Once upon a time there was a young girl—oh my! how many there were and how many there are!—a young girl who had to placidly marry a young lad" (59). This young girl is not the typical blushing maiden, however. Rather, she is "a modern young girl, a superior young girl" (59–60). A modern girl, indeed, for she pursues ac-

tivities not typically associated with women at that time; she reads
literature, attends scientific, literary, and historical conferences,
plays charades, attends opening nights, and takes a lively and
interested part in any discussion. She is too modern, in fact, to
marry the sugar wholesaler to whom she had been promised,
because "every superior girl with any self-respect must marry an
illustrious man or die an old maid" (60). (The reader must not
worry about this poor lad, however; he cried for an hour after he
was jilted, despaired for three days, was melancholy for a week
and finally married the woodseller's daughter. Some stories do
end happily.)

After a bit of searching, the protagonist sets her sights on the
"great man" of the title. This prodigy has risen from the ranks
of journalism to become a famous author and statesman; in short,
"an illustrious man, observed, studied, discussed, commented
upon and always applauded by the public" (61). The girl aggres-
sively courts him, and, as she is rich and beautiful, he descends
from "the throne of his greatness" and agrees to wed her. Thrilled
to be marrying a man of genius, she likens him to a god: "To be
the wife of this man, to carry his name, to possess his heart, to
divide his glory: that is the happiness of happiness" (63). All signs
point to wedded bliss for the modern girl and the "grand'uomo."

The conclusion, however, subverts the notion of a happily-ever-
after, at least for the female protagonist. The second half of the
short story is told through her disillusioned eyes. Their honeymoon journey across Italy turns out to be an interminable lesson
in Roman antiquities and Florentine politics—"On a honeymoon!
. . ." she writes despairingly in her diary (63). Further disappointment awaits. She discovers that her learned husband never opens
a book, wears a ridiculously beribboned nightcap to protect his
curls, and poses for hours before the bathroom mirror. His
annoying friends are constantly underfoot, and even have the
audacity to order her to "make him happy . . . because history . . .
will hold you accountable" (64). She responds, in her diary, by
wondering what business History has poking its nose into certain
private affairs. The story ends with the husband off on a diplo-
matic assignment (and possible romantic liaison), and the wife
languishing at home. "Great men . . . admire them, yes, marry
them never. . . ." she sighs knowingly in the final lines (66).

In this skillfully written short story, Serao takes on a number
of generic and thematic conventions. With her language evoking

the formulaic structure of a fairy tale, she clearly satirizes that particular genre. This is no helpless maiden who needs rescuing, but a vibrant, decisive, intelligent young woman. And the "grand'uomo" is clearly no Prince Charming but rather a posturing boor, offering his bride not a life of wedded bliss but intellectual and emotional neglect. By rewriting the traditional fairy-tale format, Serao also subverts the conventional marriage plot, writing beyond the nuptials to reveal the dullness and disillusionment faced by a woman of spirit and wit. The intelligent young protagonist, who had hoped that this marriage would result in a meeting of the minds, instead finds herself stupefied and bored after wedlock. Her husband does not treat her as an intellectual equal; in fact, he does not treat her as an intellectual at all.

Serao interjects another element into her parody of the fairy tale, for it is laced with a delightful and sometimes biting wit. The use of humor or satire was not unknown among realist authors, who often countered their portraits of humble folk with more comic or satiric descriptions of the upper classes. Serao, however, rarely used humor in her realist works, a technique precluded perhaps by her close identification with her subjects. Why, then, does she use it in this narrative? I believe she employs a comic touch to blunt the startling moral of this painful tale. Stripped of its humorous elements, the story would be a harsh indictment of marriage. Serao could hardly risk the critical (and public) censure such a tale would incur, especially at the very beginning of her literary career. Despite the story's humor, however, the message remains clear: marriage to a "grand'uomo" does not necessarily protect a woman from spiritual death and intellectual paralysis. Thus, as evidenced in "La virtù di Checchina" and "La moglie di un grand'uomo," the repression of spirit and intellect comes as a result of surrendering to the bonds of wedlock. Interestingly, the repression within a marital setting reaches across class lines, for both the lower-middle-class Checchina and the more socially elevated heroine of "La moglie" share the same fate. As will become more apparent in later texts dealing with the repression of the female spirit, Serao offers little hope and no concrete plan of action to women caught in the confines of wedlock, for in both these texts she advocates patient acquiescence rather than outright rebellion or even a more subtle resistance. Serao was aware, perhaps, of the futility of rebelling against the social and cultural matrix prescribing wifely submission.

Serao's depiction of marriage is not limited to her fictive production. A 1906 newspaper article entitled "Perchè le ragazze non si maritano?" (Why Aren't Young Women Marrying?) deplores the growing cohort of women choosing not to marry.[34] Employing a censorious tone, Serao scolds these self-absorbed women, making it clear that a woman's destiny lies in wedlock: "From when she is born, a girl is to marry. . . . This invincible, inevitable destiny . . . becomes the only moral and social objective of the girl."[35] But Serao's depiction of the trials of marriage seems to undermine the very cultural discourse that paints a rosy picture of life after the wedding ceremony. Some young women envision marriage as a liberation from parental supervision, but Serao warns them that a husband "is a master more austere, more jealous, more meticulous, more pretentious than any parent . . ." (5). This caustic description of patriarchal authority could hardly inspire a young girl to make that trip down the aisle, for according to Serao, she would be exchanging one carefully controlled space for another when she leaves her parents' house for that of her husband.

In this intriguing article, Serao also warns against paying heed to the romantic mythology surrounding the image of the married woman, advising the young girl instead to enter into matrimony with this pledge in mind: "I will not be a queen to my husband, but his companion; I will not be a capricious and fleeting lover to my husband, but the friend of all his days . . ." (5). With this creed, Serao grounds her vision of wedlock in mutual respect and the knowledge that a successful marriage is built more on the quotidian than the sublime.

How does the depiction of marriage in this journalism essay differ from that of Serao's fictive pieces? In this particular case, the author's fiction appears more conservative than her journalism, a situation atypical of her literary and fictive output. In her novels and short stories, Serao usually fails to construct a relationship based on the pragmatic and ultimately equalitarian basis of her proposed creed, for the marriages portrayed in these works are marked by a fundamental inability to empathize with or even comprehend the emotional needs of one's spouse. Tellingly, Serao appears to be casting the blame for this on the husband rather than the wife. Checchina, for example, is emotionally diminished in her relationship with the oafish and unperceptive Toto, while the unnamed wife of the second story faces intellectual neglect from the vain and insufferable "grand'uomo." The blueprint for a successful marriage delineated in Serao's article is nowhere to be seen in these fictive works. Was she unable to make the stylistic leap from fact to fiction, creating narratives that would confound both literary and social conventions by depicting a marriage founded more on respect and equality than on passionate impulses or economic interests? Or do Serao's fictive marriages reflect her fundamentally conservative and pessimistic vision of wedlock in turn-of-the-century Italy, with a particular emphasis on insensitive husbands and suppressed wives? I would argue in favor of the second interpretation, for Serao was most concerned, especially in her realist works, with presenting the world as she perceived it, rather than with creating a more idealistic landscape for her heroines. This journalism piece, with its paradoxical presentation of the institution of marriage, underscores the contradictions found in Serao's fictive output, inconsistencies that reflect not only the author's lifelong interrogation of ideologies concerning women, but also the social transitions inherent in the passage from one century to another.

Serao's bleak depiction of marriage in the aforementioned short stories is confounded by her analysis of the alternatives for nineteenth-century women: spinsterhood or the cloister. In the short story "Non più," the protagonist suffers a slow emotional death because of her unmarried state. The heroine of the novel *Suor Giovanna della Croce,* however, faces the same spiritual extinction when she is stripped of her identity as a nun. In the more ambiguous short story "Per monaca," the protagonist's decision to enter a convent can be read as either a defeat in her battle to win a husband or an endorsement of joining a closed, all-female society. The lack of a consistent and clearly articulated thesis in Serao's work indicates her lifelong struggle to both depict and question prevailing ideas about female destiny and female roles. As noted above, she grappled with this issue in both her fiction and her nonfiction. For example, in *Saper Vivere,* an etiquette manual written primarily for young girls preparing to marry, Serao also briefly discusses the advantages of remaining single. An unmarried woman (one of a certain age, at least) can travel freely, live alone, and mix easily with men in society. "Getting married is good, but it's also bad; not getting married is bad, but it's also good," she concludes, obscuring the issue once and for all.[36]

The narratives examined in this section do more than question the prevailing ideological debate surrounding the relative benefits of marriage versus spinsterhood; they also illustrate a significant theme found throughout Serao's body of work: the importance of female friendship. Her vision of female existence includes an examination of the bonds between women, a topic generally not found in male-authored texts, which tend to define female protagonists in relation to their male counterparts. The depiction of these close bonds between women adds yet another layer to Serao's careful construction of a space devoted to exploring and revealing a woman's life.

"Non più" (No Longer) is found in *Il romanzo della fanciulla,* an 1885 collection of five stories in which young girls explicate, and occasionally lament, the limitations they face in a society with strictly defined rules and roles for women. Most of these works are choral in nature, featuring a procession of young girls poised between the relative freedom of adolescence and the more restricted adult world. Paola Blelloch believes that the use of ensemble casts in these books was a deliberate strategy undertaken to enlarge the scope of the author's focus: "With these stories Serao passes from the denouncement of the suffering and oppression of a single individual to a collective pain and exploitation."[37] This choral approach not only paints a picture of the shared suffering of women, it also allows the author to depict a sweeping range of literary characters. The meticulous description of these protagonists succeeds in creating a more realistic fictional metropolis, one inhabited by individuals from every social and economic class.

Many of the young heroines in these texts eagerly embrace the values inscribed by a traditional world, but others struggle with a quiet desperation against them. Emma Demartino, the protagonist of "Non più," has assimilated the belief that a woman achieves fulfillment only through marriage and motherhood. Jilted by her lover and surrounded by married friends, she feels doomed to a life of spinsterhood and spiritual degeneration. ("Spinster" is obviously a weighted term with negative connotations, but I use it deliberately in order to remain faithful to the original Italian, *zitella*). The short story's preoccupation with the importance of marriage in a woman's life and its attendant role in the social and economic structure of her imaginary world is underscored in its opening scene. The inhabitants of a southern Italian town have turned out to watch a fireworks display in honor of the Feast of the Virgin Mary.[38] With a sure stroke of her pen, Serao succinctly describes the host of young girls gathered for the event. They are defined primarily in terms of their physical and, more significantly, financial attributes: "The three Capitella sisters each had 150 thousand lire of dowry; the two Roccatagliatas 100 thousand lire; Clelia Mesolella, wife of one year, had brought 200 thousand . . . ."[39] Serao's emphasis on the economic value of each girl reflects the highly pragmatic approach to matrimony prevalent at that time. Describing the institution, historian Michela De Giorgio remarks that "The lack of a dowry prevented young girls from entering the marriage market, from freeing themselves from the more or less coercive custody of the family or boarding school, [thus] condemning them inevitably to spinsterhood."[40] Serao's repeated emphasis on the correlation between a girl's dowry and her "value" as a bride acts as a critique of the economic aspect of marriage. This attention to the social positioning of women within different economic classes, an issue examined in "La virtù di Checchina," reveals Serao's keen awareness of the connection between gender and social and marital status.

The contrast between married and unmarried women, along with the social status ascribed to each marital state, is clearly delineated in this opening scene. At the fireworks display, Rosina Sticco, Emma's best friend, proudly shows off her new husband and, perhaps more important, her new home, symbol of her newly attained status as wife. Rosina's friends, impressed as much by the house as by the husband, are "somewhat flustered by that matrimonial atmosphere that was the reality of their dreams" (189). Serao contrasts this flock of giggling, vibrant girls with the five silent spinsters visible at the windows of the Crocco's house, women whose unmarried state is reflected in their very dispositions. The two Crocco sisters are "angry and ill-tempered," the two Caputo siblings "peacefully resigned" (192). Dominating them all is Donna Irene Moscarella, "the prehistoric spinster who everyone remembered as spinster from time immemorial, the spinster no longer either choleric or smiling, but quieted into an apathy, into an almost immobility of life" (190). Emma, watching these five women, uneasily foresees the future that awaits her. Although engaged to a young man studying law in Naples, she feels old at twenty-five, already "pale, wan, faded" (190). As the last fireworks triumphantly honor the Virgin Mary, the definitive example of motherhood and maternal sacrifice, Emma frantically pleads for divine intervention. "In your hands, Holy Virgin . . . in your hands, me and all the other girls," she prays (193). Emma asks for the answer to all of their prayers: a husband. Her supplications to the Virgin Mary are significant, for the image of this maternal icon underscores the twin duties of these young women entering the marital state—that of wife *and* mother. Emma's prayers conflate social expectations with the tenets of Catholicism, as both the prevailing social discourse and the cult of Mary converge in the sanctioning of the maternal role.

This conflation of the role of wife and mother is underscored in the second scene, which opens just after the baptism of Rosina's fourth child. Emma's inability to fulfill either of these two roles leads to her displacement from her circle of married friends and, indeed, from the narrative structure itself. As Rosina looks on benevolently from her bed, her friends bustle about, talking incessantly about their children. Maternal devotion was, for Serao, the most elevated manifestation of love, and several of her texts focus on the sublimity of the maternal instinct.[41] Indeed, in a private letter, she underscores this connection by writing, "love is worth something only when it leads to maternity."[42] Despite this rather sweeping statement, many of Serao's protagonists recognize the potential confinement attached to these roles and occasionally rebel against an existence limited to wedlock and motherhood. In "Non più," for example, Emma, who by now has been abandoned by her fiancé, articulates her struggle against the societal dictate linking female destiny with marriage. "There is no obligation to get married," she bravely tells Rosina. "Don't say that, dear. No matter how bad a marriage, it's always better than nothing," is the gentle response. "And why?" Emma questions. "'For the children, Emma,' the happy mother sa[ys] gravely and sweetly" (195). Emma can find no argument to counter these atavistic justifications. Touched by the specter of spinsterhood, she leans silently against Rosina's lying-in bed, "[e]rect, immobile," and alone (197). Serao's choice of adjectives here points to Emma's stasis, her isolation, and her increasing lack of affiliation with her female friends.

The emotional wounds caused by Emma's spinsterhood are manifested in a dramatic physical transformation, a recurrent motif in Serao's writings. As Jeuland-Meynaud astutely points out, the crushing disappointment of spinsterhood in Serao's texts reveals itself in physical ailments and a loss of vitality. Love serves as a "stabilizing factor" for women, often rejuvenating them: "Love exalts beauty, prolongs the body's youthfulness and confers a marvelous clearness to the face."[43] In "Non più," this point vividly illustrates Emma's metamorphosis. Her once vivacious eyes are now dulled, shadowed by "two bags of flabby skin, as if they were dead, already tinted by the colors of corruption and decomposition" (200). This pitiless and exaggerated description of the disintegration of a once beautiful young woman seems to reveal more than the conflation of the role of wife with the manifestation of physical beauty. This troubling tale could also be read as Serao's own critique of a social system that links a woman's value to her marital status.

The complexity of the story is underscored in the final scene, set a number of years later, as Emma is removed even farther from the textual narrative. Knitting in her room, Emma overhears the innocent flirting being carried on beneath her window by Mimì, Rosina's sixteen-year-old daughter, and Federico, her beau. Emma accidently pricks herself with a needle when Mimì reveals that she has prayed to Saint Emma to protect their love. But Emma is too anemic for the needle to draw blood, and her waning physicality symbolizes her equally desiccated soul and her "silent and dried-up heart" (203). Mirroring a stratagem used in "La virtù di Checchina," Serao uses a domestic activity—sewing—to reflect the interior condition of the protagonist. Even the most mundane activity, then, becomes transformed into a metaphor of female despair and pain. In *verista* texts, tasks are used primarily to create portraits of physical states; Serao reverses this technique and uses these activities to depict an internal condition just as real. The short story ends with the tolling of the parish church bells, announcing the death of Donna Irene Moscarella, the "prehistoric spinster" of the first scene. Emma will now take Donna Irene's place as the town's most eminent spinster.

Emma's gradual withdrawal from the valorized world of wedlock is underscored not only by a striking physical deterioration but also by her spatial displacement within the narrative itself. In the first section, Emma is center stage, watching the fireworks alongside the other young girls. Engaged to be married and eager to embark on her life as wife and mother, she enjoys the social privileges ascribed to the appropriation of these roles. By the story's second section, now without a fiancé and beyond what was then considered the marriageable age, Emma has been placed slightly outside the sphere of action, a progressive textual reality for the heroine. She sits behind a curtain in Rosina's bedroom as

the scene ends, crying softly as her married friends share confi-
dences about their husbands and children. Finally, in the last
scene, Emma is completely removed from the action, stripped of
her role as participant and reduced to the part of a silent witness.
As Mimì and Federico flirt in the courtyard and begin their own
story of love, Emma sits in her room "[b]ehind the shutter" (203).
Incapable of fulfilling her expected female role, she is denied a
prominent position in the text's spatial economy. Emma's spinsterhood leads, in effect, to an almost complete effacement of her
physical and emotional being. Serao's empathetic depiction of
Emma's physical and emotional deterioration acts as a condemnation of the social, economic, and even religious forces severely
limiting women to the roles of wife and mother.

    Like Emma in "Non più," the protagonist in the 1901 novel *Suor
Giovanna della Croce* (Sister Giovanna of the Cross) also suffers the
gradual demise of her identity. The narrative strategy in this text,
however, reverses that of "Non piu," in which the protagonist
moves from the social world to a state of isolation. In *Suor Giovanna,* it is the heroine's removal from the safe haven of her convent to the secular world outside that crushes her soul. Forced to
deny both her identity and her chosen vocation, the protagonist
gradually succumbs to a spiritual annihilation more devastating
than any physical death.

    Serao knew that the story of an elderly nun would not please
or even interest a reading public increasingly accustomed to the
sentimental novels she was inclined to write at that point in her
literary career. In the introduction to *Suor Giovanna della Croce,*
Serao defends her decision to return to the story of a "simple
soul," the subject matter of her more overtly realist works.[44] She
announces her decision to stop "seducing" those readers who de-
mand "the beauty of lines and colors, the grace of youth, the
fascination of riches. . . ."[45] Instead, Serao wants to dramatize a
real social problem in postunification Italy, the closure of half-
empty convents and the forced eviction of nuns with no means
of financial support. According to Banti, Serao's decision to write
"a novel without love, neither sensual, romantic, or psychologically
complicated, [but rather] with a religious intonation . . . was a
courageous act."[46] I would agree, and add that the subject matter
also allowed Serao the occasion to treat atypical female protagonists—women who have deliberately withdrawn from a world that
exalts marriage and motherhood.

The protagonist's connection with both the secular and spiritual worlds is illustrated by her two names. Suor Giovanna was born Luisa Bevilacqua but after almost forty years in the convent, she now identifies completely with her religious name, "suffering profoundly when her *other* name, when her *other* life presented itself in her memory . . ." (533). Renaming oneself can often take on a deeper significance in female-authored texts: "Woman's naming of self . . . is a radically defiant act that assumes a power not generally passed down through the matriarchal line"; indeed, when a character renames herself, "she rewrites history from her own perspective."[47] Upon taking her vows, at age 22, Luisa created a new identity for herself, erasing the sting of the past (she entered the convent after being jilted by her fiancé) and linking herself irrevocably to a closed community of women.

The narrative turns on the government's decision to close down the convent of the Sepolte Vive, which, although designed to house thirty-three nuns, is less than half full. The nuns, who must either return to families they have not seen in decades or support themselves on a meager government stipend, are devastated by the announcement. Not only had they taken vows of poverty, chastity, and obedience, they must now recant their most sacred promise, that of "eternal seclusion to God," an act reflected in the very name of their convent, as "Sepolte Vive" means "buried alive" (545). The nuns, in their state of isolation, of being "buried alive," have managed to erase gendered roles and feel unprepared to return to the secular world where a woman's place is clearly defined by her marital status. Suor Giovanna, whose lengthy tenure in the secluded cloister has tamed her once-tempestuous character, no longer feels any connection with her earlier life. "Who was she," she wonders in her dimly lit cell. "Not a woman, not a female creature: she was a nun, a 'buried alive'" (549). She had rejected the traditional roles of wife and mother in order to become part of a religious community, devoting herself to spiritual rather than worldly concerns. Suor Giovanna, living outside the bounds of society, has been free of its expectations. Indeed, she has ignored societal insistence on the importance of physical appearance for a woman, sporting plain religious robes, shorn hair and a wrinkled face free of beauty aids. Secure and comfortable in this all-female atmosphere, Suor Giovanna knows that her identity, as well as her world, will be fragmented by the disbanding of the convent and this all-female space.

Serao, in a chillingly brutal scene, frames the closing of the convent in terms of violation, both physical and psychic. In a space once free of gendered roles, the introduction of a male figure and his subsequent actions have the effect of sexualizing the atmosphere, abruptly plunging the nuns back into the secular world. In this scene, the serenity of the cloister is shattered by three agents of the government, whose appearance desecrates the sacred place and horrifies the nuns. The sarcastic and insensitive prefect demands that the nuns raise their veils and reveal both their faces and their secular names in order to "verify their identities" (560). The nuns refuse, anguished at the thought of revealing themselves to these cruel men. The prefect, losing his patience, appeals to the abbess to set an example. She, too, dissents. "Then," he replies with mock regret, "I will have to resort to violence" (561). He strips the veil from her face with an ironically chivalrous bow. The abbess makes no move to defend herself, and the prefect is momentarily taken aback by her "profound resignation" (561). He must do the same with the other nuns, removing their veils with poorly concealed curiosity. The graphic violation of the nuns' anonymity and privacy clearly represents psychic rape. Not only is their well-ordered, peaceful world completely destroyed and their chosen identity brutally eradicated, but the freedom of living in a nongendered setting is erased by the prefect's sadistic actions.

Just as Emma's emotional isolation in "Non più" was tracked by her spatial displacement in the narrative, Suor Giovanna's internal disintegration is delineated through a description of the nun's increasingly miserable surroundings. More specifically, Serao contrasts the security of the convent, Suor Giovanna's spiritual and emotional home, with a depiction of her subsequent places of residence, each more squalid and pathetic than the last. She moves in first with her sister Grazia and Grazia's two grown children. This first relocation has a bittersweet significance for Suor Giovanna, who, while grateful for the shelter of her sister's home, still remembers that it was Grazia who betrayed her with her former fiancé, triggering her decision to become a nun. Now, at age sixty, Suor Giovanna must return to this household, although by this point Grazia is widowed. In her new home the nun bears the jibes and insolent comments of Grazia's children and Grazia's own bitter outbursts with patience and humility. Suor Giovanna's primary concern, now that she has been thrust back into the secular world, revolves around financial considerations rather than the nourishment of her soul, for the paltry government stipend received upon leaving the convent is quickly being exhausted by living expenses. After discovering that the government will not reimburse the dowries the nuns had brought to the convent as novices, Grazia evicts her sister in disgust. Unskilled, elderly, friendless, Suor Giovanna must support herself.[48]

The move to a small boarding house represents another step in Suor Giovanna's exposure to the world at large and, increasingly, her alienation from it. It also allows Serao the opportunity to create a microcosm of the lower social classes as she peoples the boarding house with the marginalized, the poor, and the desperate. Through thumbnail sketches of these diverse characters, Serao examines various female experiences. For example, one denizen of this microcosm is Concetta Guadagno, a young woman being "kept" by her jealous and abusive lover. Initially appalled by Concetta's immoral lifestyle, Suor Giovanna gradually discovers that both women share a dependence on others for financial support. A few months later, Concetta's lover leaves her for a more socially acceptable woman, dooming her to a life of prostitution, a profession ironically reflected by her last name, which translates as "I earn" or "earnings." If this minor episode warns women not to put too much faith in lovers, the alternative—marriage and motherhood—is equally destructive, at least as it is depicted in this narrative. Another neighbor, Maria Laterza, has just suffered through a near-fatal childbirth. After a brief period of recovery, she goes insane, her madness apparently linked to the childbirth. Here, too, the choice of names is telling, for that of "Maria" is typically evocative of the maternal. With these examples Serao confronts conventional narrative patterns in which women are enclosed, and usually happily so, within heterosexual relationships. For both Concetta and Maria, such relationships have led, directly or not, to ignominy and insanity. Does this suggest that in contrast, Suor Giovanna's displacement from the traditional narrative strategy frees her from these diverse but equally harrowing fates? Textual evidence supports this, for again, it is Suor Giovanna's forced engagement with the secular world that determines her downfall.

Serao emphasizes the dire consequences of Suor Giovanna's entrance into the secular world in the next section of the book, in which the character is no longer referred to by name, but only as "the woman," emphasizing that by this point, her identity has truly been obliterated. Bent and shapeless in her tattered clothes, she slowly makes her way to her squalid hostel, a "little lost figure, in that desert, in those shadows, in that so dangerous journey" (639). In the women's dormitory, which she shares with others, her sleep is interrupted by the arrival of the police searching for prostitutes. In a scene reminiscent of the earlier episode in the convent, another all-female space, the men, again government officials, interrogate the women, demanding to know their names. Suor Giovanna, humiliated by the callous treatment, refuses to answer at first, but finally whispers, "My name is Luisa Bevilacqua. And I've never had another name" (654). Sickened with her current situation, and crushed in spirit by years of squalor and heartache, she is determined nonetheless not to besmirch her religious name by mentioning it in this squalid environment.

The final scene takes place about twenty years after the closing of the convent, when Suor Giovanna's emotional demise is almost complete. The physical setting is again significant, for here Suor Giovanna is seen completely outside of any protective walls. Instead, she is unsheltered and alone, a telling metaphor for her spiritual and psychic isolation and fragmentation. In this scene, a large group of paupers has gathered outside a parish church for the complimentary Easter meal. Serao excels in contrasting the patronizing benefactors, dressed in frock coats or fancy gowns and dripping with jewelry, and the mass of destitute people, barely covered by dirty rags, their faces marked by "a profound apathy" (658). One of the patrons, a young woman genuinely moved by the sight of this human misery, attempts to talk to "an extremely old beggarwoman" (671). At the woman's insistence, Suor Giovanna briefly describes her fall from grace. She reveals her secular name, but remains silent each time she is asked her religious name. Pressed, she finally says, "My name was . . . my name was Sister Giovanna of the Cross" (674). At the memory of her religious life, Suor Giovanna begins to cry "the most bitter tears of her life . . ." (674).

In this work, Serao does more than dramatize a tragic social issue. The depiction of Suor Giovanna's transformation from a fully self-integrated woman to a broken, nameless creature serves as an affirmation of the cloistered life. Not all critics have read the text in this manner. Jeuland-Meynaud believes in the "tacit validation posited by the author between the taking of the veil and the suppression of oneself."[49] Certainly, in the story "Per monaca," which I will discuss shortly, joining a convent takes on tones analogous to a funeral rite. But in *Suor Giovanna della Croce*, the protagonist's decision to withdraw from the social world liberates her from traditional expectations of female behavior. She is not forced to assume one of the few roles available to women—that of wife, mother, or, as a last resort, whore. Indeed, all of these roles have been examined in this text and found wanting. Grazia's marriage was unhappy and apparently marked by episodes of infidelity; Maria's experience with childbirth renders her insane, and Concetta's tragic destiny is predetermined by her poverty and extramarital sexual experiences. Suor Giovanna escapes the expectations engendered by these roles, negotiating instead her own identity, an act she celebrates by renouncing her secular name for one more compatible with her new life.

Serao's vision of the cloistered life is more problematic in "Per monaca" (The Nun), another story found in *Il romanzo della fanciulla*.[50] In this text, the author does not endorse either marriage or the monastery, focusing instead on the importance of female friendship, as Ursula Fanning has pointed out in her illuminating study.[51] As in "Non più," "Per monaca" features an assembly of girls casting about for suitable mates. With minimal description, Serao succeeds in highlighting crucial details that capture the girls' personalities and create well-rounded characters. Tecla Brancaccio, with her "virile step"[52] and masculine clothing, displays a ferocious tenacity in the face of unrequited love; Giulia Capece, noble but impoverished, relies on her beauty to attract a husband and therefore salvage her family's social status; Angiolina Cantelmo, delicate and kind, belongs to a family cursed by two centuries of violent deaths; Anna Doria, at age thirty an old maid, defiantly sports a homemade concoction of garish rouge; Elfrida Kapnist, a Hungarian, provokes a trail of scandalous comments with her mysterious background and shocking behavior; and Eugenia d'Aragona, the illegitimate daughter of a duke and a seamstress, is adored by all for her goodness and simplicity but is doomed to die in childbirth. The vivid character portrayals in this opening scene validate Serao's reputation as a masterful creator of lifelike female personalities in her city of women. She carefully and lovingly creates characters that rarely lapse into caricature, realizing her intention, as stated in the introduction to this collection, to evoke faithfully the "phantoms" of her memory.[53]

The relationship between Eva Muscettola, the protagonist, and her friends is central to a narrative that on the surface hinges on the business of heterosexual couplings. One morning, during a gathering of their daily sewing circle, Eva and her friends discuss the recent engagement of the beautiful and wealthy Olga Bariatine to Massimo Daun, an inveterate gambler in desperate need of a rich wife. Olga's friends, although aware that financial concerns form the basis of this match, nonetheless congratulate her and wish her well. Olga has successfully contracted a marriage, and her status as wife will solidify her place in society. Only Eva seems disturbed by the news of the marriage, greeting Olga's entrance by whispering fervently in her ear, "God help you, God help you, dear, dear, dear ..." (56). The frantically repeated words betray both Eva's passionate friendship with Olga and her forebodings about the marriage. Eva's own love interest comes in the form of Innico Althan, a young naval officer and the brother of her friend Chiarina.

As the narrative progresses, female friendship takes on a significance that eclipses that of male-female relationships. As the young girls in this story move from the relative liberty of adolescence to the enclosure of marriage, they turn to one another for support and guidance. The bonds among these heroines suggest an emotional, secure space offering protection from the harsh realities a young woman encounters as she enters the adult world. These friendships, then, mediate the "double life" Serao discussed in her articulation of the tenets of realism. The validation of the ties between women, rather than those between men and women, becomes apparent in a scene in which Olga and Massimo are about to embark on their honeymoon. As the girls say a tearful goodbye to their friend, they are overwhelmed by "a sense of pain" (81). Olga, this "beautiful flower raised under the Neapolitan sun," is being thrown into the harsh world "without protection, without defense" (82). While Eva hugs Olga one last time, whispering words of love and comfort, Massimo calls dryly for his bride. "'Here I am,' she answer[ed], obeying" (82). The somber mood of this scene conveys an unusually strong condemnation of marriage. As Fanning points out, "Olga is clearly leaving behind a community of love and affection, and going into a partnership not of love, as one might expect, but of patriarchal domination."[54] Bonds among female friends are apparently stronger and less precarious than those between husband and wife.

Interestingly, the strength of the ties among the young female friends does not extend to those between mother and daughter. Defined by distinct roles within the family, the mother-daughter relationship seems tenuous at best and frought with rivalry between the two different cohorts.[55] This complex portrait illustrates Serao's skillful depiction of the complexity—and the difficulty—of female relationships within a patriarchal society. The feelings of insecurity, love, and even fear that bind together these young girls weaken as they become more engaged with the adult world, a world that sanctions the bonds of wedlock over all others. Eva herself falls victim to this competition, for her own mother betrays her with her fiancé.

Unlike Emma in the short story "Non più," Eva deliberately chooses the convent over spinsterhood. Although this decision means a return to the all-female society of her adolescence, the ritual taking of the vows is described in lugubrious tones. In fact, the ceremony is presented as a grotesque version of the traditional marriage rite, inverting the anticipated happy ending between Eva and Innico. A crowd of the city's elite gathers in the church of Santa Chiara to watch the ceremony. Eva, initially dressed in a sumptuous brocaded gown and carrying a bouquet of orange blossoms, is calm but not happy, "a supreme peace was depicted on that face. Peace: not serenity" (85–86). As this citation suggests, the intimations of marital ritual soon are supplanted by those reminiscent of a funeral. Eva, after changing into the somber, plain robes of a novice, kneels before the elderly abbess in order to have her long hair shorn. A black veil is then thrown over the cropped head, now grown small "like certain dead people" (90). Eva, after pronouncing her vows and bidding farewell to the earthly world, is laid out "like a corpse," hands crossed over her breast, and covered with a black shroud (91). The funeral bells peal solemnly as the nuns recite the prayers of the dead. As Eva is admitted into the cloistered world, her female friends bow their heads and cry.

If the depiction of marriage is negative in this story, the alternative is equally bleak. Although by joining a convent Eva is entering a spiritual sisterhood, she must tear herself away from her loving community of friends. According to Fanning, even though marriage is the ultimate goal of these young women, Serao presents them primarily in their relationships with their friends rather than with their lovers: "[Serao's] female friendships are invariably more successful than her heterosexual romantic relationships—

they always provide a source of strength and support for her women characters."[56] Fanning sees the act of entering a convent as the definitive illustration of the primacy of bonds among women. This is certainly a perceptive reading of a complex text, and clearly the loving presentation of female friendship points to its importance in Serao's depictions of female experiences in general. I would suggest, however, that the funereal overtones of the final scene negate the appeal of this alternative to wedlock. The emphasis on the death of Eva's vitality and the repeated comparisons of the ritual with a funeral ceremony, although a realistic depiction of this rite, indicate an emotional death, not a victory over stifling social roles. Whereas in *Suor Giovanna della Croce*, Serao endorses the traditional female role of nun, in "Per monaca" the ambiguous ending and the primacy of female friendship undermine the value of this very role. This story points to the many-layered readings possible with Serao's works, as she struggles with traditional literary and, by extension, social roles for women, and with her own evolving ideological positions.

Serao's willingness to question the limited choices available to women reveals an attention to female concerns not generally seen in other realist texts. In these last two works, Serao has created narratives that attempt to free female protagonists from an identity wholly based on their relationships to male characters. Despite this innovative approach, she does not go farther and articulate an alternative to these limited social choices, revealing, perhaps, her inability to postulate opportunities outside the structure of a patriarchal society. This dichotomy between provocative character analysis and ultimately frustrated female ambitions was not unusual among the women writers of turn-of-the-century Italy. Antonia Arslan, who has studied the rise of women intellectuals in Italy, believes the more established writers were often unwilling to criticize a literary and social world that had, after all, embraced them and their work. These authors, and Arslan singles out Serao among others, were "hesitant and uncertain about bringing into the theoretical arena the social and emancipatory consequences that would seem logical from the cases described in their narratives."[57] Breaking into the established, male intellectual world was quite an achievement; revolutionizing it was another step altogether, one few female authors were willing to attempt.

Serao's concern with the narrow sphere of a woman's life, both intellectually and socially, is manifested in her works that depict protagonists outside traditional female spaces. In "Scuola normale feminile" *(sic)* (Normal School for Women), Serao portrays a group of girls training for teaching jobs, and young women already in the workforce are the focus of "Telegrafi dello stato" (State Telegraphists). These two short stories, found in *Il romanzo della fanciulla,* are generally cited as being among the most accomplished and illuminating of Serao's realist works. It is significant, then, that these two texts are also among the most autobiographical of her fictional works. Serao did attend a Normal School, a type of professional training school, usually for teachers, after which she worked as a telegraph operator from 1876 to 1878 while she was launching her journalistic and literary career. She apparently modeled the character Caterina Borrelli (found in both stories) after herself, and throughout her life frequently signed her personal letters "Caterina" or "Caterinella."[58] The relationship between Serao's life and its manifestation in her texts is the work of literary biographers and not the subject of this study. However, the implications of semiautobiographical writings in a woman's *oeuvre* cannot be ignored. This issue gains resonance in a discussion of Serao's realist texts, as autobiographical elements reinforce the author's symbiotic relationship with her heroines. This is not to say that male realist writers did not on occasion include such material in their works. In Serao's texts, however, the author insists on this recuperation of lived experience, broadening the definition of *verismo* to include works that fuse the "real" with the "lived," the objective description with the subjective remembrance.

These two stories are examined primarily through the lens of criticism of the *Bildungsroman,* or novel of development. A growing body of work focusing on this genre has generated interest in the differences in the social and intellectual development of the genders as they are depicted in literature. The traditional definition of the *Bildungsroman* emphasizes the young (male) protagonist's integration into the adult world after a series of experiences that serve to resolve the conflict between autonomy and social expectations.[59] The female version of the *Bildungsroman* is problematized by the protagonist's confinement to the domestic sphere. Unable to venture out into society, she misses a fundamental step in the developmental process. Indeed, some critics question whether the term *Bildungsroman* can even be applied to female-authored texts written before the rise of the modern feminist novel in the 1970s.[60] However, feminist and cultural scholars, in their efforts to reevaluate traditional literary tenets and national canons, offer a valuable framework within which it is possible to address these texts. Such scholars view the female *Bildungsroman* as an effective vehicle for discussing the heroine's negotiation of socially prescribed roles.[61] Serao's work fits well within the purview of these recent studies, for although the two short stories I examine do not fully trace the protagonist's development from adolescence to adulthood, together their representation of a young girl's negotiation of restrictive social forces merits inclusion in a discussion of the *Bildungsroman*.[62]

In her presentation of the female context of development, Serao begins with the same settings with which she opens many of her other realist works: a depiction of an all-female space. "Scuola normale feminile" centers on thirty-one students as they approach the end of their academic training and prepare to enter the world of teaching.[63] Throughout the narrative, these young women manifest their contempt for a stifling school system that seems determined to direct them toward prescribed patterns of feminine behavior. An interesting example of the students' disdain for authority is set in an atmosphere charged with the intense feelings and passions shared by these young women. As the school bell summons both day students and boarders to class, the girls gather in the corridors, many ignoring the injunction to sing the morning hymn, a preachy ode to God and country. An even greater transgression is being committed, however; despite the rule forbidding friendships between boarders and day students, the girls take advantage of the bustle before classes to arrange trysts and chatter flirtatiously with each other. The characterization of these friendships is astonishingly similar to depictions of heterosexual relationships: "[D]ay students and boarders were united in couples, in groups, so attached that no punishment could break them up; in fact it was because of this that fervent friendships bordering on passion were established . . . ."[64]

For its weighty detail and significance within the story, the passage describing the individual relationships deserves to be cited in full. While the bored and indifferent singers continue to hum along with the hymn,

> one could clearly see the impassioned stare that Amelia Bozzo, a first-year boarder, a thin brunette with green eyes, fixed on Caterina Bor-

relli . . . she of the myopic lenses that gave her a half ironic and half haughty air; and Caterina Borrelli twisted in her fingers a wilted rose that Amelia Bozzo had given her, three days earlier. Gabriella Defeo . . . with a show of airs turned her back to Carolina Mazza . . . with whom she had fought the day before. . . . Artemisia Jaquinangelo, with her hair cut short like a man, with her masculine face, was not singing . . . because Giuditta Pezza . . . no longer loved her; Giuditta Pezzo smiled at Maria Donnarumma, but in vain; Maria Donnarumma tried vainly to discover if Annina Casale had found letters for her in the mail; . . . from hand to hand passed a small bottle of scent that Clotilde Marasca had bought for Alessandrina Fraccacreta, the sentimental and flirtatious brunette. (148–149)

The metonymic symbols of these relationships mirror those of typical heterosexual couplings: love letters, gifts of perfume and flowers, petty jealousies and tiffs. Each couple embodies clearly delineated gender roles, from Artemisia and Caterina, both assertive and decidedly unladylike, to Gabriella and Alessandrina, models of femininity. The tight circle of female friends depicted in "Per monaca" has evolved in this text into separate and distinct couples. Intimate friendships, called "flames," were not unusual in all-girls' schools in postunification Italy, historian Michela De Giorgio notes, although often these relationships were viewed with suspicion by school officials and religious leaders, who feared the girls would be led to "impure" acts. However, the great majority of these relationships were apparently of an "unconscious homosexuality" and involved little or no sexual experimentation.[65]

How, then, should Serao's emphasis on intimate female friendship be read in this short story? Should her insistence on strict gender demarcations be privileged, an interpretation that, in turn, suggests that these young women are merely mimicking sexual relationships in preparation for their impending relocation to the world outside school walls? Or does the author's startling emphasis on *female* friendship imply a criticism of heterosexual relationships in general? As always with Serao's more sophisticated and better-executed works, textual evidence supports both interpretations. Perhaps more important than choosing one reading over another is recognizing Serao's desire to question conventional depictions of female protagonists and acknowledging her ability to create complex "realist" heroines who are not defined merely in relation to the male hero.

The setting of this story allows Serao to challenge traditional notions of an inherently deficient and pliant feminine intellect, beliefs inspired in part by the pseudoscientific ideology of positivism.[66] This ideology, examined in greater detail in the following chapters, helped in part to relegate women to the domestic sphere by linking their social roles to alleged intellectual weaknesses. Serao questions this premise in this short story, for in preparation for their teaching licenses, the girls must take courses in mathematics, linguistics, grammar, geography, physics, geometry, religion, French, penmanship, and the domestic arts. Some of the girls excel in their studies; others flounder. They must learn their lessons by rote and few venture to openly denounce the daunting system. Only Caterina Borrelli, an intelligent, energetic student, dares to question a professor. Called upon to recite the day's linguistics lesson, she announces serenely that she has not learned it. When asked why, she responds, "Because I'm not a parrot, trained to learn a passage of Passavanti by heart" (156). The professor marks a zero next to her name, reminding himself to discuss her attitude with the director. This brief scene not only portrays an antiquated and ineffectual educational system, but also underlines the frustration of a young girl punished for trying to use her intellect. The incident illustrates a common episode in the female novel of development, one in which the heroine finds herself frustrated in her attempts to be independent and autonomous. Frequently, these attempts are met with a forced return to the domestic sphere.[67]

Serao sets up a dichotomy between the acquisition of domestic skills and the study of more erudite material in a scene describing the students' daily sewing lesson. Ignoring the needlework at hand, the girls instead take advantage of the instructor's leniency to work on other lessons or to write notes to each other. On this particular afternoon, however, they are interrupted by the arrival of two women, "a hunchbacked, old maid of a countess and a pedantic marquise," who "inspect" sewing classes at local schools for poor girls (167). Horrified to find the students engaged in their academic studies, the marquise accuses the girls of wanting to become "too intelligent" (167). Criticizing the various needles and yarns employed by the students, the inspectors complain huffily that the students are not giving enough attention to "the importance of woman's work" (168). The students are thwarted by a system that places a higher priority on the development of traditional female skills than on intellectual proficiency, a system endorsed not only by their male professors but also by those upper-class women whose position relies on maintaining the status quo.

Given the dismal working conditions for female teachers in late nineteenth-century Italy, it is not surprising to learn of the fate Serao has penned for her pupils. She picks up the story three years after the girls have finished their training, describing in terse but eloquent terms what has happened to them. Many are living in wretched conditions, teaching overcrowded classes for long hours at a miserable stipend. Some are dead—of overwork, of illness, of poverty, or by their own hand. A few are married. Caterina Borrelli and Annina Casale, still together, work for the state telegraph office, and their story will be resumed in the following narrative. Only Isabella Diaz, a student marked by an incredibly hideous appearance, has found a satisfying teaching position as director of the biggest school in Naples. She has won prizes for her innovative teaching methods, and, the narrative continues, has decided to abolish the "old punitive methods" (185).

Serao's portrayal of stifled female intelligence realizes its foreseen conclusion in the short descriptions recounting the destinies of these young women. The author denounces the restrictive education system for squelching rather than fostering eager minds and exuberant spirits. Within the genre of the *Bildungsroman*, the importance of education in the protagonist's development, whether it is formal schooling or self-education, cannot be overemphasized. In "Scuola normale feminile," education fails to prepare these young girls adequately for the rigors of the teaching profession, but it does inculcate in them an awareness of the limitations they will face as a result of their gender. These limitations come not just from external forces, however, but also from their own acceptance of the ideal of femininity and traditional female destiny. That is why, I believe, Serao has insisted on emphasizing the intimate relationships in this all-female institution. The girls are unconsciously mimicking expected female behavior; that is, the coupling that will resolve into the marriage plot. They must do this in order to enter the adult world successfully and avoid the fragmentation and frustration that torment so many young girls in their efforts to steer through the rocky shoals of female development. Only the grotesque Isabella Diaz, whose inhuman appearance situates her in a category beyond gender,[68] can ignore societal expectations and negotiate a space within the public sphere. Serao's depiction of intelligent, interested heroines is confounded by this character who becomes successful, the author appears to imply, only because she is so far removed from the societal image of beauty and femininity.

The twin themes of female socialization and women in the workforce, both illustrated in "Scuola normale feminile," are examined in greater depth in the story "Telegrafi dello stato," which features a cast of young women employed at the telegraph office in Naples. This realist narrative is again marked by the author's empathy for her subject. Indeed, Laura Gropallo, noting the symbiotic bonds linking Serao with her subject matter, writes that the author chose the topic of telegraph workers "with all the tenderness and affection that one brings to old memories."[69] Serao flouts the conventional realist doctrine that calls for an objective text, preferring to create a document reflecting not only her concerns but her memories as well.

The connection between the two short stories is underscored by the reappearance of two central characters. Caterina Borrelli and Annina Casale (here inexplicably renamed Annina Pescara) are together again; indeed, Caterina is described as Annina's "indivisible friend."[70] However, despite the all-female setting and the close bonds evident among many of the characters, the emphasis in this narrative is on more traditional heterosexual relationships. Adelina Markò loves a clerk in the same office; Peppina Sanna desperately misses her young sailor; Maria Morra waits patiently for her fiancé to earn enough money to support a wife; and Giulietta Scarano pines for a man she is forbidden to see. These young women have become traditional literary heroines, engrossed with the marriage plot even while out in the working world.

That the working world is at the heart of this story is clear from the thoughtfulness with which Serao addresses the subject. The author succeeds in documenting the dismal and often demeaning conditions under which these women were expected to work. Knowing that Serao herself worked in such an office makes the depiction both poignant and trenchant. In this short story, the female protagonists work furiously for long hours, reaching the end of the day with only enough energy to collapse into bed. Their meager salary is reduced if they are sick or late. They must work holidays, with no extra pay. As one of the characters laments,

"They give us eighty-five lire at the end of the month? And all this work? Nothing, nothing, this is slavery" (26). Yet despite their sense of exploitation, all the employees volunteer to work extra hours on election day. Only Maria Vitale, bedridden with a severe case of bronchitis, misses the day of extra service.

The tale ends with the same melancholic hue that colors the entire narrative, emphasizing the social isolation and general despair of these young working women. It is autumn once again, a full year since the story began. Bad weather has downed telegraph lines across the country, and the workers are left increasingly stranded as one after another correspondent fails to respond to their calls. In the midst of a rather melodramatic thunderstorm, they discover that their office is now completely cut off: "Naples was isolated: the [telegraph] keys, the machines, the insulators seemed struck by a sudden death: the current was dead" (48). Just at this moment, the female director returns from Maria Vitale's funeral. This backdrop of death and isolation symbolizes the situation of these young women, who are excluded, and even prohibited, from active participation in the social world.

Serao's affectionate, if grim, depiction of working heroines, a bold choice at a time when most female characters minded the home and not the store, illustrates the obstacles facing women in the workforce. Here, as at the Scuola Normale, the protagonists are expected to obey unconditionally the patriarchal voice of male authority. In this text, it is the office director, the sole male voice in the story, who acts in this capacity. Interestingly, he uses his position of authority to distance himself from the all-female group of employees, preferring that they filter their requests through the intermediacy of the departmental manager rather than address him directly. These young heroines, then, are stymied in their attempts to assert their autonomy or independence. Awakened to the limits of their position in society, their quest for self-definition leads inevitably to the marriage plot. Indeed, the majority of characters in "Telegrafi dello stato" are more concerned with finding a way *back* to the security of the domestic sphere than they are with escaping from it. Underlying the pride they take in their work is an unstated fear of ending up unmarried and alone, still working in that cramped and dark office.

One character, however, seems eager to choose another path, her story contrasting sharply with those of her cohorts. Throughout the narrative Caterina has held herself apart from her coworkers. Untouched and even derisive of the muted atmosphere of romantic love that has so moved her friends, Caterina prefers instead to busy herself in her free time with writing a novel in her notebook. Her constant scribbling (it is to be noted that this is the character apparently based on Matilde Serao herself) and her fervent scorn for all matters of the heart, signal her resistance to traditional expectations. She wants to write her own story, a narrative that perhaps does not leave her enclosed within the domestic sphere. As was the case with Isabella Diaz in "Scuola normale feminile," Caterina in this story must ignore conventional expectations regarding a woman's sentimental aspirations in order to fulfill her intellectual ambitions. Certainly, a satisfying career and an equally fulfilling personal life seem at odds in this narrative. Tellingly, even the female office director has been stripped of her femininity. Her face has "the ivory pallor of thirty-year-old spinsters living in a . . . convent, in a natural chastity of both temperament and imagination" (16). Professional or intellectual ambitions are incompatible with a protagonist's sexuality, resulting in a splintered identity.

Whether Serao is questioning or accepting social reality with this theme, an issue complicated by the rich textual evidence supporting both interpretations, needs further exploration. More important for this study, however, is Serao's portrayal in both these stories of the heroines' (sometimes reluctant) acceptance of social expectations. Despite Caterina's attempts in both stories to articulate and satisfy her own desires, there are few rebellions. The protagonists in these mini-*Bildungsromane,* therefore, are unable to develop, manifesting a stunted maturation, a type of "growing down," rather than the growing up found in the male *Bildungsroman.*[71] Social expectations of feminine behavior, that is, the insistence on surrendering intellectual and professional ambitions to conform to more conventional roles, succeed in thwarting a young woman's development and result in a fractured sense of identity.

This portrayal of the bleak world of female telegraph workers is echoed in a newspaper article of Serao's that addresses the same topic. As with the short story, this 7 December 1886 article entitled "Le telegrafiste" examines the physical and mental hardships of this grueling and poorly compensated work.[72] The primary focus of my study is Serao's fictive output, but two elements found in this piece of journalism are especially relevant to an understanding of her literary production in general. The first element is the author's own involvement with the subject, for the article is threaded throughout with her own interjections, primarily in the form of "I remember. . . ." By weaving her own memories into the text, Serao creates a journalistic piece that exhibits her own objectives in realist fiction—relived, personal experiences. The author's stylistic manipulation of the realist text, then, is mirrored in this particular essay which, it must be noted, is devoted to exploring a specifically female experience.

The second element that links this article with the short story "Telegrafi dello stato" is the similarity between the resolutions of both texts. Both conclude with the deaths of female protagonists; Maria Vitale dies in the short story, and a brief description of the deaths of three young girls, the victims of consumption, anemia, and tuberculosis, serves as the conclusion to the article. This unsalutary setting clearly precludes any alternative resolution for the narratives of these women in either the short story or the article. Here, the author's own experience as a telegraph operator and her generally pessimistic presentation of the social and economic opportunities available to women join in what can be viewed as a single extended narrative, one presented as fiction and the other as fact.

The little-known short story "Nicoletta" (Nicoletta) is perhaps Serao's most poignant illustration of the difficulties inherent in achieving successful social development and at the same time, on a more stylistic level, it embodies her vision of the objectives of the realist text. The extremely brief tale reads as a telescoped *Bildungsroman*, following the female protagonist from infancy to death. Just as with *Suor Giovanna della Croce,* in "Nicoletta" Serao prefaces her tale with a warning to her public, alerting the readers to the unassuming (and therefore potentially unappealing) subject of her text. The authorial intervention comes within the text of the short story, however, rather than being set apart in a formal preface. This strategy serves to bridge the distance between author and heroine and, more obviously, between author and reader. In these introductory remarks, Serao cautions the reader that this narrative "is very far from being a short story, a novel, a drama, a comedy or a farce: it is the simple story of an obscure destiny."[73] "Nicoletta" is one of the rare texts in which Serao uses a first-person narrator, although only in the opening paragraph. The author claims to have found in her notebook the bare bones of this story: "the name of Nicoletta, two dates, an exclamation point, a badly designed heart, and three or four words that made no sense" (67). The author must decipher her own hieroglyphics, scribbled years before, in her youth. "[T]hen," she continues, "I got my bearings and Nicoletta's story renewed itself in my *memory*" (67; emphasis added). The use of the first-person narrative to introduce the story humanizes it, taking it from the realm of pure reportage and moving it closer to Serao's personal vision of realism. It also emphasizes the interconnection between Serao's experiences as a journalist and as an author, as already discussed in the examination of her article and short story examining female telegraph operators. Throughout her career, she did not favor one aspect of her writing over another, perhaps recognizing the importance of the influence of her journalistic training and background on her literary production and their shared stylistic and thematic characteristics. In this story, the two styles do merge, creating a superb example of a "realistic" text.

The terse, almost telegraphic style of this story emphasizes Serao's generally pessimistic view of the opportunities for female growth and development. Like "Scuola normale feminile" and "Telegrafi dello stato," this is a story of dashed hopes and thwarted dreams. Here, though, Serao has focused on an impoverished protagonist rather than the middle-class heroines of the previous tales. Again, the author makes clear that in her fictional metropolis, the frustrations faced by her female characters know no class boundaries. In this tale, Nicoletta comes from the dregs of Neapolitan society; her mother toils in a tobacco factory, her father has long since disappeared. Sent to serve as an apprentice to a seamstress, she is instead exploited as a servant. After six years of hard work, and without a single sewing lesson, Nicoletta decides to leave the seamstress and make her own way as a servant. But her first position does not last long; the mistress of the house, jealous of Nicoletta's youth and suspicious of her proximity, fires her. Hired by a woman who entertains a procession of lovers, Nicoletta "saw and heard horrible things; her nascent youth was defeated by apathy, by ceaseless work that beat her down" (72).

Following the expectations of a society that prescribes predetermined roles for women, Nicoletta marries a coachman, but the marriage fails to provide the security and material relief she seeks. Serao again overturns the myth of matrimonial bliss, pointing out instead both its physical and psychic dangers. Giovanni, Nicoletta's husband, is a drunk and a gambler, and a week after their wedding, she is back at work. She works even when pregnant, and is allowed only three days leave after each childbirth. Life with Giovanni becomes more and more brutal. He beats her regularly, usually on Saturday night, after losing the lottery. One cold winter, when Nicoletta is forty, she contracts a bad cough. The rest of her tale is summed up briefly:

> The children earned little, barely eking out a living, but they dragged along; the husband drank, played the lottery, and was the worst hackney cab driver in Naples. Nicoletta was diagnosed with pneumonia in February. She died at the Hospital of the Incurables, after four days of delirium. (74)

Nicoletta's story is one of the few from Serao's pen that follows a female protagonist through the cycle of life. The brief but haunting narrative dispassionately delineates the obstacles and hardships a woman faces throughout her life, from a restricted education, to low-paying work, to an abusive husband, to, finally, a piteous death. Like the protagonists in "Scuola normale feminile" and "Telegrafi dello stato," Nicoletta must learn to grow down, to curb her own aspirations in order to conform to the more restrictive societal expectations. Again, Serao's use of her own interpretation of the realist framework to present women-centered narratives ends in implicating the very social structure of turn-of-the-century Italy.

It seems appropriate to conclude this chapter with "Il ventre di Napoli," a text that combines Serao's gift for detailed observation with her concern for exposing social conditions for women. This text is a piece of Serao's journalism, but because of its affinities with the author's realist works it deserves inclusion in this study. Once again, I would emphasize that throughout her career, and with her vast fictive and nonfictive production, Serao consistently confounds attempts to categorize her texts by either genre or period. Recognizing this, it is important to approach her work as an organic whole rather than as a series of disengaged parts.

The text "Il ventre di Napoli" can be read as a direct ancestor of the short story "Nicoletta," for both address the role and destiny of women in a world that ignores them and limits their opportunities. The 1884 investigative report was written after a devastating cholera epidemic had ravaged Naples. Serao addressed it directly to Prime Minister Agostino Depretis, who after touring the city, allegedly declared, "Bisogna sventrare Napoli," or, "Naples must be gutted." Certainly Naples and the rest of southern Italy lagged behind much of northern Italy, which enjoyed the economic growth, social progress, and industrialization brought by the new century. The cholera epidemic only underlined the poverty and misery of Naples, especially relative to northern cities.

But despite the economic and social problems facing Naples, Serao recognized and celebrated the city's vitality and beauty. She demonstrated her own intimate knowledge of the city, using the forum of this series of articles to take Depretis and her readers behind the scenes. Serao ignores the tourist sights to explore the neighborhoods mired in poverty and despair: "There is an Alley of the Sun, called that because the sun never enters. . . ."[74] She warns against accepting the people and sights of Naples at face value, asking her readers instead to examine the social and economic factors that have brought them to this state. She points out in particular the working- and lower-class women, whose bodies have been destroyed by numbing jobs, countless pregnancies, scarcity of food, and the lack of hope. "They are ugly, it's true: they don't take care of themselves, it's very true: they disgust, sometimes," Serao writes. But she entreats her readers to look beyond this external facade, asking them "to enter into the secret of those lives, which are odes to daily martyrdom, to incalculable sacrifices, to burdens endured without a murmur" (132). The author moves easily from general descriptions of hardship and misery to more personal and specific portrayals of women she has known while living and working in the city.[75]

This text becomes critical for an examination of Serao's *oeuvre*, for it reveals the foundation of her own realism, which comes alive in its depiction of various heroines, as well as her lifelong interest in exploring different female experiences. Indeed, many of Serao's stories are rooted in the Naples she depicts in this journalistic work, from the "thin and pallid people" (126) living near the tobacco factory in "Nicoletta" to the mania for the lottery and the cancer of usury, primary themes in her novel *Il paese di cuccagna* (The Land of the Cockayne) and in numerous short stories. A fine example of sociological journalism, these essays highlight the miserable conditions faced by workers, particularly women, such as servants, washerwomen, and hairdressers; again, these characters appear in many of Serao's novels and short stories. Although Serao used Rome, Venice, or even rural locales as settings for several of her works, she felt most comfortable describing her beloved Naples, and this city became the principal backdrop for her texts.

Using this urban environment to set the scene, Serao was able to portray vividly the spectrum of social classes, from the impoverished Nicoletta to the bourgeois young women of "Non più," to the upper-class women of her romance texts. But although Serao certainly recognized and examined class structure, her repeated emphasis on the gendered expectations of women tends to efface social and economic differences. This becomes apparent in the intriguing final chapter of "Il ventre di Napoli." In this section, Serao paints a portrait of a city that must draw upon its own resources to resolve its social problems, rather than on the government in Rome. Interestingly, it is the women of Naples who step in to fill this void, demonstrating a degree of female solidarity and autonomy not seen in Serao's fictive works. In this chapter, the author describes an informal but loving network of women helping each other share the burden of poverty, ignorance, and social injustice. These women watch over each other's children, even going so far as to breastfeed a friend's baby when no other milk is available. They adopt children from the overcrowded orphanages, caring for them as if they were their own. They share medicine and food so that no one, no matter how destitute, ever goes hungry or remains ill. In short, these women act as the social conscience of the city, a feminine relief force committed to ameliorating the lives of the poor and needy.

"Il ventre di Napoli" illustrates definitively Serao's own rendition of *verismo*, one that clearly repudiates the principle of authorial objectivity. In fact, the author's interjections become an important strategy for the validation of her subject matter. Serao frequently introduces a description of a washerwoman or servant girl by saying "I remember" or "I knew her." The author's memories serve as a basis for her investigative report, pointing again to the importance to her work of lived experience. Indeed, Serao's rejection of the tenet of objectivity, so central to realist doctrine, allows space for the author's "passionate engagement" with her texts, as Darby Tench writes. "[Serao] is not 'other' to reality, but rather *in* reality, a part of the metonymical chain."[76] Serao's realism does not stop at reproducing or relating the lives of her characters; it reanimates and re-presents those lives in the light of a gender-based perspective. By doing so, she revises the genre of realism itself. The revision of a literary genre was often an opportunity for women writers to work within the male-dominated field of literary criticism and production while articulating their own narrative strategy and objectives. Female authors often manipulate literary forms as a means of self-expression. These writers must negotiate the barriers between their own desires to express their autonomy and the established literary models that act "as a brake on their creativity, their authenticity, their experimentation."[77] Certainly Serao's reworking of traditional genres allows both freedom from established literary standards and an opportunity to create a more personalized framework for her narratives.

In her texts, Serao articulates a vision of female existence not explored in other, male-authored realist narratives. Throughout these works, Serao has been faithful to the "internal drama" of her heroines, tracing their often thwarted development in the face of stifling social strictures. Reappropriating the metaphor of the fictive city of women serves to illustrate how Serao peoples her works with a vast array of female characters and their corresponding life experiences. In her realist works, Serao's metropolis is inhabited by women who work and those who remain at home; wives, mothers, and spinsters; the young and the old. Some heroines choose to enter an all-female religious environment; others rely on their friendships with other women for support and guidance in a world often blind or censorious to their psychic development. The work "Il ventre di Napoli" stands, to some degree, for all of Serao's realist narratives. In this remarkable text, Serao conflates the plight of her heroines with the fate of her beloved city, both realistically and metaphorically. The political isolation faced by Naples mirrors the personal and intellectual seclusion the author's heroines must confront in their attempt to negotiate the restrictive norms of the wider social world. Serao's realist texts, then, situate her heroines within the "cityscape" of turn-of-the-century Italy, revealing in turn the cultural and social expectations shaping their dreams and molding their lives.

2
Romantic Interlude

Matilde Serao's lifelong interest in transcribing female experience engendered a revisionary approach to her *"romanzi d'amore,"* or sentimental love narratives. By reimagining the romance, the author was able to raise a set of concerns distinct from but not divorced from her realist works. To employ again the metaphor of a literary city of women, the heroines inhabiting Serao's fictional metropolis are primarily, and fundamentally, wives and lovers. These women, representatives of classic romance fiction, appear to be defined solely within the parameters of a heterosexual relationship. But the probing social critiques embedded in Serao's work point to more provocative readings of these texts. Beneath the surface of Serao's metaphorical metropolis lies a powerful substructure that often subverts literary conventions. The heterosexual relationships portrayed in her works, for example, often threaten to destroy the female characters, as the male protagonists attempt to refashion them in the mold of patriarchal ideals of femininity. Trapped in a restricted world, the heroines' struggles to reclaim their own sense of identity is often violent and self-destructive.

In these romance works, Serao continues her exploration of the intersection of female sexuality and female destiny, a theme touched on in her realist texts. The analysis of female sexuality leads naturally to an exploration of female desire, embodied by Serao and other late-nineteenth-century authors in the figure of the *femme fatale*. By incorporating this character type into her cast of characters and by offering her a dispassionate hearing Serao broadens the boundaries of acceptable female behavior and implicitly criticizes the cultural discourse shaping this construct.

An examination of Serao's texts becomes especially appropriate in light of the ongoing polemic concerning the literary significance of the romance narrative. Modern critics are widely divided over the value and relevance of the romance genre, with some deriding it as simplistic and reactionary, and others reading in it the potential for subversive and innovative observation. In Serao's case, both interpretations are possible, for one must recognize the contradictions inherent in much of her work; that is, the fundamental conservatism underpinning her texts, an ideology broken on occasion by breathtaking examples of stylistic and thematic invention. Keeping this in mind, I have focused on the convergence of Serao's realist and romance narratives and their shared reflection of a woman's role in turn-of-the-century Italy.[1]

The innovative qualities of Serao's revision of the romance text are even more significant when placed in historical context. As with other modern literary models and genres, Italy came late to this tradition. The lack of a national language and the relatively late political and geographical unification of the country did much to hinder the growth of popular literature. Indeed, many forms of popular literature, such as the historical novel, were imported from France and England. Only a few Italian authors were both successful and prolific in this field, including Francesco Mastriani (1819–1891), who wrote immensely popular *"romanzi d'appendice,"* a form based on the French *feuilleton,* or serialized novel.[2] Mastriani, known today primarily for the 1869–1870 novel *I Misteri di Napoli* (The Mysteries of Naples)—the title inspired by Eugène Sue's 1843–1844 opus *Les Mystères de Paris* (The Mysteries of Paris)—shared with Serao a symbiotic relationship with the city of Naples and a facility in capturing its essence through the use of realistic settings and characters.[3]

As was the case with many authors throughout Europe at that time, most of Serao's early works were published first in installments in newspapers before being reissued as books. The extremely accessible format of the serialized narrative facilitated the process of generating a loyal reading public, an audience that came increasingly from the middle classes. In fact, Antonio Gramsci hailed the serialized novel as a means of stimulating the imagination of the less learned classes, and he was one of the first critics to discuss, albeit briefly, the varying, gender-oriented reactions to popular literature, reporting its success with female readers, especially young girls.[4] Other critics have delved more deeply into the implications of gendered differences in both writing and reading the romance. I emphasize this point to underline again the relationship between literary production by women and its critical reception. How was the connection between female authors and the romance narrative viewed by a traditional, male-dominated literary establishment? Suzanne Clark links the romance's critical devaluation implicitly to the genre's popularity with women writers. Women were believed to have an innate affinity with the genre, which therefore removed it from the more pragmatic (and critically acceptable) realm of realist literature: "[W]omen writers were entangled in sensibility, were romantic and sentimental by nature, and so even the best might not altogether escape this romantic indulgence in emotion and sublimity."[5] Even the term "sentimental," once used as a term of approbation for eighteenth-century romance narratives, eventually acquired negative connotations, a semiotic transformation Clark calls both deliberate and persistent: "The disparagement has served, indeed, to repress the fact that writing women were beginning to dominate the history of writing and that their domination was far from being a sign of escapism."[6] Clark was writing specifically about the tradition in the United States and England, but I believe an equivalent situation existed in turn-of-the-century Italy.

The devaluation of the romance text has recently been questioned by critics who see in it potential for revolutionary revisions. Romances, long thought to describe and defend the traditional social order, can instead be read as socially political texts. Fredric Jameson, for example, writes that romances reflect the desires of marginalized groups oppressed by gender or ethnic heritage.[7] Feminist critics have reclaimed many of these texts, recognizing a forum that describes uniquely feminine experiences in an idiom accessible to all readers.[8] Even the Harlequin romance and the soap opera, derided by many as formulaic fodder for bored housewives, may offer alternative and subversive readings.[9] Clearly, the once denigrated romance narrative needs to be reread in light of these new and diverse interpretations.

Several of these innovative approaches help to locate Serao within the tradition of the romance narrative. A valuable critical strategy is found in Diane Elam's *Romancing the Postmodern,* an analysis of the romance text and postmodernism. This study of Serao's works is not concerned specifically with postmodern texts or tenets, but Elam's comments on the romance genre are illuminating. She recognizes the instability of generic categories, pointing out that the line between romance and realism is often blurred, as characteristics of each genre regularly cross over into the other. Romance itself is an elusive category, confounding generic conventions with each new text. In a definition recalling Jameson's notion, Elam sees the revolutionary potential of the romance:

> Romance may also act as the site of a struggle with the politics of the representable, as locus for the articulation of cultural groups that are not simply minorities within a homogeneous field, a small percentage of that population, but are radically excluded from the representable population, *a priori*.[10]

While Jameson focuses primarily on groups marginalized by political or ethnic makeup, however, Elam points to the romance narrative as a vehicle especially suitable for gendered responses to traditional literary discourses. It comes as no surprise, then, that she identifies the romance as "*the* female genre."[11]

Elam's main points—the elusiveness of fixed generic conventions and the romance's focus on female desire—are instrumental in an examination of Serao's texts. Certainly Serao's romances, many of which were written after the demise of the *movimento verista,* borrow heavily from her schooling in realist techniques. Even texts featuring upper-class protagonists and *milieux* contain elements of realism in their meticulous descriptions of settings, characters, and social customs. In an indication of the author's fluid approach to genre, Serao was one of the few writers who moved easily and often between the different stylistic demands of "high" and "low" literature; that is, canonically approved texts and more popular literary fare.

In order to distinguish, then, Serao's romance works from the rest of her literary production, it is necessary to set up a broad two-part definition, a stratagem that acknowledges the difficulty of classifying texts by genre and recognizes the complexity and internarrativity of her work as a whole. First, Serao's romances are marked by a change of cast, as it were, as they typically feature only one or two female protagonists, rather than the ensemble casts found in so many of her realist works. Male characters, often paired with the female protagonist, play a more visible role in these texts. The second characteristic of Serao's romance texts is perhaps an obvious one: the primacy of love in the narrative. While heterosexual coupling remains a dominant theme in her realist works, other issues, such as the importance of female friendship or the difficulties faced by working women, often complicate the "love story." In Serao's romances, the love story is central.

This chapter continues an exploration of female experiences in Serao's works, here defined almost exclusively in light of the relationship with a male partner. Along with this examination of female destiny, the chapter analyzes the articulation of female desire. Contemporary critics were uncomfortable with this subject, attacking many of Serao's texts not only for literary shortcomings but also for their alleged indecency.[12] Indeed, critics frequently were unable to distinguish between the artistic merits of a work and its moral content. Anthony M. Gisolfi has discovered that at least one contemporary translator even rewrote Serao's more suggestive passages, toning down or deleting references to the female body and female sexuality to avoid offending (or perhaps arousing) the sensibilities of impressionable readers. According to Gisolfi, these alterations "do not detract in any way from the merit of a translation that has caught the spirit and the poetry of Serao's writing."[13] But he has not recognized that this act of censoring Serao's texts effectively silenced her depiction of female protagonists and their experiences, especially the manifestation of their sexuality.

Other Italian women authors were also exploring the issues of female destiny and desire through the forum of the serialized romance text. Carolina Invernizio, and Liala, for example, were both immensely popular and prolific. Invernizio (1851–1916) wrote roughly 130 novels, most adventure-filled romances and period novels with strong moral overtones. Liala, pen name of Amalia-Liana Cambiasi Negretti (1897–1995), continued the tradition begun in part by Serao and Invernizio, creating narratives that featured young women and their amorous involvements. These authors are generally considered the leading exponents of an emerging category of romance narrative, the *romanzi rosa,* which corresponds loosely to the Harlequin romance.[14] Because of the perception that the *romanzo rosa* suffers from a "monotony, schematism, and repetition of content and language" the genre has long been ignored or denigrated.[15] Modern critics, however, especially those working in feminist and cultural studies, have begun to revive these texts as a means of analyzing the construction of femininity in a patriarchal society. Serao's romance texts, more linguistically sophisticated and better crafted than those of Liala and Invernizio, examine a number of fundamental issues addressed by other contemporary women writers, including suicide, adultery, and sexuality. Looking beyond the fascinating facade of costume and custom in these novels, the discerning reader discovers a serious attempt to create a more profound and perceptive starting point from which to address cultural debates concerning women.

Serao's innovative reworking of the romance text reveals how even a purely stylistic interpretation creates a space for subversive readings. The author often used the romance as a forum to explore nonconventional resolutions for her female protagonists. Her articulation of female destiny, for example, frequently subverts more traditional portrayals of the fate scripted for many heroines. Many nineteenth-century romance narratives conclude with a description of the female protagonist's marriage or death. A heroine who successfully negotiates the minefield of socially prescribed female behavior is "rewarded" by a legally sanctioned relationship. Female protagonists who act inappropriately, however, such as by expressing their sexuality outside of the marriage bond, are punished by death. But some women authors often "write beyond the ending," refusing to penalize their protagonists for their sexual activity.[16] In the process, these authors also free their heroines from what they see as the often stifling institution of marriage.

The process of refashioning narrative strategies did not always prove easy, demonstrating how firmly embedded were those conventions in cultural and literary discourses. Serao herself reveals the difficulties inherent in challenging literary conventions regarding fictive resolutions for heroines in the fascinating short story "Paolo Spada" (Paolo Spada). The narrative, found in the collection of stories entitled *Fior di passione* (Passion Flower), focuses on the literary accomplishments of the title character, a talented young author. However, although his initial efforts promise an illustrious career in letters, he never fulfills this early potential and soon begins the descent into obscurity. The reason for this declining popularity revolves around Paolo's unconventional treatment of his female characters; in short, he finds himself unable to sentence his heroines to the fictional demises dictated by literary usage. Instead, he rescues them from fictive extinction in the most unartistic of ways:

[T]he one destroyed by consumption . . . found a miraculous medicine, and married her doctor; the one stricken by meningitis took a strong quinine treatment and was cured; the one who because of a love betrayed . . . wanted to die, consoled herself for no reason in the world. . . .[17]

Paolo is fully aware that by flouting literary custom and creating alternative endings for his heroines, he is destroying not only his works but also any hope of being accepted by either the critics or the public. He even admits to a friend, "Art tells me: Fulvia must die. And I, crying, scream: I don't want her to die! Art tells me: Kill her. And I, consumed by pain, scream: I can't because I love her" (42). The agonies suffered by this young author as he struggles in vain to create new and different literary plots suggest just how entrenched literary conventions can be.

Even more intriguing is the correlation between the protagonist of this short story and Serao herself, a connection that raises a series of questions about the role of a woman author writing in a world of male-scripted literary conventions. While Paolo Spada is male, I contend that he does to some degree stand in for Serao herself. I would be reluctant to make this assumption if it were not for two provocative links to the author. First, Serao used a number of pseudonyms during her tenures at various newspapers, including that of "Paolo Spada."[18] It would seem likely, then, that Serao has appropriated this male persona in her fiction as well as in her journalism. It would not be the first time she employed a male protagonist to bridge the world of literature and journalism. Her novel *Vita e avventure di Joanna Riccardo* describes the travails of the title character, a young man striving to succeed in the arduous world of journalism. In the case of "Paolo Spada," Serao perhaps employed a male protagonist to legitimize the amorous feelings the novelist feels for his heroines. But the use of a male character also protects her to a degree, for it removes her from the text and, therefore, from the explicit challenges to the literary establishment that it raises.

By using a male protagonist in this short story and in the journalistic novel, two among the very few of Serao's texts that address the public rather than the domestic sphere, she displaces her own uneasiness with the rigidity of literary structures. This strategy of male impersonation was not uncommon in texts by eighteenth- and nineteenth-century female authors, who often used male protagonists as a means both of acquiring male power and of realizing their own forbidden aspirations.[19] In the case of the short story "Paolo Spada," the male protagonist mediates the (female) author's own difficulty in reimagining the conventions of the text, while at the same time questioning the authority of these very narrative patterns.

The second reason I would assert that this male character represents Serao lies in the very description of Paolo's heroines. For Paolo, these fictive women are extraordinarily lifelike; indeed, when they visit him in his dreams it is as if they are women of flesh and blood:

> They came to him, sat down, narrated their life stories, crying, laughing, leaning their head on his knee, humming a melody, murmuring verses full of pain, playing a tarantella on the harp, plucking some flowers, then, like Ophelia, leaving so they may return. He knew them, he called them by name, he knew about their lives. (36)

I include this passage to emphasize my point, which is the marked similarity between Paolo's inspiration for his female characters and that of Serao herself. As was noted in the preceding chapter, Serao often used as the prototype for her heroines the memories of her school chums or other young women she had known. She claimed a symbiotic relationship with them, an understanding of their lives, their thoughts, and their aspirations. In "Paolo Spada," the protagonist does the same, expressing in the above-mentioned passage an easy and comfortable intimacy with these women, a familiarity that would ultimately preclude him from executing their expected literary demise.

If these two points are accepted, that is, if Paolo Spada does represent Serao to some degree, what then is the reader to make of this short story? I would suggest that it turns not only on the question of literary conventions, but also on that of authorial anxiety, indicating Serao's profound frustration with literary tenets, especially those concerning female characters. In more general terms, how can a female author in turn-of-the-century Italy work with literary traditions that severely limit the artistic and social opportunities available to her heroines? What if these authors do not wish to either marry or kill off their heroines? I would argue that in Serao's case specifically the intimate relationships she developed with her heroines—women based, as she claimed, on her own friends—prevent or at least impede a strict observance of literary tenets. But she is also keenly aware of the dangers of not conforming to literary conventions, for the protagonist in "Paolo Spada" is ridiculed and ultimately left to languish in literary obscurity for his attempts to challenge the rules of construction of a novel or short story. Although Serao has left behind few writings discussing the role of the female author, "Paolo Spada" offers a rare, reflective examination of the issue of working with the conventions established and championed by a cohort of literary men.

Serao's familiarity with those literary conventions and her skillful manipulation of romantic archetypes becomes apparent in the following two texts, both of which question traditional narrative closures and explore the expectations of female behavior within a romantic discourse. The 1905 novel *Tre donne* (Three Women), set in the rarified air of an upper-class setting, focuses on the women in love with don Francesco, described repeatedly as "the beautiful, indifferent and discourteous prince."[20] He epitomizes the image of the brutal romantic hero, keenly aware of his sway over women, yet himself impervious to all human emotion. The two female protagonists, donna Clara and Miss Daisy, embody the classic romantic trope mandating the juxtaposition between a "dark lady" and a "fair lady."[21] However, the raven-haired donna Clara, while more visibly emotional than the "placid, motionless" and blond Miss Daisy (12), is not the exotic temptress often represented by the traditional dark lady. And Miss Daisy, a sedate Englishwoman, proves to be just as susceptible to passionate feelings as her dark counterpart. Serao often either ignored or subverted this binary depiction of women, a topic addressed in greater detail in the final section of this chapter.

Serao's metonymic representations of love place the narrative squarely within the romantic tradition, while simultaneously illuminating the romantic properties of each character. The significance of flowers in the courtship ritual, for example, is emphasized throughout the narrative. At a fancy ball, don Francesco flirts with both donna Clara and Miss Daisy, entreating each for a flower from her corsage or bouquet. Both women are reluctant, keenly aware of the significance of such a gift. Although the floral offerings mean nothing to don Francesco, donna Clara and Miss Daisy figuratively pledge their devotion with this token, as well as signal erotic accessibility, as flowers have traditionally symbolized both love and sensuality. Don Francesco's subsequent actions belie the sincerity of his request, for he abandons both women to meet the beautiful and mysterious donna Maria di Lanciano. That Serao is questioning these romantic archetypes becomes apparent through their self-referentiality. At one point, don Francesco accuses Miss Daisy of being, along with all other women, "incorrigible." When she asks why, he responds, "Because you take life as a romance novel, where 'love' rhymes with 'always'" (25–26). With this brief passage, don Francesco sketches a stylized evocation of romantic mythology, linking women explicitly to amorous sentiments and idyllic illusions. By extension, he represents those contemporary male critics who derided the romance narrative as maudlin and frivolous, in part because it was viewed as a woman's genre. But Miss Daisy and donna Clara seem also to participate in the promulgation of this romantic mythology. The Englishwoman confides that she once refused an offer of marriage because the suitor in question was not really in love with her. "[Y]ou have to act out a romance when you get married?" donna Clara asks her. "Yes," Miss Daisy replies, adding that she would rather remain a spinster than marry without love (65). Like don Francesco, these two female characters appear to subscribe to this gendered ideology linking women to the romance.

But a close reading of the rest of the novel casts this very ideology into doubt, for it endows the female characters with an unusual degree of subjectivity and creates alternative resolutions for the romance text. In this latter half of the novel, the female characters give voice to their own narratives and formulate their own fictive resolutions. Both donna Clara and Miss Daisy write long epistles to don Francesco. These letters, expressions of their feelings, outline plans for a future that epitomizes a destiny that is decidedly a subversion of the traditional romance narrative strategy. Donna Clara, although in love with don Francesco, will wed an elderly German prince she hardly knows "because it is my duty to do so. . . ." she writes (83). Donna Clara, whose family is facing financial ruin, has always known she would have an arranged and economically advantageous marriage. Marriage in this text clearly does not represent the happy ending found in traditional romance narratives. Instead, donna Clara sacrifices her own happiness and acts as a pawn in the financial bargaining between this prince and her family in order to restore her family's fortune. Serao undermines the conventional closure of donna Clara's story by questioning the institution of marriage and a woman's role in it. Marriage here does not represent a "reward" for good behavior (in a strictly narrative sense), but rather is depicted as a cold economic transaction. With the story of donna Clara, Serao offers a harsh denunciation of the economic value of a woman and its role in the socially sanctioned rite of wedlock. She moves beyond her critique of the perils of the marriage market found in "Non più," for in *Tre donne* the author frames the discussion of the issue within the forum of the romance proper; that is, within a space specifically devoted to an analysis of the institution of marriage, or, on a broader level, relationships between men and women. Donna Clara's fate becomes a more pointed indictment, then, of wedlock, for not only is she allowed no voice in the matter of her own marriage, she is reduced to a mere instrument in the financial maneuvering of her family.

If donna Clara's marriage is described more as an affliction than a reward, the subversion of Miss Daisy's destiny provides yet another reality of the paths marked by conventional narratives for women. She, too, is in love with don Francesco, but she chooses suicide, rather than marriage, to conclude her story. Although her fate is death, Miss Daisy does not typify the romantic heroines who are killed off at the text's resolution in order to punish them for untoward sexual behavior. In this work, Miss Daisy is the epitome of purity; indeed, the only overt expression of her desire was the reluctant gift of a flower to don Francesco. Rather, she *chooses* to divorce herself completely and irrevocably from the conventional resolutions of romance narratives. Miss Daisy embraces the thought of death, subjectively scripting her own resolution and ultimately declaring agency: "I want to die *thoughtfully,* tranquilly, if it is possible, on the day, at the time *that I have fixed*" (113; emphasis added). The method of death Miss Daisy chooses is itself an act of rebellion, "a moment of protest" not uncommon for many texts ending with the heroine's death.[22] The protagonist's dramatic suicide dissociates her once and for all from images of female passivity. Instead of a decorous suicide by poison or sleeping draught, she will fling herself off a mountain, a melodramatic ending certainly, but one that allows the heroine to soar briefly and triumphantly in a finale of her own design.

Donna Clara resigns herself to a loveless marriage; Miss Daisy kills herself. Although both heroines offer a challenge to their conventional script as women, can Serao envision a more positive resolution for the female character ensnared in a romance narrative? Only in the portrayal of the third female figure, donna Maria di Lanciano, does the reader find a strong woman in control of her own sexuality and destiny. Hers is the third and final letter of the novel, a brief note to don Francesco asking him to bring her a rose, a request that recalls his own request of donna Clara and Miss Daisy. Clearly, the tables have been turned. It is the male figure's sexuality, represented by the flower, that will be the currency of exchange in their relationship. And, in fact, the besotted don Francesco responds by bringing not one rose but a carriage full of fragrant blooms in an illustration of hypersexuality and availability. Maria professes to love him, but her cold and disinterested tone contradicts her words, and the narrative ends with the sound of her sardonic laughter. With the figure of Maria, Serao lapses into the stereotypical depiction of the manipulative, eroticized *femme fatale*. The portrayal of this character is so brief and cryptic as to make analysis of her almost futile. However, the inclusion of such a figure points to Serao's continual struggle (and occasional failure) to depict heroines freed from literary stereotypes.

The dualistic nature of the romance text's conventional closures for female characters—either marriage or death—continued to interest Serao throughout her literary career. In the 1889 short story "La grande fiamma" (The Great Flame), which portrays the unexpected demise of a passionate love affair, the author manipulates both these fictive resolutions while creating an innovative one of her own. In this work, Serao draws heavily on the romantic trope that invests love with the power to enslave and consume. Many of her romance narratives circle around this theme, as she endows the emotion of love with extraordinary powers. But although many critics have recognized love's centrality in the narrative economy of Serao's works, they often fail to read beyond this framework and examine the often negative manifestations of the emotion.[23] In "La grande fiamma," Serao examines the disintegration of that very emotion, a task that informs her exploration of fictive resolutions. The two central characters are the elegant and rich Grazia, who is stricken by an "impassioned fever" whenever she thinks of Ferrante, an equally elegant young man who is equally in love with her.[24] But he lives in Rome and she in Naples, and despite exchanging daily letters, both have become desperately unhappy with their situation. Surrendering to their passion, they decide to run off to Venice. The trip becomes less a romantic and carefree lark, however, than a grim voyage signaling the demise of their love. Everywhere they turn they see manifestations of death, from the cemetery they glimpse on the journey, to the gondola-led funeral procession in Venice itself. Indeed, the very city of Venice evokes feelings of death: "It seems like a tomb," Grazia murmurs upon seeing it (333). Grazia and Ferrante encounter Giorgio, a mutual friend, himself making a pilgrimage to Venice, the site of the few days of happiness he once spent with his now dead lover. After listening quietly to Giorgio's woeful tale of love and heartbreak, the lovers return silently to their hotel, conscious of their own petty passions. They say a cheerless and final goodbye: "In both, the great flame was extinguished" (346).

With this text, Serao rejects outright conventional resolutions for her heroine. Grazia's narrative does not end in death or marriage, endings consonant with conventional portraits of love. Instead, it defiantly ends in indifference. In a fascinating illustration of literary virtuosity, one that clearly reveals her manipulation of the genre, Serao alludes to both traditional resolutions. Grazia, a widow of three years, has been framed once within the marriage plot, the fictive ending most commonly found in romance narratives. The alternative of death serves as an atmospheric backdrop for the narrative, and touches several characters; Grazia has lost her husband, Ferrante his child, and Giorgio his lover. This last death does, in fact, correspond to the traditional "punishment" for the overt expression of female sexuality. The woman involved was married at the time (to a brute, but married nonetheless) and died tragically after running off with Giorgio. But while she is "punished" for her behavior, Grazia is not. In this text, then, while cleverly acknowledging the marriage/death motif, Serao deliberately scripts a different ending for her female protagonist, an anticlimactic, open ending that confounds traditional literary tenets.

Both "La grande fiamma" and *Tre donne* can be read as illustrations of Serao's desire to experiment with literary tenets, specifically with alternative endings. In these texts, she exemplifies a fundamental characteristic of those authors who creates new and even revolutionary resolutions; that is, the "desire to scrutinize the ideological character of the romance plot (and related conventions in narrative), and to change fiction so that it makes alternative statements about gender and its institutions."[25] Certainly in the short story "Paolo Spada," Serao's pushing of the boundaries of romance conventions indicates a genuine concern about the limitations of the established literary tenets. In her romance texts she continues the project begun during her schooling in the precepts of realism. By freeing her narratives from conventional resolutions, Serao not only rewrites the stylistic principles of the romance text, she also implicitly critiques the cultural discourses linking female behavior to women's (literary) destinies.

In the next series of texts I discuss, Serao moves beyond a stylistic rewriting of literary tenets to a more penetrating investigation of the depiction of female identity as framed within the romance narrative. In these works, she examines the difficulty heroines face in creating their own sense of self outside the bonds of heterosexual relationships. Instead, the world of romance becomes fraught with danger, a struggle between female protagonists, who must extricate themselves from destructive relationships, and their male counterparts, who seem intent on refashioning them into a paradigm based on restrictive notions of feminine behavior. The heroine's struggle to reclaim her own sense of identity becomes the subtext of three of Serao's works. That the heroines frequently fail in this endeavor should come as no surprise; Serao's often grim narratives reflect her awareness of the very limited situation of women in conservative, late nineteenth-century Italy. These texts serve as cautionary tales, warning of the physical and psychic perils of heterosexual coupling. And unlike the works discussed in the previous chapter, in these texts there are no compensatory relationships, such as adolescent friendships or those found in a secluded community of women, to mitigate the social pressures.

The works under consideration in this section, although traditionally evaluated for their realist attributes, contain many elements of the romance, including an insistence on male-female relationships, and merit examination as romance texts. Even more important for the purposes of this study, both the novel *La ballerina* (The Ballerina) and the short story "O Giovannino o la morte" (Oh Giovannino or Death) trace the construction, and the destruction, of female identity. The little-known short story "Livia Speri" (Livia Speri) further investigates this issue—with a more radical resolution—within the framework of a more conventional romance narrative.

The intersection of identity and agency can be a vexing one

when working with noncontemporary texts, for one cannot assume a universal validity for these concepts, whose meanings often depend on different cultural and historical conditions. In recognition of the complexity of this issue, a bipartite approach will clarify the use of these difficult terms in analyzing Serao's texts. First, I define the concept of identity as a sense of internal coherency that is exterior to or preexists cultural expectations and social roles.[26] In other words, even when the female protagonists are portrayed initially as being outside the confines of a heterosexual relationship, they are self-contained and even conscious of their condition. The second arm of this approach rests on the notion of agency, a fundamental tenet of feminist theory and other humanistic and philosophical disciplines. I use "agency" in the broadest sense to include both (self) control and (self) determination. The concept of agency also implies an ability to act, to find within oneself the inner resources needed to assert a sense of identity. Under this particular interpretation of female identity, Serao's heroines must feel free of the restrictions imposed by hegemonic, normative culture while manifesting a sense of autonomy. By doing so, they embody the characteristics of authentic, integrated selfhood. The issues of identity and agency add another layer to Serao's fictive production, for she significantly deepens her portrayal of women in the social world through an analysis of their motivations.

For many of these fictional heroines, the threat to their sense of self comes not only from their male partners, but, on an even broader level, from their own economic situations. For example, the 1899 novel *La ballerina* chronicles the amorous experiences and tragic circumstances of Carmela Minino, a third-rate Neapolitan ballerina.[27] The move from chaste heroine to defiled protagonist in this text acts as a narrative reflection of Carmela's loss of both internal coherency and autonomy. Tellingly, Serao attributes this loss to the various male characters, representatives of agency and social norms, each responsible for a further lapse in the (wayward) heroine's behavior. Even more significant is the correlation Serao draws between female identity, a heroine's economic status, and her subsequent destiny. Carmela's behavior at the hands of the men intent on refashioning her identity is explicitly linked to her penurious state. Serao had explored the connection between class and (female) gender in other texts, notably *Suor Giovanna della croce* and "Per monaca," but this novel introduces a third

element, that of masculine manipulation and exploitation. In
La ballerina, Serao has created an even more complex picture
of female experiences, exploring how a heroine must confront the broad prescriptions established by both class and gender
while negotiating the more specific expectations of her male
counterpart.

In *La ballerina,* poverty and class origins are underscored as
markers of identity in the novel's opening pages, as Carmela
counts the few coins in her tattered purse and buys flowers for
the grave of her godmother, the famous dancer Amina Boschetti.
Carmela, the illegitimate daughter of a maid who worked for
Amina, was doomed to a similar life of servitude when the kindly
ballerina interceded, paying for dance lessons and finding her a
position with the San Carlo Theater ballet company. But Carmela
lacks both talent and beauty, and since her protector's death six
years earlier, she has been relegated to the back row of dancers.
Carmela's poverty derives from more than her mediocre dancing
skills, however, for unlike the other dancers in the troupe, she has
chosen to reject the customary and lucrative relationship with a
wealthy benefactor. Though this choice is described as the cause
of her impoverishment,[28] her refusal to compromise her religious
principles and trade in her primary capital—her virginity—for
economic security stems not only from a recognition and appreciation of her chastity, but also and more importantly, from her
control over it. Carmela exercises her autonomy precisely by not
following the example of her colleagues, many of whom have
parlayed their sexual liaisons into economic stability. Serao depicts
the backstage world of the San Carlo Theater, a potentially inclusive, all-female space, as a locus of economic transaction, a "market
of beauty and youth" (44). Rather than the embodiment of female
friendship or solidarity seen in many of Serao's realist texts, the
women in *La ballerina* are not supportive of Carmela, scoffing
openly at her chastity.[29] One, the seductive Emilia Tromba, warns
her not to waste any more time in securing a lover: "You're not
beautiful, it's useless to tell lies and you know it; if you don't profit
from your youth, no one will ever want you . . ." (49–50). Emilia's
blunt words illustrate the commodification of these young women.

Carmela's virtue, and thus her identity, faces even more pre-
sumptive attacks from three male characters, each representative
of various social classes. Roberto Gargiulo, a young clerk just
starting out in the world, remains interested in the virtuous, if

homely, Carmela, despite her continued rebuffs of his offer to walk her home from the theater. Her virtue is also under siege by don Gabriele Scognamiglio, a wealthy, middle-aged pharmacist who flirts cynically with her. The aristocratic class is represented by Ferdinando Terzi di Torregrande, an idle, elegant young man who frequents the theater to watch his lover, Emilia Tromba. While these men represent different social classes, they are tied together by their manipulation, deliberate or not, of the unsexualized identity Carmela has carefully constructed for herself. The emphasis on the social status of these male characters is a deliberate strategy, serving to indict masculinist behavior in a very broad way. These men act from a position of power bestowed by gender and class, a locus of power that underlines Carmela's own lack of authority. They succeed in preying upon her precisely because of the relatively ineffectual and marginalized position she has been placed in, both as a woman and as a member of the working poor. Clearly, in a move reflecting the inherent pessimism that colors Serao's vision of turn-of-the-century Italy, the economic status of the women in her fictional works can undermine their sense of agency and identity.

The precariousness of Carmela's position, combined with the repeated overtures by both Roberto and don Scognamiglio, eventually erodes her resolve, a resolve further weakened by continued exposure to the depravity contaminating the theater world. Her scruples are finally and completely undermined, however, by the aristocratic Ferdinando. Because of the vast difference in social class between Carmela and Ferdinando, their paths rarely cross. Throughout the narrative, however, it becomes apparent that Carmela is increasingly drawn to him, while realizing that he remains outside the limits of her aspirations. This is made clear to her by a careless comment of Ferdinando's that targets the identity she has constructed for herself. One evening Emilia introduces the two, and then whispers loudly into his ears, "[She] is still a spinster" or, in other words, a virgin (52). Ferdinando, fixing Carmela with a scornful gaze, responds cruelly, "What a fool!" (52). Carmela, faint with mortification, impulsively allows the waiting Roberto to escort her home, the first step in her capitulation to the prurient demands of the novel's male characters.

The protagonist's subsequent exposure to sexual experience acts as the catalyst for the erosion and eventual collapse of her self-identity, an identity built on the tenets of chastity and virtue.

These psychic changes are underlined by a drastic physical transformation, a narrative maneuver already seen in "Non più" and
Suor Giovanna della Croce. In *La ballerina,* Carmela's transformation signifies both her appropriation of the symbols of female
sexuality and an acquiescence to her lover's wishes. Thus, she
wears heavy stage makeup and cheap costume jewelry to please
Roberto, who has refashioned her into an eroticized persona that
corresponds to his image of femininity. Carmela, who by now is
too ashamed of her behavior to go to her once-cherished parish
church, gradually realizes that her capitulation was "her first and
her biggest mistake" (66).

Tellingly, in this tale of woe among the lower classes, the taking
of a lover does not lead to financial security for Carmela; instead,
she finds herself in increasingly straitened circumstances. She
must spend her meager savings on restaurant meals, as Roberto
does not like her to roughen her hands by cooking, as well as on
new clothes and baubles, so she can be appropriately dressed
when the two go out. Even more damaging is her internalization
of Roberto's disdainful attitude toward her; she even blames herself when he breaks off their relationship. Carmela's acceptance
of the prevailing social ideology prescribing gendered differences
in sexual behavior is exemplified by her own exoneration of Roberto. The young man, after all, "had played his game, the one
all men play, to see if they win: for the woman, it all boils down
to not entering into this masculine game!" (73). While Roberto
will move easily from one conquest to another, Carmela's life will
be irreparably changed. Homely, unskilled, and now bereft of her
only valuable asset, her virtue, Carmela can only continue on the
downward path begun under Roberto's tutelage. Indeed, a short
time later, she reluctantly agrees to dine in public with the persistent don Scognamiglio, a clear sign of the direction their relationship has taken.[30] As with the depiction of the affair with Roberto,
Carmela's new liaison with the wealthy pharmacist is set against a
culinary backdrop. Avoiding graphic displays of sexuality, Serao
instead displaces the construction of sensual appetites onto depictions of food and eating. It is indicative of Carmela's profound
unease with all matters physical that she appears extremely uncomfortable when dining with these men. Her reluctance to eat
parallels her inherent distaste for the physical union between men
and women, a union she succumbs to "as a punishment for her
sin" (67–68).[31]

The liaison with don Scognamiglio further effaces Carmela's sense of personal integrity. Only at the end of the text does she regain her faculty for agency, the second element in my definition of integrated selfhood. In *La ballerina*, the female protagonist acts in a daring and public way, reclaiming her lost sense of identity while constructing a relationship consistent with her own code of conduct. The forum for this dramatic scene is, appropriately, the San Carlo Theater. As the young dancers prepare for that evening's performance, rumors circulate backstage about a young, unnamed nobleman who has committed suicide. The news disturbs Carmela, who begins to feel "a nervous restlessness, a need to move, to talk, to act" (85). During the ballet's last act, the dancers whisper to each other the identity of the suicide: Ferdinando Terzi.[32] Upon hearing the name of the man she loves, Carmela abruptly abandons the performance and runs offstage. Changing into street clothes, she roughly wipes off her heavy makeup, "wanting to put back on her everyday face" (89). By doing so, she erases all traces of artifice, renouncing the frivolous, sexualized persona created first by Roberto and later reinforced by don Scognamiglio.

The once passive Carmela, who obeyed Roberto's demands and don Scognamiglio's orders, finally rebels. Throwing off the shackles of her passivity and firmly breaking off the relationship with her lover, she doggedly tracks down the real object of her desire: Ferdinando. She finds him in a squalid hotel room, lying on the bed in blood-stained evening clothes. In this scene, Carmela rewrites the rules of romance, for she acts as pursuer rather than pursued. This subversion of literary tenets is all the more striking given the protagonist's humble social status and Ferdinando's elevated standing and given the limitations attributed to her gender. She finds heretofore unsuspected fonts of strength, convincing the skeptical hotel clerk to let her watch over Ferdinando's body that night: "[T]hat corpse was hers, for an entire night, in a strange and lonely room" (100). Carmela takes possession of Ferdinando, not as Roberto and don Scognamiglio once took possession of her, but in a chaste union. She emphasizes the spiritual nature of the relationship between the two when she places her rosary on Ferdinando's bloodied chest and tenderly, chastely, kisses his forehead. Through this short-lived and even macabre relationship, Carmela can finally reclaim a sense of internal coherency. But it is only through Ferdinando's death, and therefore his rather obvious removal from any reciprocal exchange of love, that Carmela can create an unsullied, nonerotic relationship that allows her to figuratively regain her former virginal status. She herself comments on this irony, whispering to Ferdinando, "[O]h my dearheart, only in death could I kiss you!" (101).

This conclusion, and indeed the novel as a whole, acts as strong condemnation of the difficulty Serao's young heroines face in creating a relationship free of gender-coded expectations. Certainly Carmela's powerlessness in the face of her lovers' demands is directly tied to her gender. However, her social and economic status also play a fundamental role in her story, an analysis best served by comparing Carmela's destiny with that of the protagonist of the short story "La virtù di Checchina." In *La ballerina,* Carmela's inherent morality appears to parallel the initial scruples of Checchina, as both women compromise their virtue by turning to relationships outside the bonds of marriage. However, one notable difference distinguishes the two. Checchina's aborted liaison with the marquis represents an act of rebellion against an increasingly stifled existence. Carmela, on the other hand, does not so much rebel as succumb to her destiny. Joseph Spencer Kennard calls Carmela's love for Ferdinando the catalyst for her capitulation to Roberto: "The overmastering passion, so enslaving the will that the entire life drifts like a rudderless boat to final wreck, is the characteristic trait of all of Matilde Serao's women."[33] But Kennard's analysis overlooks the financial situation of the heroine, for surely her impoverished state significantly contributes to her decision to take a lover. Serao's repeated emphasis on the economic status of her protagonists clearly calls for a reading that combines a consideration of both gender and class. In the novel, poor, homely, and untalented Carmela has few options in a world that limits a woman's social roles to either wife or lover. She seeks more than love; she wants the stability ensured by a liaison with a financially secure man. But after these relationships have failed, Carmela realizes she has lost not only all hope of security but also her tenuous position in the social world. Checchina can always slip back into the protected, if dull, bourgeois circle ensured by her marriage, but Carmela's destiny is as inevitable as it is bleak.

In the 1889 short story "O Giovannino o la morte," the multifaced aspects of identity plot out a rich landscape, charting the movement from the heroine's gradual loss of self to a dramatic conclusion in which she reclaims what had been lost. As in *La ballerina,* this story, which unfolds in the environs of a middle-class Neapolitan neighborhood, also explores the economic issues underlying sentimental relationships. Like Carmela, Chiarina, the heroine of this tale, is an orphan and must rely on her strong moral principles to guide her through the tricky waters of post-adolescence. But several noteworthy differences set apart the two texts. Chiarina, although orphaned, has a "protector" in the guise of her stepmother, donna Gabriella. She still lives within the bosom of a family, albeit an unusually controlling one, and is not forced to make her own way in the world like Carmela. Even more striking is the difference in temperament between the meek and modest heroine of *La ballerina* and the protagonist of this text. Chiarina, although described as "a kind and good creature," is nevertheless marked by an indomitable sense of resolve and strong passions; indeed, these attributes, along with an ardent religious faith, constitute her sense of identity.[34] All of these traits unite into a hearty loathing and disgust for donna Gabriella, her stepmother, who controls and occasionally destroys her neighbors through her profession as a usurer. Chiarina's strong will is repeatedly tested by donna Gabriella, who refuses to allow the young girl to see Giovannino, an unemployed young man who lives in the neighboring building. Chiarina stubbornly defies donna Gabriella, asserting bravely, "You know: either Giovannino or death" (235). Clearly, her love for this young man is matched by her tenacity and resolve.

But these two figures, donna Gabriella and Giovannino, soon manifest a strange complicity, designed to erase the heroine's spirit and sense of integrity. Donna Gabriella makes the first dent in Chiarina's principles, using her consent to an engagement between the two sweethearts to emotionally blackmail Chiarina. After giving her blessing to the marriage, she insists that her stepdaughter address her as "Mamma." Initially refusing, Chiarina finally gives in, feeling, however, that she is betraying her own dead mother by using this term of affection for a woman she despises. This capitulation, arising from her engagement to Giovannino, threatens to diminish her most marked personality trait, her "ancient fierceness" (256).

More important is the evolution of Chiarina's relationship with Giovannino, which soon turns on financial as well as sentimental matters. Even at the onset of their relationship, before Giovannino receives permission from donna Gabriella to officially court Chiarina, he has made it clear (to the reader, if not to her) that he is as attracted by her financial assets as he is by any others. He rebuffs her suggestion that they elope by saying, "Without money, you can't do anything" (244). Despite Chiarina's happiness with her engagement, she feels a growing sense of alienation from Giovannino, a psychic uneasiness that manifests itself in strange dreams. The nightmares also reflect Chiarina's fundamental moral conscience, an important element in her makeup and one that contributes significantly to her sense of self. For example, donna Gabriella's gift of luxurious fabric for Chiarina's trousseau provokes only feelings of horror, as she realizes the cloth came out of her stepmother's usury business. She confides her disgust to Giovannino, who ignores her scruples. That night she dreams she is wearing "a fantastic shirt made of tears, a skirt made of blood" (260). Clearly, the blood and tears of those indebted to her stepmother weigh heavily on Chiarina and presage her doomed relationship with Giovannino. Ignoring these presentiments, Chiarina continues to look upon her upcoming nuptials as a liberation from her stepmother's domination.

Serao casts the story in the ideology of the most classic of romance texts: the fairy tale, in which the handsome young hero's function is to rescue the young heroine from the controlling grasp of the evil stepmother. But the author soon subverts the fairy-tale ending in another example of her continual engagement with literary forms. In this text, Chiarina's dreams of freedom and happiness are shattered by a series of betrayals initiated by both her stepmother and Giovannino. With these betrayals comes a heightened sense of the protagonist's own powerlessness to act in the face of such dominating forces. First, Chiarina learns that despite her imprecations, not only does Giovannino plan to work for donna Gabriella after they are married, but they will continue to live with her as well. Giovannino's explanation is based on financial concerns, as he lacks the resources to go into business for himself. In this section, Serao conflates Chiarina's economic and sexual value, with physical favors standing in as the unit of currency. In this telling scene, Giovannino attempts to appease Chiarina's anger and despair by asking for a kiss, the first time in their courtship that he has made such a request. Chiarina refuses, however, recognizing finally that his interest in her is not entirely romantic. By doing so, she retains control of her physicality, even while allowing her principles to be compromised. Here Serao reverses the situation of Carmela in *La ballerina,* who compromises her virtue but retains a sense of emotional autonomy. Giovannino, however, knows where to turn for that kiss, and one evening Chiarina returns early from church to find him in a compromising position with her stepmother. With this act, Serao weds the economy of desire to that of wealth as Giovannino realizes his dream of financial and sexual profit.

Chiarina's suicide on the heels of this scene (she throws herself into a well) has traditionally been attributed to her despair over Giovannino's betrayal.[35] Another interpretation, however, reads it as an example of those fictional suicides that are presented as constructive acts, deliberate attempts by the characters to control their destinies. A classic instance is Edna Pontellier's death in Kate Chopin's 1899 novel *The Awakening.* Marianne Hirsch, while recognizing the purposefully ambiguous description of this scene, believes Edna's suicide is the final and logical step in her gradual awakening: "Death becomes an escape from female plot and the only possible culmination of woman's spiritual development."[36] Another example, one more closely mirroring the situation found in "O Giovannino o la morte," is found within Serao's own work— that of the female protagonist's suicide in the romance novel *Addio, amore!* (Farewell, Love!). In this work, which will be discussed at greater length at the end of this chapter, the female protagonist kills herself after her husband betrays her with her sister. The suicide in this text is a desperate act by a woman destroyed by love and desire. How, then, should Chiarina's death in "O Giovannino o la morte" be read? Is it as positive and deliberate an act as Edna's suicide in Chopin's novel or, rather, is it the result of heartbreak and betrayal as in *Addio, amore!?* I would argue that Chiarina's dramatic suicide, although seemingly a reaction to the duplicity of her beloved, can also be understood as an attempt to recuperate the sense of integrity and agency that had been steadily eroded throughout her engagement. By choosing to end her life, she also frees herself from a situation that ties her assets to financial and sexual attributes.

Not all of Serao's heroines must struggle so desperately to assert their autonomy in the face of their lovers' gendered expectations. In the short story "Livia Speri," the female protagonist explicitly rejects her lover's attempt to contain her within the hegemonic world he represents. Throughout this narrative, Serao plays with the expectations of gendered behavior in the context of the romance novel. Although the character of Livia remains deliberately ambiguous, her actions undermine her lover's characterization of her as a helpless, high-strung woman. The very elusiveness of Livia's character suggests a heroine far removed from the typical representation of female protagonists, for she falls neither into the camp of virtuous virgin nor into that of *femme fatale*. By creating such a character, Serao experiments with traditional literary tenets; more important for the purposes of this study, she also envisions a heroine released from the prescriptions engendered by those fictional and, by extension, social codes.

Livia's voice is not heard at all in this short story; rather, it is the voice of her lover that shapes the tale. The brief descriptions of her actions, then, become extremely important, semiotic manifestations of the identity she has succeeded in creating for herself. The short story is composed almost entirely of a letter to Livia from Roberto Fiore, who writes to break off their relationship, confessing that he no longer loves her. The long epistle is encumbered with flowery phrases and sentimental commonplaces, illustrating Roberto's adherence to romance codes and the appropriateness of his last name. He is most concerned with her reaction to his abandonment, describing in almost perverted detail her anticipated collapse and berating himself for the pain he will cause. Indeed, he rather sadistically compares himself to an "executioner," and Livia his "poor, poor, beloved victim. . . ."[37] Livia, however, does not exhibit the anticipated deathbed agonies upon receiving this news but reveals instead a disposition that subverts the conventional depiction of a woman destroyed by unrequited love. Nor is she his defenseless "victim"; she does not collapse prostrate with despair upon reading his letter but returns calmly to her novel. Indeed, Roberto seems much more distraught than she, droning on about the agony *he* feels at their separation. The ambiguity of the gender-oriented roles is reflected in the title itself. Although the story was first published in the 1918 collection *La vita è così lunga* (Life is So Long) under the title "Livia Speri," a second version published two years later was entitled "Una Vittima" (A Victim). Just who Serao considered the victim in this deliciously enigmatic story remains open to interpretation.

Serao not only reverses conventional depictions of gendered behavior in this narrative, she also gently pokes fun at the romance tradition in general. Livia is reading a romance novel as the story opens, an act that symbolizes her independence. Reading by females was carefully regulated in nineteenth- and early twentieth-century Italy by parents, clergymen, and teachers, who considered amorous situations in novels to be potentially corrupting.[38] In Serao's works, however, female protagonists often discover the world of eroticized relationships through the reading of forbidden texts.[39] Livia's alleged innocence is called into question by her exposure to these novels. The reference to reading in "Livia Speri" becomes even more pointed when the author that so engrosses the heroine is revealed, for she is reading Paul Bourget's novel *Les détours du coeur* (The Meanderings of the Heart). Bourget (1852–1935) was perhaps best known for his highly popular sentimental novels, although he was also a poet, literary critic, playwright, and travel writer.[40] He was a close friend of Serao, who often reviewed his books for various newspapers.[41] Critics unhappy with Serao's gradual abandonment of orthodox realist principles often blame Bourget, attributing her growing interest in romance texts to his influence. By mentioning Bourget in this cryptic story, Serao acknowledges her debt to the French author and his work and offers a tongue-in-cheek parody of the romance genre as well. Serao implicitly contrasts Livia's unperturbed reaction to the letter with the more traditional female protagonists in Bourget's works.

Livia manifests her sense of agency not just by reading forbidden texts, for she also subverts the feminine attribute of vanity. For example, after reading Roberto's letter, she pulls out a hand mirror, scrutinizing herself not to gratify her sense of vanity but to ascertain that she is not, in fact, the "ideal lover" described by Roberto (51). As was noted in the discussion of "La virtù di Checchina," studying oneself in a looking glass represents a significant act of self-conception and self-knowledge. When Livia holds up her mirror, she looks beyond the surface to verify her perception of self based not on Roberto's romanticized portrayal but on an inherent sense of autonomy. Unlike Carmela and Chiarina, Livia avoids being defined solely by the archetypes of femininity advocated by her male partner. Heterosexual relationships, whether outside the marriage bond or within acceptable social parameters, are potentially lethal for the first two of these female characters. They become subsumed within a male-created persona, whether it is the highly sexualized creature Carmela must finally slough off or the morally compromised person Chiarina must literally kill. Livia's identity is more fluid, however. Her ambiguous character is symbolized by her smile, "a mysterious smile" that appears at the beginning and end of the narrative (45).[42] Livia's destiny, too, seems wrapped up in that metonymic mark, gloriously ambiguous and open-ended. With this enigmatic conclusion, she is freed from constricting literary norms that mandate narrow categories for heroines and from the social expectations that link behavior to specific gendered codes.[43]

Livia's ultimate liberation originates in part in her elevated social and economic status. Certainly, in *La ballerina* and "O Giovannino o la morte," the heroines' loss of identity is directly related to their relative powerlessness, which stems not only from their gender, but also from the circumstances conferred by their class. In "Livia Spera," the bulk of the story is devoted to Roberto's letter, but symbols of the protagonist's elevated social position abound. Indeed, the very reading of the letter becomes a stage on which Livia can display these very relevant signs of her wealth. As the tale opens, Livia, idly reading among the myriad of cushions on her chaise longue, is interrupted by a servant bearing Roberto's letter on a tray of Japanese bronze. She opens it with a golden letterknife, and as she reads it, her beautiful, jewel-laden hands play with the string of diamonds resting on her chest. This short, extremely cryptic story suggests that the impotency of gender—female gender, in particular—can be mediated by the authority bestowed by economic class and social status. Carmela and Chiarina seemed doomed to succumb to the psychic manipulations of their lovers, but Livia is empowered by her wealth and therefore able to reject a similar stratagem by her former lover. Once again, Serao's texts paint a portrait of a metaphorical city in which women are caught in a web of social expectations based as much on their gender as on their position in this very stratified world.

As the above analysis illustrates, Serao's manipulation of the romance genre creates a focus for the examination of assumptions, both literary and social, about female sexuality and desire. Even though erotic longings simmer beneath the surface of many of Serao's realist works, the theme is more deliberately and thoughtfully probed in her romance works, which revolve, after all, around heterosexual couplings.[44] The narrative strategy of the three preceding texts, although structured around amorous relationships, originates in an examination of the heroines' sense of self. In the three works examined in this section, however, the expression of female desire actually shapes the destinies of the heroines. In *Cuore infermo* (The Sick Heart), the principal female character dies of an overabundance of love; in *Addio, amore!*, the heroine kills herself because of unrequited love; and in *Fantasia* (Fantasy), Serao's most critically acclaimed romance novel, one female protagonist commits suicide after the other runs off with her husband. I look at these texts not on the basis of the coupling of heroine and hero but rather, according to their articulation of female sexuality, which is located in the figure of the *femme fatale*. This stock literary character crosses national and generic boundaries that occur in texts by Dickens, Sue, Keats, and Wilde, among others. Variations range from the man-eating Black Widow to female vampires, but all share an aggressive eroticism and almost magical powers of seduction and entrapment.[45] The increased use of this figure in nineteenth-century literature can be traced in part to a growing acceptance of the tenets of Darwinism and its insistence on an instinctual, irrational female nature. This ideology manifested itself in both literature and art in depictions of women as highly sexualized creatures threatening the rational, manmade order. Such convictions eventually led to even more negative beliefs in women's subhuman attributes and, indeed, many references to these female characters include comparisons with animals and the natural world.[46]

Various manifestations of the *femme fatale* inhabit the pages of Italian literature, both male- and female-authored. The raven-haired Ippolita in Gabriele D'Annunzio's 1894 novel *Il Trionfo della morta* (The Triumph of Death), for example, is pale and seductive, while La Lupa (The She-Wolf) in Verga's short story of that title exhibits the dangerous, animal-like characteristics typical of many *femmes fatales*. For their part, Italian women authors more often observed, rather than challenged, the often reductive tenets of the literary system that had accepted them. Serao, although relying heavily in her romance texts on the figure of the *femme fatale*, did attempt to revise, or at least question, this fundamentally negative characterization of womanhood.[47]

One of Serao's first attempts to integrate the character of the *femme fatale* into her literary works occurred in the 1881 novel *Cuore infermo*, a text that ostensibly revolves around the story of an upper-class married couple but is overshadowed by the figure of the *femme fatale*. Indeed, the erotic energy emanating from this character serves as the impulse that underlies the narrative, as she manipulates both the male and female protagonists in a bizarre triangle of passion, jealousy, and repulsion. The novel's structure satisfies many of the elements associated with the genre, including unrequited love, overwhelming passions, a wedding, and a funeral. The plot, too, is relatively straightforward. The heroine, Beatrice Revertera, marries Marcello Sangiorgio out of a sense of duty rather than any emotional attachment. Marcello, although desperately in love with his unapproachable wife, eventually begins a liaison with the seductive Lalla D'Aragona. Beatrice, discovering that she does, in fact, love Marcello, enjoys a passionate, if brief, interlude with him before dying. The character of Lalla, however, threatens to upset the principal plot, that is, the relationship between wife and husband. It is Lalla's embodiment of eroticized female desire and its role as a disruptive force that must be explored, for it reveals Serao's manipulation of conventional literary depictions of women and demonstrates her revision of this tradition.

In this exemplary novel Serao has turned her two diametrically opposed protagonists, Beatrice and Lalla, into the embodiment of the "angel in the house" and the "monster," the traditional representation of female characters. The first archetype symbolizes selfless sacrifice and purity, the second, destructive sensuality and rebellion. These two paradigms, pervasive not only in literature but also in cultural discourses of the nineteenth century, had to be confronted by women authors depicting the feminine.[48] Many female authors did not create characters free of sexual or gender-based stereotypes, whereas others appropriated the positive traits of the *femme fatale,* seeing in the character's freedom and energy a model of creative power.[49] Serao's works embody an interesting intersection of these two approaches. She often questioned negative images of women, especially the *femme fatale,* in a literary context but she frequently failed to present any positive alternatives. Perhaps the relatively rigid demands of the romance text, particularly in the matter of character type, precluded more radical revisions, although some experimentation is clearly evident.

In *Cuore infermo,* for example, the two female characters initially appear to embody the attributes of classic romantic heroines. Beatrice, who evokes Dante's famous namesake, personifies the attributes of the archetypal virtuous heroine—passivity, inaccessibility, and rectitude. A telling description emphasizes these traits: "[H]er beautiful figure settled into a secure calmness, in a reflexive tranquility. . . . Her entire face was closed, silent, serene in its indifference. . . ."[50] By contrast, Lalla is endowed with the typical attributes of a *femme fatale*—illness, passion, and irresistibility. A description of her emphasizes the contrast between her and the placid Beatrice, for Lalla is marked by "a bizarrely passionate heart" (54) and a turbulent and exotic demeanor. As one character comments, "She is really the modern woman, the passionate woman, strange, maybe superficial, delicate, sickly, nervous, capricious, of various appearances that seduce everyone; a woman made for pleasure for the restless and refined modern youth" (113). Even Lalla's physical appearance expresses her inherent eroticism: "She had a pair of excessively black eyes. . . . A mouth with lips so thin and vivid that it seemed like a bloody scar" (59). This striking image, with its vampiric imagery, points to Lalla's rapacity and her destructive powers. Indeed, her mysterious past includes an incident suggesting just those powers. She was briefly married, but "It seems that those two loved each other too much, and one is dead of it" (54). Lalla's voracious capacity for love carries with it fatal consequences, underscoring the potency of her charms and the underlying connections among sensuality, appetite, and death.

This superfluity of sexuality in Lalla's character spills over, threatening a social order that bases its existence and perpetuation, in part, on gendered order and rigidity. Serao examines this aspect of the *femme fatale* as she underscores the affinity between the two female characters, even as the physical and psychic differences between them become more pronounced.[51] Here Serao portrays the *femme fatale* not only in relationship to the male protagonist, the traditional beginning point in the romance text, but also through her connection with the other female character. For instance, Lalla's seductive power, the *femme fatale*'s calling card, manifests itself in her glance, a traditional attribute of male characters and one that carries with it intimations of active agency. She is endowed with this attribute because of her supersexualized femininity, which makes her the representative of excess and therefore positions her beyond the reach of the controlled social order. In the following scene, which demonstrates Lalla's rapacious and nongender-specific appetite, her glance initially encompasses *both* Marcello and Beatrice. As Marcello and Beatrice leave on their honeymoon voyage, they notice a solitary figure in the carriage of an adjacent train: "[A] young woman, alone, with a dark, thin, ill and made-up face ... She fixed a long and dark look into the newlyweds' carriage; for one moment those three characters stared at one another" (36). All three characters participate in this moment, but as Ursula Fanning has pointed out, the two women will eventually engage in a relationship that excludes Marcello, despite his liaison with Lalla.[52] Indeed, even as their affair intensifies, Lalla becomes almost obsessed with Marcello's wife, interrogating him about Beatrice and even attempting to instigate a meeting between the two of them: "During the morning [Lalla] walked in the park, with the hope of meeting her" (148).[53] The two women finally come face to face at a friend's salon, and Lalla again demonstrates her fixation with Beatrice. She stares openly at her lover's wife, smiling at her, "turning her head to her, as if she wanted to talk with her" (174). Lalla goes so far as to confess to a would-be suitor, "I even love the Duchess Sangiorgio." "You love too much, Countess," is his reply. And her telling response: "It is my defect. Ask Marcello about it" (176). The exchange reveals how Lalla is as engaged with Beatrice as she is with Marcello. As Nancy Harrowitz astutely points out, Beatrice is the "absent yet primary object of love" for both Lalla and Marcello.[54] She functions as the fulcrum around which the other characters revolve.

Ultimately, Lalla serves as the catalyst for a dramatic change in Beatrice, illustrating both the *femme fatale*'s sovereignty in matters of the heart and the allure of her sexuality. As the lives of the two women intersect more frequently, Beatrice draws from Lalla a strength and a passion she had previously lacked. Beatrice's growing determination to win back Marcello is intrinsically linked to her budding sensuality, a sexual awareness that has been awakened by another woman, rather than by her husband. This passion manifests itself in a standard romantic trope: music. Beatrice's piano playing becomes more and more intense as she sinks deeper into despair about Marcello's infidelity. In a scene shot through with irony, Beatrice serenades Lalla and Marcello one evening during a tryst at Lalla's adjacent villa. Tellingly, while Marcello is oblivious to his wife's transformation, Lalla recognizes in the melancholy but powerful chords a change directly inspired by her example.[55]

The turning point in this triangular relationship is set against the tumultuous strains of the opera being presented at the San

Carlo Theater one evening. Initially mortified upon spying Marcello sitting in Lalla's box, Beatrice soon recovers and even manifests a strange and new vigor: "A strong desire to fight, to act, came to her . . ." (214). Later that evening, intuiting the lovers' plan to run off together, she confronts Marcello. Dressed portentously in her wedding frock, Beatrice declares the love that had slowly been growing within her: "Don't you see that I love you? . . . I'm your Beatrice, your bride; I'm wearing my white dress. I love you" (223). With these words, she reminds Marcello of her sanctioned role as his wife, a role he is only too happy to endorse, for he confesses that his liaison with Lalla was the only antidote to the intense feelings he had toward his heretofore unresponsive wife. Beatrice's entreaty appeals not only to Marcello's feelings, but also to his awareness of their position in the social world. Serao underlines this point deliberately, I feel, for a significant attribute of the *femme fatale* is her status as outsider. This figure, often depicted as foreign, as Other, is an intrusive element threatening the established order. Lalla, with her obscure origins and ambiguous position, remains outside the countenanced social world. It is this marginalization, perhaps, that generates such sexual energy, as the *femme fatale* becomes freed from restrictive expectations of female behavior. Must, then, the expression of female sexuality be articulated *only* in the figure of the alienated *femme fatale*? Serao refuses to fall into this trap, endowing even her "angels in the house" with a fluid sensuality not typically found in other nineteenth-century texts.

The sexual energy and power intrinsic to the *femme fatale* often correspond with physical weakness, and in this text Lalla's relationship with Beatrice turns not only on a sense of sexual energy, but also on a diseased corporeality. Igino Ugo Tarchetti's title character in the 1869 novel *Fosca* perhaps best illustrates this trope in nineteenth-century Italian literature. This female protagonist, despite a repulsive appearance and sickly constitution, nevertheless succeeds in captivating the heart of the hero. In another example, the seductive Ippolita in D'Annunzio's *Il Trionfo della morta* is epileptic, an attribute shared by many women of dangerous sexual powers. In *Cuore infermo*, Serao invests Lalla with seductive powers exactly at the moment when her body is at its weakest. Described as "sickly" and "consumptive" (54), Lalla becomes dangerously ill with an unnamed ailment early in the narrative. Despite their brief acquaintance, Marcello rushes to her bedside, where she lies as still and pale as a corpse. He pleads with Lalla to speak, but the only word she can utter is his name, an implicit confession of her love (108). By doing so, Lalla effectively uses her illness as a tool to ensnare Marcello, conflating sexual appetite with illness.

The association between passion and illness is even more marked in the case of Beatrice, whose mother had died of heart disease, a condition apparently caused by excessive emotion and reflected in the very title of the novel. Alarmed by her mother's untimely and peculiar death, Beatrice had rid her own life of any emotional disturbance in an attempt to avert this hereditary disease. But provoked by Lalla's example, she finally gives up the charade of living without love and reveals a sexual appetite unimaginable up to that point. No longer the "gentle beloved," she becomes "the imperious, hot-tempered, capricious, impassioned, jealous lover . . ." (253) in a description evoking that of Lalla. Indeed, Lalla's illness underlines the affinity between the two female characters in this novel and, significantly, exposes the capacity for sexual desire inherent in even those characters who stereotypically represent feminine virtue. Beatrice expresses her sexuality with even more abandon than Lalla. As in Lalla's case, illness and sexuality are once again linked, for Beatrice becomes progressively weaker as her love for Marcello grows more passionate and is expressed with even greater abandon.

The parallel between Lalla and Beatrice reverses the conventional closure in which the male protagonist is ruined by his liaison with the *femme fatale,* as Lalla's lethal powers ultimately lead to the destruction of Beatrice, rather than Marcello. Again, Serao seems more interested in exploring the dynamic between the two women than the heterosexual affair around which this narrative would traditionally revolve. One afternoon, while arranging flowers in her arbor, Beatrice glimpses Lalla, "bent" and "pallid," walking slowly down the lane (269). Disturbed by the sight of her former rival, Beatrice collapses and dies. She lies surrounded by flowers, emblematic of the sensuality awakened by Lalla. A circle of sun is painted on her lips, reminiscent of the Sphinx-like smile symbolizing the seductive powers of the *femme fatale.* Beatrice's appropriation of Lalla's sensuality may be fatal, but the final image of this once-repressed and passive woman is strikingly moving, suggesting a spiritual, if not a corporeal, liberation.

By closing with a dysphoric ending, the novel fails to conform to conventional structure. It continues in an intriguing epilogue that again emphasizes the presence of the novel's *femme fatale* rather than its heroine. In this scene, a grieving Marcello visits Beatrice's grave, where he encounters Lalla, "pale, a little older, but with that ever magnetic glance" (286). She, too, is clad in mourning, underlining her own peculiar relationship with Beatrice, a relationship she evokes when she reminds Marcello, "There were three of us who loved each other" (287). But despite the connection among the three protagonists, Lalla's status as an outsider is again emphasized. While Marcello remains bowed over his wife's grave, Lalla slowly walks off, alone and excluded. However, when set against the conventions of fictional resolution in which unsanctioned sexual behavior is often severely punished, the originality of Serao's text becomes clear. In this narrative, one female character, whose sexuality is freely expressed but contained within the sanctioned bond of marriage, dies. The other female protagonist, one whose sexuality is generated and satisfied outside of the laws of society, is rescued from textual extinction.

Lalla is portrayed as an outsider, disrupting the social order with an excess of erotic energy, but what happens to both the narrative structure and, indeed, the very image of the *femme fatale* when this figure works her magic from *within* the sanctioned world? Serao addresses that question in the 1883 novel *Fantasia,* which offers an even more complex and thoughtful portrayal of female sexuality. The author's depiction of unchecked desire in this text clearly disturbed those accustomed to equating female sexuality with procreation and limiting it to that function. Indeed, contemporary critics, while praising the novel's literary merits, were shocked by its overtly erotic content and apparent disregard for an unequivocal moral conclusion. Enrico Nencioni, for example, believed the text lacked "the idea of the conscience and of human responsibility. . . ."[56] In response to this pervasive attitude, I would argue that the literary establishment was incapable of distinguishing (or unwilling to distinguish) between the subject matter of a text and its female authorship. Women writers were not only expected to emulate conventional, male-constructed literary standards, they were often held to a higher moral standard in the execution of these tenets. Texts such as *Fantasia,* which dealt with adultery and erotic impulses, were judged on a moral as well as an aesthetic basis. However, despite (or because of) critical grumbling about its content, *Fantasia* was wildly popular with the public, establishing Serao's reputation as an important literary figure as well as a chronicler of social mores.[57]

On one level, the novel reads as an intensified version of *Cuore infermo*, published two years earlier. In *Fantasia*, the *femme fatale* not only steals away her best friend's husband, destroying her friend in the process, she escapes unpunished. But there are significant differences between the two in their portrayal of female desire, which in turns lead to an important reconstruction of the very idea of female sexuality. A brief summary of the narrative reveals a text substantially more sophisticated and balanced than that of *Cuore infermo*. In *Fantasia*, Caterina Spaccapietra, a placid and gentle Neapolitan, is married to the robust outdoorsman Andrea Lieti, and her best friend, the seductive Lucia Altimare, has wed Alberto Sanna. The novel begins with a description of the two women as young students, but it soon focuses on the liaison between Lucia and Andrea and finally ends with the death of Caterina, who commits suicide after discovering the double betrayal. The inclusion of four characters rather than three has led to simplistic analyses based on the differences between the two men and the two women and their relative positions along the spectrum of conventional literary paradigms. The exotic Lucia, for example, is often dismissed as being simply a foil to the angelic Caterina, rather than being acknowledged as a complex character in her own right. The sensitive portrait of this character, however, reveals how Serao both acknowledges and subverts the traditional depiction of a *femme fatale*.

Even as a young woman, Lucia demonstrates characteristics traditionally attributed to that of the *femme fatale*. Her excessive religious devotion, hinting at untold depths of feeling, distinguishes her from her classmates. She is easily moved to tears by both prayer and music, an indication of a heightened sensitivity and emotional susceptibility. The first section of the novel, set in a local Catholic boarding school, does more than illustrate Lucia's eccentric behavior, however; it establishes her countenanced status within a community. By depicting her as an adolescent, Serao endows Lucia with a history, an attribute denied most *femmes fatales* and one that confers on this character a clearly delineated past. Lucia does not materialize from nowhere or arrive mysteriously from some exotic land, like the enigmatic Lalla in *Cuore infermo*. Instead, she has a past and a family, albeit an unhappy one. But despite being a legitimate member of the Neapolitan bourgeoisie, Lucia clearly feels alienated from it. Perhaps this alienation stems from an acute awareness of her own position in the social world, a position severely circumscribed by her gender. Even as a schoolgirl, she recognizes both the limited engagement women have with the intellectual and cultural domain and the social expectations that tie them to the hearth. "If I were a man, I would go to Africa to explore unknown regions," she tells Caterina. "If I were a man I would become a missionary monk in China, in Japan, far, far away. But I am a woman, a weak and useless woman."[58] Unlike many *femmes fatales* who revel in the trappings associated with their gender and operate on a plane of exaggerated femininity, Lucia sees, instead, its limitations. Are her subsequent sexual transgressions an attempt to cross into a province traditionally forbidden to women? Is the expression of female sexuality the result of the suppression of social and cultural opportunities for women? Is this then the origin of Lalla's excess eroticism in *Cuore infermo*? If this were indeed the case, then the erotic impulse would serve as a source of power and liberation for the *femme fatale*, endowing her with an authority heretofore denied her. This interpretation is an intriguing one, and Lucia certainly enjoys a degree of authority denied more conventional heroines, but I am reluctant to attribute to Serao such a radical revision of the figure of the *femme fatale*. The author was certainly cognizant of the limited opportunities for women, but I suspect she would not have compensated for those limitations (or indeed, superseded them) through the manifestation of hypersexuality. However, I do believe that Serao's portrayal of Lucia hinges on the suppression of the character's aspirations and of her explicit uneasiness with social expectations.

Lucia's alienation from these expectations results in occasional attacks of nerves and illness, physical manifestations of her emotional and spiritual condition. Illness or physical weakness has historically been the domain of the *femme fatale*, even though a striking number of nineteenth-century texts are inhabited by invalid or sickly heroines who do not otherwise manifest traditional attributes of this character. In these works, sickness often symbolizes a woman's dis-ease with contemporary society: "Illness becomes a way to resist the sexist norms of nineteenth-century society, a specifically feminine form of revolt against male control, and a sign of *real* health in a *sick* world."[59] A debilitating illness becomes not only a rejection of societal prescriptions, but also an escape from them. It is ironic, then, that Lucia decides to marry her sickly cousin Alberto, despite earlier avowals that she would never wed. Despite the dis-ease she may feel with the expectations of her world, she is helpless to escape them. With this neat and effective plot development, Serao further underscores both Lucia's sanctioned position in the social world and the negation of her own aspirations. The marriage transforms Lucia's heroic vision of explorer and missionary into the more acceptable roles of wife and nurse.

But although Lucia is ensconced in these sanctioned roles, she cannot escape her own erotic desires. Serao encodes Lucia's sexuality in metaphors linking her to the natural world, a common trope in depictions of the *femme fatale*. Lucia is described at various moments as a "slender mermaid" (56), a "serpent" (86), and a "tiger" (98), and she is repeatedly compared to a variety of flowers. This association with nature along with its attendant erotic symbolism are emphasized during several scenes that unfold at an agricultural exposition, scenes in which Lucia and Andrea acknowledge the strong sexual and emotional attraction between the two of them.[60] In one such scene, the two visit the animal barn, where Lucia is overcome by the pungent odor of steamy horses. In the flower hall, surrounded by the scent of exotic blooms, it is Andrea's turn to feel faint. Later, the pair confess their love and desire in the verdant surroundings of a lush garden, chaperoned (in what surely must be an ironic touch) by a small statue of Venus. Although the connection between the natural world and erotic desire is a literary commonplace, these scenes and others reveal a deliberate recasting of the traditional aggressivity and sexual appetite of the *femme fatale*. Although Lucia is clearly a woman of dangerous charms—she is repeatedly described as being "a witch" and "a sorceress"—she remains reluctant to betray Caterina and Alberto.[61] She tells Andrea that their love would be "a sacrilege," (174), "a grave danger," (175), and "a folly" (175). Lucia's sexuality is more pronounced than that of Lalla's in *Cuore infermo,* but she is less willing to succumb to her own libidinous desires if it means losing her husband and her best friend.[62]

In a fascinating device that further removes Lucia from the conventional image of the *femme fatale,* Serao displaces the character's sexuality onto the artistic realm. Even as a student she had showed signs of an exaggerated romantic sensitivity. After Caterina cursorily recites the life of the Roman noblewoman Bea-trice di Tenda during a history lesson, Lucia embroiders her version with lurid descriptions of passion and death. Her teacher promptly chastises her for having "too much fantasy" (17). As another example, Lucia's fertile imagination, although stifled by a pedantic education system, is manifested in even the most inno-cent of domestic skills: sewing. She joins a myriad of Victorian heroines for whom needlework served as a metaphor for unex-pressed desire. This apparently innocuous activity, explicitly linked to the domestic and feminine sphere, offers the potential for unchecked creativity.[63] In this novel, Lucia weaves a richly colored tapestry, "all of fantasy," containing a bizarre collection of the natural world to which she is connected: stars, animals, fruits, and vegetables (181). Again I ask, is Lucia's creative energy, as reflected in her tapestry and celebrated in the very title of the novel, a sublimation of the inappropriate endeavors she dreamed of as an adolescent? In this instance, I would answer that Serao is indeed displacing Lucia's frustrated ambitions into a "safer," more domestic sphere. In an even more significant manifestation of Lucia's creativity, the reader learns that along with her needle-work, she is also writing a novel. This novel, described as being "all of fantasy, all of creation, which certainly would have super-seded those of all the Italian authors," is not what it appears to be (182). It turns out to be Lucia's diary, in which she has re-counted the development and the details of her liaison with An-drea. As her husband cries out upon finding the work, "Oh, there are magnificent passages of description, there are beautiful things, narrated inside it. It is an instructive and interesting read-ing" (249). By writing this text, Lucia places her sexuality onto the written page, authenticating her experience by immortalizing it. Her narrative, rather than the adventures she sought in her younger years, becomes an extension of her sensual desires. By transcribing her sexuality, Lucia literally makes the flesh word. The act of writing also allows her to narrate and interpret her sexuality herself, in a subjective act.

As the novel draws to a close, Lucia reveals the more destructive attributes of the conventional *femme fatale*. The text's resolution, however, is significantly different from that of *Cuore infermo*, which saw the dissolution of the romantic liaison and a reaffirmation of the *femme fatale*'s status as outsider. In *Fantasia*, the *femme fatale* gets her man, as it were, albeit at quite a price. By running off with

Andrea, Lucia destroys both her sickly husband, whose condition worsens dramatically, and her best friend, who commits suicide. As a symbol of this act of perfidy, Caterina clutches in her lifeless hands half of Lucia's broken rosary, a reminder of the vow of eternal friendship the two had pledged before leaving school. Despite Serao's statement in a private letter that Lucia "ends by sacrificing all the characters in the novel to her own egoism," she remains an intriguing and not entirely unsympathetic character.[64] Her very excesses—mysterious illnesses, strange eating habits, heightened sensitivity to music and nature—almost seem a clever parody of the traditional *femme fatale*. Serao rescues her from caricature, endowing her with unfulfilled aspirations, a family history, and a solid social standing. Even more arresting is the emphasis placed on Lucia's artistic endeavors and their connection with her erotic impulses. In this text, female desire and sexuality are driven in part by creative forces, an intriguing reading of the conventional, typically negative portrayal of the *femme fatale*.

Serao continues her project of questioning conventional depictions of female desire in her novel *Addio, amore!* (1890). But unlike *Cuore infermo* and *Fantasia,* the locus of desire in this narrative is found not in a character who trespasses on the marital covenant, but rather in a female protagonist who is "both morally good and sexually passionate."[65] With Anna Acquaviva, the heroine of this novel, Serao succeeds in creating a female character who integrates the attributes of both the "angel in the house" and the *femme fatale*. Anna defies categorization, an astonishing accomplishment if one considers the scores of stereotypical heroines inhabiting the pages of nineteenth-century literature. Even more significant for the purposes of this study are the implications conveyed by this character, for through her portrayal Serao enters into the debate surrounding the correlation between gender and intellect, nature and culture. In other words, she questions the very assumptions concerning the construction of Woman.

At the outset of the text, Anna is established as the representative of unbridled longings, desires that manifest themselves not only physically but also in the startling action they propel her to take. In the opening scene, Anna is slipping out of bed to meet Giustino Morelli, the impoverished young man with whom she has fallen desperately in love. Like Lucia in *Fantasia,* Anna's passion becomes associated with strange and exaggerated physical symptoms, as Serao underscores the somatic effects of unchecked desire. Indeed, the mere thought of Giustino generates an intense reaction in Anna: "[A] fire climbed from her heart to her brain, spread through her blood, burning her veins, increasing her pulse rate, burning her flesh, increasing the throbbing of her arteries so excessively that she could not follow the precipitous movement."[66] In short, she tells Giustino, she is "consumed by passion" (19).[67] But Anna's passion is left unconsummated, for despite their plans to elope, Giustino, keenly aware of the class differences between them, eventually refuses to marry her. After his rejection, Anna is struck by a debilitating illness that is explicitly linked to her frustrated desires: her blood was "too rich, too ardent, too impetuous . . ." (51). As was the case with Lalla in *Cuore infermo*, whose illness helped to ensnare Marcello, in *Addio, amore!* Anna's malady serves as the instrument with which she secures the man she loves. It is no longer Giustino, however, for during her long illness she has transferred her desire to Cesare Dias, a cold, stern man who has served as guardian for Anna and her sister since their parents' deaths. He, however, ignores or ridicules Anna's avowals of love until she sickens unto the point of death, and the exasperated Cesare finally agrees to marry her.

This is hardly an auspicious beginning for a marriage, and Serao soon emphasizes the inherent differences between the two, differences that will eventually point to a crucial split in gender-constructed behavior. Expecting the marriage to serve as an outlet for her passion and sexuality, Anna is soon frustrated. Cesare's indifference toward her continues long after the wedding vows, as do, Anna suspects, his earlier liaisons. Her pitiful attempts to turn his coldness into love are met with derision, and she is forced to transfer her longings onto her husband's possessions. While waiting for Cesare one evening, for example, she picks up his gloves, kissing them "with a crazy outburst of passion," and passing them over her breast in a vivid illustration of her unhappiness and frustration (201). Anna's increasing misery and loneliness continue for months, reaching their climax one evening when she discovers Cesare kissing her sister Laura. After hysterical scenes with Laura and her husband, both of whom dispassionately deny Anna's right to Cesare's love, she kills herself.[68] Even Anna's method of suicide symbolizes the intensity of her passion, for she shoots herself in the heart, targeting the very source of her anguish. She does not obtain the serenity usually granted by death, however, for the author notes that her face is marked by "the sorrow of they who were Passion and who were killed by Indifference" (300).[69] By casting Anna as the very personification of Passion, Serao appears to encourage an essentialist reading of the character; that is, one reduced to the most fundamental (and typically negative) attribute of the *femme fatale*. I would posit, however, that the author instead has created a complex, atypical heroine, one both virtuous *and* passionate, and by doing so has opened up the portrayal of this figure and of female sexuality in general.

This is all by way of an introduction, for underlying Serao's portrayal of Anna and the resulting examination of female desire and traditional literary characterizations of women lies an even broader issue. In *Addio, amore!*, Serao addresses the nineteenth-century scientific and cultural debate that casts women as the embodiment of instinct and men as the representatives of the intellect. Cavalli Pasini, in her examination of the scientific influences on the nineteenth-century novel, explores the contemporary belief in a "woman's intuition." This supposedly inherent faculty stemmed in part from a woman's close connections with nature, exemplified primarily by the reproductive process. Men were considered more removed from this process and from nature in general and became associated with intellectual activity. "[O]ne can note," Cavalli Pasini writes, "that during the *fin de siècle* the idea of an antagonism between cerebral activity and procreation, the first reserved exclusively for men, the second typical of women, takes hold with force."[70] Serao engages in this debate through her presentation of the principal protagonists in *Addio, amore!* In his role as guardian, and later as husband, Cesare endeavors to master both Anna and her instinctual drives. After Anna's failed elopement with Giustino and during her subsequent illness, he takes advantage of Anna's weakened state, when her spirit is "malleable as wax" (60). Cesare attempts to eradicate "the flame of passion" (57) and, indeed, under his tutelage, Anna appears obedient, resigned, and humble. But Cesare's endeavors to subdue his wife's passionate nature are not completely successful. Despite a new-found passivity and a willingness to temper her earlier fervor, Anna has not changed: "She knows only how to love and obey love" (132).

Cesare's attempt to domesticate Anna rests on a linguistic motif that underscores Serao's interest in the culture/nature polemic. In order to be fully socialized into the sanctioned social world, the female protagonist must recognize not only the folly of her desire, but also the supremacy of the male model of discourse. The phrase *"avere ragione,"* or "to be right," is used repeatedly to emphasize Anna's apparent acceptance of Cesare's mastery. During her illness, the once assertive Anna passively submits to Cesare's indoctrination: "She would have only said yes, Anna Acquaviva: since she had been wrong and the others, all of them, were right" (63). As Elisabetta Rasy points out, Cesare acts as an omniscient teacher, and Anna is cast as his pliant and somewhat obtuse student.[71] This dynamic between an older male protagonist who educates a neophyte young woman is a common trope in Serao's works, according to Isabella Pezzini. She has found that male characters are often described as the "depositary of the law" and the "depositary of reason."[72] Indeed, in *Addio, amore!* Cesare tells Anna, "The opinions of girls don't count, my dear. You're very intelligent, there's no doubt; but you understand nothing" (102). Cesare instructs Anna not only to forget her earlier passions, he also teaches her a more general lesson. He inculcates in her the widespread nineteenth-century valuation of gendered roles and capabilities. Anna must learn to accept the hierarchy established by Cesare, who acts as the mouthpiece for hegemonic cultural and scientific beliefs. Woman, as the personification of the sentient and physical world, is "naturally" inferior to Man.

Anna negates this rhetoric by revealing the vapidity and destructiveness behind Cesare's discourse. In the climactic scene with her husband, she rejects his *"ragione,"* overturning the hierarchical valuation of gendered roles:

Oh how you are right, always, all your life: from since I have known you until today, how you've always known how to put yourself on the side of reason! You're right in your egoism, in your perfidy, in your perverseness, in your fearful corruption. . . . (286)

The final scene, in which Anna chooses to kill herself rather than live without her husband's love, can be read on one level as the rather hollow victory of Intellect over Emotion. With the depiction of Anna's suicide, then, Serao portrays the sociocultural polemic concerning gendered attributes in nineteenth-century Italy, as well as the symbolic struggle of the doomed destiny of women.

Serao's presentation of female desire in these three texts evolves, then, into an examination of fundamental cultural stereotypes concerning women and their role in society. Lalla, in *Cuore infermo,*

despite her rather peculiar relationship with Beatrice, incorporates most of the traditional attributes of the *femme fatale*, from
her outsider status to her exaggerated sensuality. Lucia is a more
integrated character, both within society and within the text
proper, playing a central role in *Fantasia*. Despite the familiar
trope of illness, Lucia's established position within society demonstrates Serao's desire to move away from purely negative portrayals
of an eroticized female protagonist. This project reaches its fru-
ition in *Addio, amore!*, for Anna is perhaps Serao's most fully integrated portrayal of female desire. After her first, unfulfilled love
for Giustino, Anna's desire is expressed (if not reciprocated)
within the marital bond. Her rectitude, moreover, is in no way
compromised by her desire, creating the portrait of a literary
heroine endowed with both integrity and sensuality. This complex,
almost philosophical study moves beyond the traditional romance
novel to examine the underlying cultural debates concerning a
woman's role in society.

Serao's romance texts address fundamental nineteenth-century
cultural and literary debates, including the primacy of marriage
in a woman's life, the construction of female identity in a patriarchal society, and the gendered valuation of social roles. Her works
exemplify Massimo Romano's thesis that even popular literature
serves as a reflection of ideological beliefs. The *romanzo d'appendice*,
for example, is important not only for its literary value, but "as
much as a sociological phenomenon, an indication and a reflection
of custom, of the ideology and of the imaginary universe of a
given historical period."[73] The use of romance texts and popular
literature in general as guides in the study of a particular time
and place, validates the exploration of a genre generally devalued
by literary purists. More specifically, the romance text appears
especially appropriate for an examination of the construction of
femininity and female roles. Even seemingly traditional heroines
and conventional love plots can question prescribed paradigms of
female behavior.[74] Deanna Shemek notes that "Serao's love novels
present a fictional world where women's passionate desires constitute a positive force struggling within a repressive and enclosing
society."[75] Serao employed the romance text not only as a vehicle
to further shape her fictive city of women, but also as a forum to
examine, and occasionally reject, contemporary orthodoxy concerning the female character and her place in society.

In order to address these issues, Serao had to contend with

entrenched literary traditions concerning the structure of the romance proper. In the texts *Tre donne,* "La grande fiamma," and particularly in "Paolo Spada," one can see the concern and even anxiety with which Serao confronted these traditions. If she failed to deviate in any radical sense from conventional narrative patterns, she did successfully question their value. Serao's desire to write beyond the traditional closure of conventional love stories led her to explore the stifling consequences of heterosexual relationships in such works as *La ballerina* and "O Giovannino o la morte." Again, even though these works reveal her fundamental observance of conventional literary narrative structures, she did succeed in creating the enigmatic and provocative "Livia Spera." Perhaps an even greater legacy of Serao's romance texts, however, is her exploration of the expression of female sexuality. In these works, Serao reconfigures the character of the *femme fatale* in a way that celebrates her special attributes, a potentially subversive literary maneuver. By questioning fictive portrayals of female desire and sexuality, Serao simultaneously points a finger at the cultural ideologies that shape such literary assumptions. She significantly expands her depiction of female experiences, then, by examining not only conventional male-female dynamics but also the very social matrix within which those relationships are formed.

3

Family Gothic

Within the forum of the Gothic text, Matilde Serao continues her project of depicting female experiences in a threatening and oppressive world, but in these works, the danger often comes from within the domestic space. Although she does make use of the Gothic tenets that emphasize the perils inherent within the family circle, Serao often moves beyond that schematic to explore the dynamics of the family structure itself. Again, as noted in the examination of her realist and romance texts, Serao's insistence on observing, and occasionally challenging, the status of women in turn-of-the-century Italy reaches across the boundaries of literary genres. When she writes in the Gothic genre, for example, the framework becomes an opportunity to delve even more deeply into the intricacies of historically overlooked female experiences, specifically, that of the bond between mother and daughter. If, to continue the trope begun in the introduction, Serao is constructing in her texts a metaphorical city of women, her Gothic works illustrate not only the worldly environs of her heroines and their relationships with lovers, but also their domestic spaces, where familial bonds take center stage. The reader is no longer backstage with the ballerina Carmela or in the noisy bustle of Caterina's telegraph office, but has been drawn into the intimate world of parent and child, husband and wife. Serao builds yet another edifice of meaning in her imaginary metropolis, revealing the construction of family life, a configuration that both reflects and reinforces the gender-based hierarchical structure of the world outside the family.

In their examination of familial ties and roles, these works uncover the problematic construction of female identity and subject formation. Linked to these issues, which she previously examined in the romance texts *La ballerina*, "O Giovannino o la morte," and *Tre donne*, is the topic of female anxiety and the creative process.

In her Gothic-influenced works, however, Serao more explicitly confronts these themes and more conclusively weds them to her own often contradictory attitudes toward female roles in turn-of-the-century Italy. Perhaps she recognized that the relative latitude of the Gothic framework, with its bigger cast of characters, looser narrative structure, and wider range of subjects, allowed for greater stylistic experimentation and thematic innovation than did the more rigid precepts of the romance text. Serao's reshaping of conventional narrative strategy as well as the very literary and cultural assumptions upon which it rests, although at times eclipsed by the convoluted plotting of the Gothic work, do suggest a deliberate and clearly discernible attempt to address gendered roles, both in the construction of the literary text and in the many depictions within such a work. Certainly in these Gothic texts, Serao's reworking of the conventions of the genre reveals her evolving ideological position on the various social and familial roles of women.

Serao's innovative thematic approach to these works corresponds to a stylistic evolution, as she gradually extricates herself from restrictive genre tenets. These works, four lengthy novels and two short stories, reject a single-genre strategy to blend realist techniques and romantic subplots with the conventions of the mystery, the detective story, and Gothic fiction. The effect of this overwhelming mixture of genres has not always resulted in a positive assessment of the author, for with the exception of the novel *Il paese di cuccagna,* acknowledged as one of Serao's masterpieces, these works were largely ignored or dismissed by contemporary critics. This critical neglect may have stemmed not only from the frustration Serao provoked by creating texts that eluded genre categorization, but also from a more generalized disdain for popular literature. In other words, these Gothic works suffered the same fate as many of Serao's romance texts. They were compared (unfavorably, in most cases) with her realist works rather than being examined either within the context of contemporary popular fiction or by means of an investigation of the author's contribution, through these generic reworkings, to a national literature.

The Gothic narrative itself has a long and illustrious pedigree. Born in late eighteenth-century England, the genre was in part a reaction to the sentimentalism in works by such authors as Samuel

Richardson and Lawrence Sterne. Gothic structure and themes reflected the increasingly popular exercise of self-exploration. The realist novel calls for an engagement with the social world, whereas "Gothic and romantic writing usually lead the reader to consider internal mental processes and reactions."[1] The Gothic can be read as an inversion of the romance, its world ruled by fear and terror rather than by love. With this definition of the Gothic as a basis, it becomes apparent that Serao uses this particular genre to articulate and even to criticize the cultural discourse that defined and dictated female behavior.

The archetypal Gothic flourished in England between 1764, when Horace Walpole's *The Castle of Otranto* was published, and 1820, when Charles Robert Maturin's *Melmouth the Wanderer* appeared. This brief period saw the publication of a number of classic Gothic texts, including Ann Radcliffe's *The Mysteries of Udolpho* (1794) and *The Italian* (1797), Matthew Lewis's *The Monk* (1796), and Mary Shelley's *Frankenstein* (1818). The genre was so popular it even generated a series of parodies, including Jane Austen's droll *Northanger Abbey* (1818). The most celebrated Gothic works share a number of conventions and themes, such as a forbidding castle; a Medieval setting in Italy or an equally exotic locale; a moral struggle between good and evil, represented by a romantic if passive hero and a sadistic but not entirely unattractive villain; and a reliance on ghostly apparitions, doubles, dreams, masking, and insanity.[2] Later narratives, such as Edgar Allen Poe's short stories, Henry James's *The Turn of the Screw,* Carson McCullers's *The Ballad of the Sad Cafe,* Daphne du Maurier's *Rebecca,* and even Anne Rice's vampire novels, often incorporate and modernize these conventions.[3]

Because of its focus on female experiences, the Gothic, in both its original and its modern forms, has provided a rich theater of study for feminist and cultural critics. Indeed, it has become almost a commonplace to say that women writers, using the Gothic as a vehicle to express anxiety about female social roles, have dominated the genre.[4] In a sensitive study that sheds light on this phenomenon, Leonard Wolf concludes that feelings of female oppression and frustration are actually encoded within the Gothic:

Despite the triumphs of Lewis and Maturin, the Gothic novel was something of a cottage industry of middle-class women—as if women, oppressed by needlepoint, whalebone stays, psychic frustrations, shame and babies, found in the making and consuming of these fictions a way to signal each other (and perhaps the world of men) the shadowy outlines of their own pain.[5]

In this analysis of the origins of the female Gothic, Wolf links the trappings of the domestic space with the production of Gothic literature. His observations are shared by those who see the Gothic as a unique forum for both revealing and indicting social restrictions on female development and behavior. Also, it is a genre that lends itself to a variety of gender-based strategies in its construction and its intent. Early male Gothicists, for example, focused on "horrible spectacles of sexual violence, gore, and death, locating evil in the 'other'—women, Catholics, Jews, and ultimately the devil," writes Kari J. Winter. She continues, "In contrast, female Gothic novelists uncovered the terror of the familiar: the routine brutality and injustice of the patriarchal family, conventional religion, and classist social structures."[6] A heroine's safety, the woman-authored Gothic tells us, is threatened from within her known world, rather than by the nameless, external terrors of many male-authored texts. By setting these works in a menacing, gloomy castle, the female author emphasizes the horrors of a woman's restricted life and reveals that it is the negotiation of internal, rather than external, spaces that becomes perilous and threatening for women. It is through this examination of institutional patriarchy that female practioners of the genre also investigate such themes as the alienation and silencing of women.

In the Gothic, it is the heroine's position as Woman that marks her in particular and that gives rise to uniquely female concerns. Juliann E. Fleenor, in her thoughtful essay on the genre, writes that the Gothic generates powerful emotions that turn on those issues specifically related to women, such as procreation, the expression of female sexuality, and the positioning of women within the familial and the social worlds. She adds, "At the center of the Female Gothic is the conflict over female identity."[7] It is this conflict that Serao examines in many of her Gothic narratives. By depicting these themes, and I include as well the mother-daughter bond as a female-centered Gothic topic, Serao reveals women's experiences in turn-of-the-century Italy while constructing her own portrayal of sisterly solace in an often forbidding social landscape.

In Italy, as in other parts of the Continent, the English Gothic tradition gradually evolved into the historic novel in the tradition of Alessandro Manzoni.[8] Precise distinctions among these various genres are not always possible, however. Fredric Jameson, for example, points out that Manzoni's novel *I promessi sposi* (The Betrothed) actually encompasses two narratives, one, with Gothic overtones, describing Lucia's story, and a second, similar to an adventure tale, following Renzo's exploits.[9] The novel's structure, with its dual focus, combines the traditional female- and male-focused narratives, one examining an interior space and the other depicting a more public sphere. But few Italian authors penned narratives in the manner of the classic English Gothic, as the novelistic tradition came relatively late to Italy.[10] One short-lived school of artists, however, did incorporate Gothic elements into its works. The *Scapigliatura*, the name a loose translation of the word "bohemia," was a Milan-based group of authors and artists who were popular between 1860 and 1880. The movement, which included Emilio Praga, the Boito brothers, Arrigo and Camillo, and Igino Ugo Tarchetti, drew on foreign literary models for inspiration rather than on Manzoni's Christian realism. These authors were particularly influenced by E. T. A. Hoffmann's fantastic stories, devising their own brand of Gothic tale, or *racconto nero*. By writing narratives that incorporated the supernatural, alchemy, dreams, and ghosts, the authors of the *racconti neri* created an intriguing body of work that acted as a type of "fairy tale for adults."[11] Serao's texts, however, seem more clearly influenced by the traditional English Gothic novel rather than the *Scapigliati*'s texts and their metaphysical focus. Despite the occasional intimation of supernatural phenomena in her Gothic works, she rarely abandoned her journalistic training or her background in realist precepts to create texts as fantastical or fanciful as those of the *Scapigliati*.

Although texts written by traditional Gothicists and the *Scapigliati* often depict imaginary worlds, they typically do so against a backdrop of specific cultural and social events of eighteenth- or nineteenth-century Europe. The quest for scientific knowledge, for example, becomes a dominant literary theme in a century that saw the birth of Darwinism and positivism, massive industrialization, and the institutionalization of the medical profession, as well as significant technological advances. The dangers of overreaching mortal limitations also figures as a motif throughout late Gothic literature, as exemplified in such texts as Mary Shelley's *Franken-stein* and Hoffmann's "The Sand-Man" (1816–1817).

One of Serao's most intriguing works, the 1890 short story "Un inventore" (An Inventor), incorporates elements of this theme while also articulating her vision of the creative drive. Like the earlier works, the tale cautions against challenging divine powers and warns of the dangers of usurping procreative faculties. "Un inventore," which chronicles the adventures of a toymaker whose designs become progressively more fantastic, both conforms to and breaks with traditional Gothic technique. For example, the tale is set in Nuremberg, an exotic foreign locale, rare in Serao's predominately Neapolitan-based narratives. The choice of setting is of course deliberate, for it accentuates the tale's strangeness; indeed, Nuremberg is described as a "Gothic city, with fantastic and bizarre architecture."[12] But Serao lightens the narrative's atmosphere, creating a melancholy tenor, rather than the men-acing mood found in most Gothic works. She also bypasses the traditional Gothic technique of multiple narrators, hidden manu-scripts, and explanatory letters, preferring a more direct nar-rative. Perhaps Serao's straightforward style, found in even her most structurally complex narratives, originated in her journalis-tic work. As discussed in this study's introduction, the line between Serao's literary and journalistic styles and techniques was ambigu-ous at best. Even in her most fantastic tales, such as this one, the author utilized clear and unembellished prose. Her approach to the craft of writing stemmed as much from her training in the trenches of journalism as in her lifelong experiments with various genres and literary techniques.

This experimentation becomes apparent in "Un inventore," for Ulrich, the inventor of the story's title, is one of the few male protagonists in Serao's almost entirely female cast of principal players. The choice of a hero rather than a heroine seems deliber-ate, both in light of the author's practice of featuring female pro-tagonists and in the theme underlying the story. Ulrich is another in a long line of literary characters—all male—endowed with the ability to create a bastardized form of life, thereby usurping fe-male procreative faculties for their own warped ambitions. This gendered difference in a character's involvement with his or her world was a critical element of Gothic texts, as William Patrick Day points out: "All the male protagonists . . . share the qualities of egotism and monomania; they seek to dominate their world, rather than accommodate themselves to it as the female characters do."[13] In Shelley's novel, for example, Victor Frankenstein, who as a young lad desired to learn "the secrets of heaven and earth," creates a gruesome monster capable of both reason and sentiment.[14] In the "Sand-Man," Professor Spalanzani, with the assistance of the mysterious watchmaker Giuseppe Coppola, constructs the beautiful automaton Olimpia in yet another instance of male procreation.

In "Un inventore," Ulrich also creates "life," as it were, fathering a series of dolls and endowing them with human attributes: "Everything consisted in giving an element of soul to the toys, in imparting a breath of life to them . . ." (231). But even though Ulrich's ambitions, like those of Frankenstein and Spalanzani, seem caught up in a self-destructive drive to create life, Serao subtly reshapes the more Gothic elements of this text. First, Ulrich is driven by artistic impulses rather than a twisted urge to generate his own progeny. In other words, even though he fashions lifelike objects, he is not coopting the divine ability to create life, but rather delighting in producing "a cheerful and honest work" (233). Ulrich directs his efforts not toward himself, but toward the infinite number of children who take pleasure in his toys. Frankenstein, on the other hand, is concerned with satisfying his own egotistical lust for knowledge, realizing only belatedly that with his scientific prowess he has unleashed a vengeful madman.

Although his motivation may be different from that of the protagonists of *Frankenstein* and "The Sand-Man," Ulrich eventually does exceed his reach, damning himself in the process. Clearly, the urge to transcend natural human limitations spells only doom in the eyes of these authors. Ulrich becomes obsessed with concocting increasingly fantastic toys and in the process becomes more and more removed from reality: "He walked with his head in the clouds, an artist in love with art, an incorrigible dreamer . . ." (234). Despite warnings from his supervisor to simplify his inventions, Ulrich creates "an extraordinary toy"—a miniature farm, complete with animated farmers, workers, and animals (237). Here he creates not only life-like figures, but an entire universe in which they can live and work. His toy is too sophisticated and complicated for children, however, and his nephew breaks it in frustration. Ulrich's delight in designing entertaining playthings has become lost in his obsession to surpass his earlier creations. Although Ulrich originally had no pretensions to be anything but a simple inventor, his artistic gifts carry him to almost immortal heights. From these heights, however, the descent is steep. Like Nathanael in "The Sand-Man," who falls under the hypnotic spell of the automaton Olimpia, Ulrich is eventually driven mad. As he stares at the moon, in an explicit reference to his insanity, Ulrich thinks obsessively about "the grandiose and unformed idea of a monstrous, gigantic, impossible toy" (239). He has become the epitome of the Gothic antihero: a victim of his own genius.

As an exercise in reinterpreting literary conventions, "Un inventore" is an entertaining example of the author's manipulation of the Gothic text. Serao's recasting of Gothic conventions creates an intimate, melancholy tale, free of the terror and despair of more traditional Gothic literature. She borrows settings and themes, but revises atmosphere and motivations in a move similar to her reworking of conventional realist tenets. By eliminating or diluting some of the more fantastic Gothic elements, Serao's preoccupation with the creative process itself, here linked explicitly to procreation, moves more readily into the foreground. The work may not be as harsh in tone as some earlier Gothic texts, but Ulrich's eventual downfall indicates the author's profound uneasiness with the notion of male procreation. Serao warns of the consequences of coopting divine powers and of appropriating procreative faculties traditionally associated with women. Motherhood, the author writes in both her fictive and nonfictive output, is a woman's greatest gift and highest duty. This ideology may have had a foundation in Serao's religious or cultural beliefs or even in her physiology, but perhaps she recognized as well the importance of designating a site of authority and creativity that would be available only to women. The resolution of "Un inventore" reveals Serao's anxiety about and even aversion to a male figure who, in his efforts to create objects bordering on the lifelike, usurps a female prerogative.

The anxiety inherent in relinquishing the female domain of procreation is mirrored in another source of apprehension, this time hinging on the construction of female identity. Serao confronts this topic in the enigmatic short story "La donna dell'abito nero e del ramo di corallo rosso" (The Woman in the Black Dress and with the Red Coral Brooch).[15] This 1890 work addresses many of the same issues, such as madness and the female double, examined in Charlotte Perkins Gilman's semiautobiographical text "The Yellow Wallpaper," published in the same year. Both stories deal with the very origin of female madness, attributing it to the psychic alienation women feel in a patriarchal society. Female Gothic authors often use the topos of madness to reflect a heroine's sense of frustration and estrangement. Lacking a socially sanctioned outlet for their creative impulses, female protagonists often manifest their despair and frustration in ways that trespass upon conventional standards of behavior. Given this scenario, literary madness is often represented by a psychic splitting of the self, as the character wrestles with, and finally surrenders to, the struggle of reconciling two distinct personae. In "La donna dell'abito nero," the psychic separation of the main character originates in feelings of anxiety about both literary and cultural constructions of femaleness. Serao uses the relative freedom of the Gothic forum, a genre that often generates probing analyses of the female psyche, to examine the difficulty in creating integrated heroines and to address the turn-of-the-century conundrum surrounding a woman's inherent "nature."

The tale is colored by feelings of rage and despair as the protagonist battles firsthand with literary and social images of women. The powerful first-person narration, stripped of all extraneous descriptive elements, bares startlingly raw emotions. Serao seldom used this technique, preferring works diffused in part by unobtrusive narrators removed from the text proper. But the first-person narration works very effectively in this gripping text, for it immediately focuses the narrative on the principal female protagonist while not diminishing the power of her tale through authorial asides or lengthy descriptions. The narrator, an unnamed woman writing from an insane asylum, vehemently directs her readers to listen to her "frightful secret" (105). She is, in her own words, "possessed" by a second self, a woman who overpowers the desires of the first self and in the process destroys her very world. Although neither of these two figures is described in any detail, the second self embodies the physical characteristics of the conventional *femme fatale*. The woman's deathly pallor and dark clothes reflect her predatory attributes, and her jet-black eyes and crimson mouth point to an inherent eroticism. The narrator, on the other hand, while perhaps not the conventional "angel in the house," is depicted as the other woman's opposite. As the tale progresses, it become apparent, as in "The Yellow Wallpaper," that the two female figures are indeed one woman. What happens, then, when the two personae are joined in one body? The result is disaster, as the second figure forces the first to act in ways contrary to her desires.

Under the sway of this second persona, the narrator finds herself swearing eternal love to a man she detests and treating another, one she truly loves, with contempt. As Ursula Fanning points out, by placing the narrator's duality against the backdrop of male-female relationships, the author emphasizes the explicit interconnection between female literary stereotypes and the manifestation of sexuality: "Serao seems to imply that the romantic male-female relationship leads to a sense of duality and, ultimately, of crisis for the female."[16] Indeed, the narrator feels happiest and most free when she is unfettered by amorous attachments: "[I] did not love anyone at that time . . . I did not love, I did not have regret of love, I did not have the desire for love" (109). The narrator is not bound by conventional images of women, which insist on enclosing them within the bonds of a relationship, but succeeds in maintaining a sense of integrity and autonomy although alone.

Even more interesting is Serao's examination of female madness, which arises from the duality of a woman's role and which is a traditional element of the Gothic. The narrator, although faced with a growing sense of internal fragmentation and estrangement from the social world, insists on her sanity: "It is not true that I'm crazy; I live, I feel, I remember, I reason" (106). The narrator's impassioned assertion reveals the frustration felt by female characters doomed to be both misunderstood and mistreated. This duality, Serao implies, is not madness but, instead, the natural consequence of attempting to reconcile two contradictory sets of female attributes.

I would go farther and posit that with this text Serao also examines the Darwinist-influenced psychiatric and medical beliefs prevalent in turn-of-the-century Europe. Under these assumptions, female physiology marked women as different, both physically and mentally. Women were assumed to be inherently and fundamentally inferior to men, their duty relegated to serving as men's helpmates rather than acting as their equals. The medical establishment conveniently utilized these allegedly scientific beliefs to justify and preserve a socioculturaleconomic system that denied female intellectual abilities and kept women rigidly con-

tained within a specific and narrow set of roles, primarily that
of wife and mother.[17] How do Serao and her nameless narrator
confront this restrictive notion of what it means to be female? In
the short story, the narrator scoffs at the diagnosis of insanity
inherent in the above definitions of womanhood and decries the
rough treatment suffered by the inmates of insane asylums: "I
am not crazy. . . . [T]he padded room, the hot bath, the constant
watch are useless" (106). The narrator is not only not insane, she
writes that she "has never possessed such lucidity, such soundness
of mind . . ." (106).

   By depicting a narrator who writes, Serao examines the position
of the female author as well as women in relation to the creative
impulse. It is interesting to note that this narrator demonstrates
such powers of rationality at the moment in which she is compos-
ing her narrative; indeed, the very act of writing confers lucidity.
By framing this figure in the setting of the asylum, Serao comments, albeit indirectly, on the difficulties with which women authors struggled in order to be heard and understood in a world
accustomed to negating female intellectual endeavors. This character not only writes, she articulates the source of her inspiration
and the objective of her narrative: "I am writing my secret," she
says, "so that one knows the truth of my case" (106). Her creative
process stems from a desire for the invention of self rather than
the creation of life, like Ulrich and Dr. Frankenstein. Rather than
self-glorification, this artist wants to share her story with other
women, using her narrative and indeed her very life as a cautionary tale. In "La donna dell'abito nero," Serao employs the Gothic
theme of madness to explore psychic fragmentation and literary
representations of women as well as the anxiety inherent in producing female-authored texts in a sometimes hostile literary and
social environment.

   Serao turns from the scientific doctrines underpinning literary
depictions of femaleness that are explored in "La donna dell'abito
nero" to a more pointed examination of the construction of female identity and sexuality in the 1893 novel *Castigo* (Punishment).
The novel, a sequel to *Addio, amore!,* is more overtly Gothic than
its precursor, colored as it is by an atmosphere of revenge and
guilt and laced with insinuations of supernatural happenings.
Even the title reflects the novel's general air of mystery and despondency. And like the stylistic strategies of "Un inventore," the

Gothic elements in *Castigo* are used almost as window dressing, both softening and camouflaging acute social commentary. By using a Gothic forum to continue the tale begun in *Addio, amore!*, Serao was able to impart a more caustic message, veiling it behind intricate narrative complications and the dazzle of other-worldly phenomena. The Gothic, like the romance text, proves fertile ground on which to examine female sexuality, a topic addressed in both these novels. The sequel, however, allows Serao to depict from yet another perspective the sexuality of her heroines. In this Gothic work, Serao uses the conventions of the genre to underscore the relationship between the enclosure of women in the domestic sphere and the expression of their sexuality. She augments her depiction of the *femme fatale* in the romance texts by manipulating the tenets of the Gothic to expose and demystify female sexuality, bringing it out of the hidden domestic space around which the genre pivots.

Serao underscores the narrative links between the two novels, for *Castigo* picks up just hours after the conclusion of *Addio, amore!*, which ends with the suicide of Anna Acquaviva, who has killed herself after discovering the double betrayal of her husband, Cesare, and her sister, Laura. At the center of *Castigo* lie two seemingly unrelated mysteries: Was Anna the lover of Luigi Caracciolo, in whose home she killed herself? And who is Hermione, the enigmatic Englishwoman with a strange predilection for the macabre and an uncanny resemblance to Anna? Both mysteries become closely linked with the construction of female identity within heterosexual relationships, a theme presented in Serao's earlier realist works but here dealt with in a particularly Gothic fashion. In other words, the threat inherent in these relationships is both more explicit and more destructive, underlining the fragility of female protagonists within the Gothic forum.

In *Addio, amore!*, Anna's identity was based in part on her passionate nature, a disposition that rejected her husband's gender-based assumptions about male and female discourses. In *Castigo*, Serao returns to this topic, focusing on the expression of Anna's sexuality. The author raises this issue immediately, using the particularly Gothic device of the veil as a metonymic symbol of the character's sexuality. Veils and masks reveal as much as hide, and often hold sexual connotations: "[T]he veil that conceals and inhibits sexuality comes by the same gesture to represent it, both as a metonym of the thing covered and as a metaphor for the system of prohibitions by which sexual desire is enhanced and specified."[18] In *Castigo,* the wedding veil enshrouding Anna as she lies on her funereal bed points beyond wifely devotion to suggest unsuspected depths of passion. When Cesare, in his lonely vigil, finally lifts the veil, he is shocked to see "a stupefying and terrible spectacle."[19] Anna's face is not marked by the serenity typically granted in fictional deaths, but by "an intense, profound expression of regret . . ." (27). What does Anna regret? Is it her perfidious betrayal by Cesare, or some desire never fulfilled? The veil serves to obfuscate not only the regret and reproach depicted on Anna's face, but also her own sexual appetite.

Tellingly, a veil is not worn by Laura, the duplicitous sister, at her wedding to Cesare seven months after Anna's death. Serao's careful note of the omission underscores the significance of this motif in *Castigo.* In Laura's case, there is presumably no longer any mystery attached to the expression of her sexual desires as her liaison with Cesare has already been consummated and, with the wedding, legitimized. She needs no veil to suggest hidden desires, for her once-forbidden passions have become contained within the socially accepted bonds of marriage.

It is Anna's unsanctioned passions, however, that constitute both the crux of the novel and its narrative structure. As discussed in the preceding chapter, the expression of female sexuality often serves as the cornerstone of Serao's nonrealist narratives. In *Castigo,* however, it is the dead female protagonist whose erotic desires are under question, rather than those of the living heroine. Interestingly, as the character of Anna becomes more sexualized, at least in the eyes of her former husband, she becomes endowed with an authority not present in the first novel. The mere intimation of sexuality confers a degree of power, even in a character no longer active in this world. Through the examination of her alleged sexual activities, Anna, one of the more submissive spouses in Serao's cast of subjugated wives, becomes in death a powerful figure. As Nancy Harrowitz writes, this sequel "can be read as a rewriting of [Anna's] female passivity."[20] Indeed, Serao, in both an acknowledgment of Gothic tenets and a recasting of Anna as a more dynamic figure, has her haunt the novel's other characters, speaking the language of revenge from beyond the grave. The memory of Anna and a growing sense of guilt about their betrayal threaten the stability and happiness of Cesare and Laura, now newlyweds. Cesare's growing obsession with his first wife's faithfulness manifests itself on his (second) wedding night, a singularly gloomy occasion. Sitting in what he calls his "house of the dead" (141), surrounded by memories of Anna, Cesare avoids Laura's advances and the two at last retire to their separate rooms. In death, Anna finally manages to destroy the relationship between her husband and her sister, an act she was powerless to do while alive. Her own burgeoning sexuality, real or not, negates that of Laura and Cesare.

The mystery of Anna's behavior—did she or didn't she?—turns into an obsession for Cesare, although it soon becomes apparent that it is the appearance of betrayal that most offends him, rather than the actual deed. Serao, always careful to ground even her most melodramatic narratives in a foundation of realist detail and social observation, here explores the consequences of marital infidelity in late nineteenth-century Italy. Cesare, who after all has betrayed his wife with her own sister, still feels not only obligated to but morally justified in defending his own tarnished honor, even though he has no evidence of Anna's deception. His exaggerated sense of honor leads to a duel, or rather, to two duels, with Luigi Caracciolo. Cesare's musings on the eve of the first duel reveal the gendered differences in social expectations of fidelity: "He was the injured one; he was fighting because his wife had gone to Luigi's home; perhaps she had betrayed him there, but the *perhaps* was not important, even the law would have agreed with him, the appearance of betrayal amounts to betrayal" (154). Only for the husband, apparently, as Cesare's own adulterous behavior escapes both comment and consequence. Cesare wounds Luigi in this duel but feels no vindication or, in modern parlance, no sense of closure. He gets another chance with a second duel at the close of the novel, and this time he is mortally wounded. Before dying, however, Cesare learns that Anna was innocent and entirely undeserving of his suspicions.

I am inclined to read Cesare's death as a vindication for his own betrayal while Anna was living and for his suspicions after her death. I make this claim in part because his death mirrors hers, as he is stabbed in the exact spot—the heart—that Anna chose for her fatal bullet wound. Even more significant, however, is the fact that Serao actually kills off the faithless and overly suspicious Cesare, one of the few male characters to die in her works, an *oeuvre* littered with the corpses of her less fortunate (and better behaved) heroines. Cesare's exaggerated sense of honor, especially ironic in light of his own guilt, points to a grossly unfair standard of morality. The ultimately senseless duels do not avenge Anna's alleged guilt, but they do underscore an archaic social code.

If Anna's sexuality reconfigures her identity, even after her death, what happens to a character who bears an astonishing likeness to her? Is Lady Hermione, the duchess of Cleveland, able to circumvent the refashioning of her identity? The difficulty inherent in negotiating the social and psychic expectations of male lovers, a topic addressed in works such as *La ballerina* and "O Giovannino o la morte," becomes even more critical in *Castigo,* as Hermione risks complete obliteration when her lover conflates her identity with that of another woman. The underlying question becomes not whether Hermione is the reincarnation of Anna but, rather, whether she escapes the persona projected onto her.

Hermione is certainly an enigma, not least because she is a foreign woman traveling unescorted by her husband. Her bizarre taste for the macabre marks her as an archetypal Gothic character; she speaks constantly and all too knowingly of death, her hands are icy cold, and she mysteriously leaves no footprints when walking in the snow. But what marks her and spells her doom is her remarkable resemblance to Anna. Indeed, when Luigi first sees Hermione he literally cannot believe his eyes, referring to her as a "shadow," (94), "a specter" and "a dream" (95). Luigi had been in love with Anna since before her marriage to Cesare in the novel *Addio, amore!,* but despite Cesare's infidelities, she never reciprocated his feelings. Through this male figure, the lines defining Hermione become cloudy, blurred by the man who wants desperately to believe his beloved Anna is still alive. When Luigi confesses his feelings to Hermione, he also reveals his continued and confused assumption about her identity, even calling her "my dear dead one," (241). His obsession with Anna, paralleling Cesare's preoccupation with his wife's alleged betrayal, prevents him from acknowledging Hermione's identity. Both men insist on reconfiguring these two women, denying one her very identity and imputing to the other perfidy and sexual licentiousness. Again with this novel, Serao underlines the fragility of "womanhood."

Hermione's problem is framed within the peculiarly Gothic preoccupation with female identity, for the heroine of such texts must defend and protect her sense of personhood: "Gothic romance is especially a woman's genre because . . . it is about the nightmare of trying to 'speak I' in a world in which the 'I' in question is uncomprehending of and incomprehensible to the dominant power structure."[21] Hermione's fate in *Castigo,* however, suggests an inability to express that "I." She is, of course, neither a ghostly apparition nor the projection of Luigi's fantasies and desires, but when it becomes apparent that she is unable to convince him of this, she leaves Italy, sailing on her yacht, appropriately named *Chimera.* Harrowitz writes that Hermione "is not herself a passive victim of love,"[22] but I would argue that the resolution of her story speaks to an ultimate failure to carve out her own space. The yacht sinks as it nears England, and Hermione drowns, her watery and ultimately invisible grave a telling symbol of a woman denied an identity.

How then does Serao resolve this question of female identity within the context of the Gothic text? I believe she moves significantly beyond the discussion of this issue in her romance works to present an even more discouraging portrayal of male-female relationships. The characters of Carmela in *La ballerina* and Chiarina in "O Giovannino o la morte," for example, are forced to assume an overtly sexual persona. So must Anna in *Castigo.* The difference, of course, is important, for in the romance works both heroines are allowed to confront and eventually cast off this persona and regain their original autonomy and identity, although at a high price. In *Castigo,* this is clearly impossible, for although Anna's name is vindicated by the end of the novel, it is through a male agent, Luigi, rather than by her own doing. She is removed by her death from Cesare's reconstruction of her identity and from its eventual reinstatement. Despite the active role she takes in the dissolution of Cesare's relationship with Laura, Anna remains a cipher. Unlike Anna, Hermione is decidedly not a cipher, but within the Gothic framework, with its affinity for the supernatural, her identity remains under question and under assault. By shifting the analysis of the negation of female identity from the romance to the Gothic novel, Serao points not only to the universality of this issue across literary genres but also to its very entrenched position within these narrative structures.

Serao appropriates the tenets of Gothic fiction in order to explore the dynamics of the patriarchal family in the 1891 novel *Il paese di cuccagna.* This text has been categorized with the author's realist works, but Serao integrates various elements that allow multiple readings, in the tradition of the Gothic. This novel, which describes the lethal effects of the lottery as it destroys those from all levels of society and corrupts the very soul of Naples, is loosely related to Serao's journalism essays collected in *Il ventre di Napoli*, a work that also deplores the poisonous pastime. In this sweeping fictive piece, however, Serao incorporates one characteristically Gothic element—a virginal heroine tested by improbable trials— as the foundation upon which she can base her vision of the family structure. This is a decidedly unique perspective among Serao's large cast of female characters, allowing as it does an analysis of the daughter's position in this world. In *Il paese*, the young hero-ine's tribulations are framed by her struggles with her cruel father and her memory of her beloved mother. Her relationships with both parents, in Serao's rendition of the familial plot, become crucial markers in the development of the young girl.

In *Il paese*, this figure is embodied by Bianca Maria Cavalcanti, an innocent young girl who lives with her domineering father in their decaying family mansion. Like most Gothic heroines, she is motherless, entering her adulthood as a *tabula rasa* waiting for the eventual inscription of her adventures.[23] In *Il paese*, the heroine's double name "Bianca Maria" suggests not only an inherent purity, but also an allegiance with the ideal Mother, a dynamic that will be addressed below. Bianca Maria is blessed with all the moral and physical attributes of a true Gothic heroine, and she exhibits a mystical connection with the spiritual world. This is not, how-ever, the exaggerated sensitivity arising from the eroticism of the *femme fatale*, an attribute manifested, for example, by Lucia in *Fantasia*. Rather, in Bianca Maria's case, it is her very innocence, a virtue soon to be abused by her father, that allows her to hear conversations when in a dead faint and to see ghostly visions.

Significantly, it is both Bianca Maria's innocence and her gender that mark her as a conduit for spiritual revelations. The union of purity and femininity in this character creates an untainted vehi-cle for other-worldly communications, a gift denied those more firmly planted in the material world. Tellingly, the visions that Bianca Maria sees refer back to her dead mother, unveiling a relationship between the two women that extends beyond the physical world and linking her innocence to that of the maternal figure. By removing the mother from an active role in the text, Serao participates in a maneuver familiar in female-authored works. I rely here on Marianne Hirsch's extensive work on familial structures in the nineteenth- and twentieth-century novel, particularly the mother-daughter relationship. Hirsch writes that the absence of the maternal figure acts as a critical narrative strategy "which creates the space in which the heroine's plot and her activity of plotting can evolve."[24] In *Il paese* and in the two novels to be examined subsequently, the absent mother becomes a significant figure in her own right, working inside the text to prompt narrative resolution and outside the narrative structure to represent Motherhood.

In *Il paese*, the mother, Beatrice, continues to act as teacher and guiding spirit for her daughter, even from beyond the grave. That the mother is cast as a mentor is clear from her very name, with its Dantean evocations of spiritual guidance. In Serao's text, however, Beatrice does not lead the protagonist to salvation, but rather to destruction. The mother's legacy of passivity and obedience, cornerstones of the maternal role, serves to inculcate debilitating family and social roles in her daughter as she sacrifices not only herself but her own daughter to prevailing ideologies.

If the mother's role is to preserve the structure and advance the interests of the patriarchal family, which in turn acts as a mirror of the social world outside it, who is the villain of this Gothic text? In Serao's vision, he is not the cruel stranger of many Gothic novels but the heroine's own father. The Gothic family, typically patriarchal in structure, becomes an extension and instrument of the father's authority, allowing him a space in which to wield his power.[25] Evil resides within the domestic sphere, embodied in the family patriarch who acts at various times as lawmaker, disciplinarian, and master. In *Il paese*, this evil resides, cloaked, in the figure of the Marquis of Formosa, Bianca Maria's father, a man haunted by his own obsessive greed. He intends to exploit his daughter's mystical inclinations, at the risk of her own delicate health, in order to win the weekly lottery and restore his family's squandered fortune. The author uses this text to describe the family's role, executed in particular by the father, in socializing and containing the daughter.

Serao challenges the traditional Gothic persona of the villain by locating him within the family circle, and she subverts the genre's setting to further advance her commentary on the family. The castle, a powerful symbol in Gothic ideology, entraps the heroine in a world beyond the domain of the rational.[26] In *Il paese*, the castle is transfigured into the family's house, as Serao chooses the mundane domestic world as the site of terror. Persecution is located within the family home, the very familiarity of the setting intensifying the atmosphere of betrayal and menace. The once stately Cavalcanti manor has become a "cold and solitary house," and the scene of Bianca Maria's increasingly nightmarish life.[27]

Along with other female authors, Serao structures the heroine's struggle as a conflict within the domestic sphere, a struggle that stems explicitly from her role as daughter. Serao recognizes the difficulty of this role, for a young girl must balance her own developing sense of self with the abnegation required by the traditional hierarchal family structure. Indeed, in *Il paese*, Bianca Maria is torn between compliance with her parents' wishes and her own sense of self-preservation. Before she dies, killed in part by her husband's neglect, Bianca Maria's mother entreats her daughter to love and revere her father despite his bizarre and increasingly cruel behavior. But the fragile young woman, tormented by her father's demands, wants desperately to escape the pattern of her mother's miserable life and early death. "Oh mother, mother, I have disobeyed you!" she cries. "You knew how to die for my father, but I do not know how to imitate you!" (235). By urging her daughter to acquiesce to her father's wishes, Beatrice is enforcing the patriarchal law that demands absolute filial obedience. Nor is this doctrine uncommon, and the mother is commonly held responsible for transmitting and upholding patriarchal ideology.[28] In *Il paese*, Beatrice is merely fulfilling the dictates of her maternal role in maintaining the traditional family structure. Bianca Maria's story literally becomes one of life and death as she struggles to control her own destiny in defiance of her mother's wishes and her father's increasingly sadistic demands. Indeed, the resulting physical and psychic ordeals awaiting Bianca Maria rival those of any Gothic heroine, as her father deprives her of both sleep and food. It is her role as daughter, a position signifying complete submission and allegiance to the father, that allows the marquis to exploit her. And like other Gothic heroines, Bianca Maria is unable to disobey even the most absurd demands of her father, time and again capitulating to his wishes. It is not unusual for Gothic heroines to participate in their victimization, as active rebellion is typically beyond the powers of these young women, many of whom are marked by unthinkable extremes of passivity and compliance.

Bianca Maria, however, does demonstrate a moment of unsuspected resilience and resistance, battling both parental persecution and the typhus that ostensibly kills her. For three days and three nights she lies in a delirium, murmuring over and over a piteous refrain, "I don't want to die, I don't want to die, save me, save me . . . I don't want to die . . . " (422). Bianca Maria places the blame for her plight squarely on her father, indicting the entire patriarchal familial system: "It's my father," she tells Dr. Antonio Amati, "he has killed me" (421).[29] She refuses to let the marquis enter her sickroom, claiming, if only briefly, her own space in the family structure. But despite Dr. Amati's devotion and skill, Bianca Maria dies, invoking her mother with her last words: "Mamma, I don't want to die, I don't want, I don't want, Mamma dear!" (424). The cry, which accuses as much as laments, serves as a reminder of the mother's often passive acquiescence in the oppressive family sphere and reveals again the relative powerlessness of the maternal discourse within the familial structure.

In the novel's resolution, Serao turns from the mother-daughter relationship, evoked by Bianca Maria's cries, to that between father and daughter. The text closes with a sentence that critics have called melodramatic, introducing, as it does, the Shakespearean representation of the father-daughter relationship. Informed of his daughter's death, the marquis pauses at the threshold of her room "asking pardon, like the aged Lear before the body of the sweet Cordelia" (425). The literary allusion may seem an anomaly in what has been a relatively straightforward narrative.[30] But I would argue that the reference to Shakespeare's mad king and patriarch reinforces Serao's project, which is to depict the potential oppressiveness found in the family unit. Cordelia and Bianca Maria, both victims of paternal domination, embody the ultimate Gothic heroine, threatened from within their domestic world. The familial structure, then, suggests an arena of persecution for the Gothic heroine. By paralleling the domestic sphere with the conventional Gothic symbol of entrapment, the castle, Serao appropriates the genre's tenets to articulate her own vision of the familial structure.

Gothic literature provides the ideal forum for analyzing the construction of female identity, including not only the various social roles expected of women, but also the cultural ideologies on which those roles are constructed. The positions of the mother and daughter in the family structure, as examined in *Il paese di cuccagna,* underline the supremacy of the father figure and, by extension, the patriarchal social system. As Serao continues to experiment with Gothic tenets, she gradually magnifies the importance of the mother figure, moving her from her offstage role in *Il paese di cuccagna* to the foreground in her later texts. The maternal figure is rarely found in Serao's narratives, as many of her protagonists are either orphaned or under the protection of a mother substitute, such as the conniving stepmother in "O Giovannino o la morte" or the beneficent dancer in *La ballerina.* As these two examples attest, the depiction of the mother figure is problematic in Serao's works, for the author presents contradictory and even problematic interpretations of the maternal role. Perhaps these inconsistencies stem from Serao's own, sometimes ambiguous thinking about just how this role was, or should be, defined. In the following two novels, for example, the mother is granted a more prominent position in the text, adding another dimension to Serao's increasingly complex metaphorical city of women. Her emphasis on the maternal discourse falls neatly within the sphere of Gothic fiction, for the Gothic narrative often turns on questions of matrilineal lines.[31]

Serao's examination of family dynamics is multilayered, for in the portrayals of her female characters she is questioning the socioliterary frameworks on which they are constructed. This sociological approach reveals Serao's understanding of the interconnections between literature and the social world, and it also allows her the opportunity to devise an innovative reworking of the principles of her genres. For example, in the 1908 novel *Il delitto di via Chiatamone* (The Crime on Chiatamone Street),[32] Serao uses the Gothic structure to explore the prevailing cultural discourse that ties female identity to the expression of sexuality. She is returning to familiar ground here, for this is a topic explored in many of her romance works, including *Addio, amore!, Fantasia,* and *Cuore infermo,* among others. In her Gothic works, Serao refashioned prototypical character types such as the chaste heroine to articulate her own version of female identity.[33] She continued the undertaking, begun in her romance narratives, of creating more realist female characters who are not bound by cultural stereotypes.

In *Il delitto,* Serao continues her analysis of the cultural debate surrounding female identity, by casting the two female protagonists as antithetical archetypes of womanhood. This strategy generates cultural critique and a thoughtful examination of familial relationships, as the novel's two heroines gradually appropriate attributes of the opposing figure. Serao carefully introduces both these characters in a way that is calculated to demonstrate their affinity with specific Gothic character types. The modestly dressed Teresa Gargiulo appears out of the shadows of a deserted Neapolitan street one November night in "that treacherous and inauspicious autumn of 188—".[34] Upon boarding a tram, Teresa discovers she lacks the money for a first-class ticket. She refuses to compromise her virtue, however, by accepting the few pennies offered by a kind young sailor. Instead, she takes her place in the second-class compartment, where, a few moments later, she is shot. Teresa Gargiulo, her young life imperiled by a mysterious hand in the novel's opening pages, has joined the ranks of Gothic heroines. Serao underscores Teresa's vulnerability and reinforces her rectitude, as her first words in the hospital after awakening from a coma are to call not for a doctor but for a priest. In this opening scene, Serao employs Gothic tactics designed to ensure that Teresa's integrity is innate and indisputable.

The author uses the same technique in the presentation of the second female protagonist, for if Teresa displays characteristics typical of a vulnerable and chaste Gothic heroine, it soon becomes apparent that her counterpart, the courtesan Anthonia d'Alembert, embodies the attributes of the sexually experienced woman. Teresa's quiet entrance onto the novel's stage contrasts sharply with that of Anthonia, who is first seen on display, as it were, sitting alone in her box at the theater. Serao draws attention to the fact that Anthonia is on exhibit, underscoring her physical attributes as well as her function as spectacle. The faces of the theater-goers are turned toward her, drawn by her seductive red mouth and flashing dark eyes, symbols of her sexual availability and eroticism. Anthonia, who at age twenty-two has already amassed a fortune from judiciously chosen liaisons, is clearly not chaste; indeed, she mockingly calls herself "a wicked woman . . . outside the law" (1:32). But just like Lalla in *Cuore infermo*, Anthonia hopes to legitimize her position in society, and when the duke Giorgio San Luciano visits her box, she dares him to sit openly beside her. He declines the scandalous challenge despite his desire to consummate their embryonic relationship. San Luciano's refusal underlines the vulnerability of the *femme fatale*, doomed by her erotic energy to remain outside acceptable societal circles.

Despite these introductory scenes, with their carefully delineated character sketches, Serao quickly disassociates Teresa and Anthonia from more stereotypical literary heroines.[35] Teresa, for example, soon demonstrates an erotic sensibility not typically part of the Gothic heroine's code of behavior. Her fiancé, Carlo Altieri, has taken to visiting her apartment each evening. Carlo is actually San Luciano in disguise, intent on robbing Teresa of the fortune she will inherit on her twenty-first birthday.[36] Teresa, who knows nothing of this fortune, trusts Carlo completely, and each evening begs him to stay later, moved by "a wave of passion" (1:219). These passionate feelings are soon fully satisfied, a turn of events not usually allowed Gothic heroines. Even more important is the fact that while Carlo clearly acts as seducer in this liaison, Teresa participates fully and willingly. The author paints the scene not in terms of defilement, a maneuver that would exonerate the defenseless young heroine, but rather reveals how Teresa colludes in the act. As a portentous storm thunders outside, Teresa feels "the dark ardor of passion climb from her heart to her head, in breath-taking tumults" (1:227). That evening, her scruples are overcome by "a great languor . . . a slow dizziness . . . a flame" (1:236). Serao's revision of Gothic mythology allows even her most virtuous heroine a degree of sensuality.

If Teresa is capable of carnal love, Anthonia is equally capable of renouncing her own sensuality, pointing to the fluidity inherent in Serao's depiction of female sexuality. Throughout this narrative, Serao continues to strip away conventional expectations of feminine behavior, creating more complex characters who succeed in laying waste to traditional depictions of heroines. As Ursula Fanning notes, Serao "reveals the angel/monster polarization of women as a male construct which she then allows Anthonia to challenge, and ultimately, to deconstruct."[37] The author does this primarily through a discussion of the protagonist's erotic impulses. Anthonia, who began life as the humble seamstress Antonietta Duguè, is not, in fact, the sensual, predatory courtesan she pretends to be. Indeed, this charade has cost her the one man she truly loves, the young sailor Gennarino Esposito, who is, however, not only hopelessly in love with Teresa, but repulsed by Anthonia's licentious past. Although realizing her love will never be reciprocated, Anthonia decides to mend her ways and return to her original life of chastity and simplicity, becoming a "penitent sinner" (1:308). Anthonia/Antonietta even agrees to help Gennarino save Teresa from the conniving Carlo/San Luciano.[38] In order to do so, she must resume temporarily the persona of the seductive Anthonia d'Alembert. By helping to rescue her rival, Anthonia expiates her sins and becomes an active figure. Serao extricates and examines sexual attributes found in both these heroines of *Il delitto*, challenging the cultural validity of traditional, binary images of women, specifically those of the angel and the *femme fatale*.

Serao uses these fictive constructions of womanhood as a point of departure to examine the mother-daughter relationship, here recasting the maternal figure as the key to her daughter's salvation. Unlike Beatrice in *Il paese di cuccagna*, the mother figure in *Il delitto* cautions her daughter about the perils of the familial institution, in particular, the maternal role. Serao creates an analogous narrative between Teresa and her mother, underlining a sense of foreordained repetition in the fulfillment of the female role. Cecilia, Teresa's mother, was seduced, impregnated, and abandoned by Francesco Vargas, a wealthy nobleman and San Luciano's uncle. In an attempt to protect her daughter from becoming another Gothic victim, Cecilia warns Teresa to avoid her fate, even giving her just before she dies a medallion inscribed with the words "Fear the lion." The lion, depicted on the Vargas coat of arms and evocative of patriarchal forces, represents the villains of Cecilia's past and Teresa's future.[39]

But Teresa ignores both the precedent set by her mother's life and the warning implicit in the medallion, a narrative strategy illustrating the authoritative power of maternal absence in the text. This absence traditionally ensures the daughter's obedience of patriarchal laws, for the heroine, forced to navigate the rocky waters of maturation alone, often repeats the mother's mistakes.[40] In an interesting narrative maneuver that underscores the traditional path for heroines, Teresa moves from the role of daughter to that of mother, for she too is seduced and impregnated. Tellingly, Teresa seems bereft of maternal feelings, explicitly favoring her lover, by this time unmasked as San Luciano, over her child: "The poor one was not a perfect mother, since the maternal instinct was not very well developed in her. . . . she loved that innocent little creature, but she loved her Giorgio even more" (2:229). Serao deliberately removes Teresa from the iconography of the

Madonna, dissociating the heroine from the maternal archetype and creating a mother whose sexual identity proves more potent than her maternal instinct.[41] After the painful birth of their son, San Luciano marries Teresa in a rudimentary wedding ceremony that is performed in a makeshift chapel inside the gloomy, isolated manor where he has installed her.[42] Teresa, still weakened by the ordeals of childbirth, collapses at the end of the ceremony and eventually dies. While her death may be viewed as the traditional punishment for trespassing on societal sanctions, Serao's depiction of the young woman's destiny indicates a more general caution on the potential dangers of the maternal role.

Again, it is the familial roles of wife and mother that threaten disaster, just as Bianca Maria's role as obedient daughter proved fatal in *Il paese di cuccagna*. Both these young women are doomed by their gender. Bianca Maria's father believes explicitly that her femininity makes his daughter more susceptible to communications from the spirit world, and to facilitate those communications, he endangers her life by depriving her of food and sleep. In *Il delitto,* San Luciano deliberately imperils Teresa's life by impregnating her. "You are killing me," she murmurs to San Luciano during their first night together. His reply is telling: "Yes: I want to kill you" (1 : 237). Nor is he lying; if Teresa dies in childbirth, her fortune will be his. On another level, the act of procreation in this text promises not life but death for the heroine, as she had been forewarned that her fragile health would not withstand the trauma of childbirth. Teresa's destiny is predetermined by her mother's fate and by her own femaleness. In this character, the mother-daughter dyad becomes conflated into one doomed figure, a maneuver that speaks to the conflicted readings of motherhood in Serao's works.

While Serao's depiction of the maternal figure in this text is problematic, it points to her revision of Gothic resolutions as she reverses the destiny of the two female protagonists. At the end of the novel, Teresa, the presumed young heroine, dies, too weak to withstand the double shock of discovering that her beloved Giorgio is not only her first cousin, but that he had engineered the shooting attempt on her life that opened the novel. The narrative includes marriage and maternity, the traditional "rewards" for such heroines, but both experiences prove destructive. Anthonia, on the other hand, is a survivor, another of Serao's *femmes fatales* allowed to live on in a literary world that traditionally punishes

such characters for their transgressions.[43] Although her story is
tied to the romance plot, she is granted a rare independence, for
she decides to give up her way of life and humbly follow Gennarino on his travels. Serao closes the novel on a note of ambiguity,
a decidedly un-Gothic turn of events. Most such works conclude
with an ending that is happy as well as tidy, but Serao leaves unresolved the destiny of Anthonia and Gennarino, who is still in love
with the dead Teresa. The rare "open ending" emphasizes Serao's
reworking of the conventions of the genre.[44] It also frees one
of the female protagonists from becoming entrapped within the
domestic space or the marriage plot. As in the short story "Livia
Spera," the unresolved ending of *Il delitto* removes the female
protagonist from literary expectations, allowing her personal autonomy which creates a certain textual energy.

I will conclude the discussion of Serao's Gothic revisions with
an examination of the 1912 novel *La mano tagliata* (The Severed
Hand), a text that weds many of the motifs of earlier works to
even more trenchant commentary on female experiences. The
author explores, as she did in *Il paese di cuccagna,* the dynamics of
the patriarchal family, focusing again on the potentially perilous
relationship between father and daughter. The bond between
mother and daughter, briefly delineated in *Il paese* and *Il delitto
di via Chiatamone,* here moves into the foreground. Also central to
La mano tagliata is the Gothic motif of the mad scientist attempting
to transgress mortal limitations, a theme examined in "Un inventore." But although this novel may read as the archetypical Gothic
text, Serao also incorporates elements of the detective format,
a subgenre considered to be a direct descendent of the Gothic
narrative.[45] By borrowing stylistic and thematic elements from
other genres, Serao shapes the narrative in a way that emphasizes
the role of women within the family structure and within the
social world in general.

The physical and psychic victimization of women is epitomized
in the experiences of Maria Cabib, whose fragmented body becomes the pivot around which the novel's mystery revolves. Her
very physicality serves as the site on which male figures act out
their scientific and erotic impulses. The severed hand of the title
belongs to Maria and serves as a grisly reminder of the megaloma-
nia of Marcus Henner, the novel's prototypical villain. Henner
exemplifies the attributes of the mad scientist and represents the

dangers of trying to surpass the limits of human knowledge. The son of a doctor and a sorcerer, he uses a strange mixture of science and necromancy to control others through hypnosis. The opposites of scientific-medical ideology and supernatural belief, a motif found in *Il paese,* are joined in this single figure, and Serao denounces both aspects. In *La mano tagliata,* Henner attempts to usurp divine powers, claiming to be "the man who has stolen from God the secret of dominating human will."[46] But in an interesting narrative stratagem, Serao conflates Henner's lust for knowledge with physical lust.

The object of Henner's desire, Maria Cabib, is the epitome of Gothic virtue, stoically undergoing ordeals as terrible as the horrors faced by the heroines of classic Gothic literature. In this text, Maria functions as a female subject of experimentation, for her body, mind, and spirit are continually under attack. Does Serao intend to suggest through the portrayal of this character's plight that sociocultural forces conspire to oppress and imprison women? Certainly Maria's situation is a dramatic illustration of the extreme vulnerability and powerlessness of female characters. The Gothic heroine, then, serves as an example, sometimes extreme, of the position of women in society—forced to contend with a world predicated on the sovereignty of men and the inferiority of women.

Nowhere in Serao's work is this made more clear than in the case of Maria Cabib. Fifteen years before the novel opens, Henner had used his command of science and witchcraft to steal Maria away from her husband, Mosè Cabib. She fell into a death-like trance, which he was forced to break by inflicting agonizing pain. He did this by cutting off her forearm, which had the anticipated effect of waking her from her catalepsy but also, understandably, earned him Maria's undying hate and disgust. Since then, Maria has been held prisoner in his house, leading a monastic life in a tiny, bare room next to the lavishly appointed bedroom Henner hopes she will eventually share with him. But Maria proves to be his equal, for her steadfast resistance to his nightly entreaties and threats, along with her ability to withstand his experiments in hypnosis, counterbalance Henner's pseudoscientific experiments and the power engendered by his position as patriarch.[47]

The result of Henner's most horrific experiment, Maria's severed hand, becomes an object of desire and appropriation.[48] In *La mano tagliata,* this fragmented body part has been read as a critique of the traditional, idealized portrayal of the female body[49] and as a religious relic, pointing to the intersection of gender and religion in this text.[50] Both of these readings provide valuable insights into the novel, but I would posit that the severed hand acts more as a literary and social critique of male-constructed portrayals of female characters. In *La mano tagliata*, both Henner and Roberto Alimena, a young man who accidentally comes into possession of the embalmed limb, want to possess Maria, although their desire is typically coded in the terminology of romance narratives. Roberto's discovery of the hand, however, is described explicitly in terms of sexual violation. Curious about the contents of an intriguing box he finds on a train, Roberto opens it by forcing the intricate lock: "[H]e tried to penetrate it with a small shaft in the opening; but he found a soft resistance" (30). Maria's body, or rather, her limb, becomes both fragmented and objectified and, through Roberto's attempted violation, the object of sexual desire. He falls in love with the hand and, by extension, the woman who lost it, and devotes his life to finding her. In her Gothic text, then, Serao explores not only the physical and psychic mutilation of women at the hands of unscrupulous men, but even more specifically, the fragmentation of the female body.

Serao points to the universality of female persecution, represented in its most extreme form in the torture and imprisonment of Maria, by complementing her story with that of her daughter, Rachele. The author employs the same narrative stratagem here as she did in *Il delitto di via Chiatamone*, which saw the mother and daughter realizing similar life stories. In *La mano tagliata*, Rachele's oppressor is her own father, indicting once again the deleterious effects of a patriarchal family structure. Initially, Rachele's fate mirrors that of Bianca Maria in *Il paese di cuccagna*, whose very life becomes consumed by the fulfillment of the daughterly role. But while the fragile and submissive Bianca Maria dies in the act of obeying her father, Rachele demonstrates the strength of character necessary to liberate herself from hers. Mosè Cabib strictly controls his daughter's movements and demands that she marry the powerful and wealthy Marcus Henner, a man Rachele abhors. (Henner, although in love with Maria, proposes to marry Rachele because of the eerie similarity between them.) Rachele refuses: "You can break my life, but not my will," she warns her father (126).

The chain linking Rachele to her father is counterbalanced by the loving, supportive bond she shares with her mother, a woman she had long believed dead. In this text, then, the savior is Rachel's own mother, a "feminine, maternal deliverer" at odds with the male hero of both romance and Gothic narratives.[51] Indeed, Serao's use of the maternal figure as the heroine's savior completely subverts the narrative structure of the Gothic text. The author employs a similar strategy in *Il delitto di via Chiatamone*, portraying Cecilia as the potential savior of Teresa. But Cecilia's removal from the text proper makes her guiding hand much less effective. In *La mano tagliata*, although Rachele and Maria do not meet during the course of the novel, the two establish a close relationship born of mutual pain and carried out in that classic Gothic terrain, the subconscious. Maria appears to her daughter in visions and dreams, directing her to become a Christian in order to protect herself from Henner. Maria, a converted Jew, is trying to save her daughter from the very man who has persecuted her for years. Through the magic of Gothic fantasy, she even leaves a crucifix in Rachele's hand one night, dispelling her doubts. Maria even indirectly effects an introduction between Rachele and Rainieri Lambertini, a young man she meets in church. With the strength forged from Rainieri's love, her mother's support, and a new-found faith, Rachele is able to free herself from her father's domination.

But it is the mother-daughter bond that proves to be the strongest factor in the resolution of Rachele's story, as Serao casts the novel in a way that empowers the female roles. By doing so, the author takes on not only conventional Gothic tenets, but also the structure of the traditional patriarchal family. After a misunderstanding with Rainieri, Rachele sequesters herself in a Neapolitan convent, mirroring the monastic life led by her mother. But she decides against taking religious vows after receiving a posthumous letter from Maria who, after years of withstanding Henner's psychological warfare, has finally fallen victim to his powers of hypnosis. Rachele follows her mother's advice, seeking out Rainieri and telling him, "My mother wrote me to come to you, to love you faithfully, until death. Here I am!" (434). The union between Rachele and Rainieri, and indeed the happy ending conventionally found in Gothic fiction, is orchestrated by the mother rather than the hero, who is strangely incapacitated throughout much of the text. The maternal figure is endowed with an astonishing degree of authority, which is made even more significant by the fact that she must direct her daughter's actions from beyond the grave. This maternal power is still bound to conventional euphoric fictive closure, but it does offer an alternative characterization of motherhood, one perhaps more multifaceted than those presented in earlier texts by Serao.

What does one make of Serao's depiction of motherhood, a theme explored not only in *La mano tagliata* but also in *Il paese di cuccagna* and *Il delitto di via Chiatamone?* Considered chronologically, often a speculative process with an author who continually reworked themes, these texts manifest an interesting evolution. The mother figure takes on a progressively more substantial role in the narratives' proceedings, becoming less and less ephemeral and eventually superseding the role of the male hero. In *Il paese*, Bianca Maria's mother, although dead long before the novel begins, continues to exert an influence on her daughter even though this influence is primarily a negative one, as it is because of her mother's dying injunction that Bianca Maria refuses to leave her increasingly sadistic father. The mother's role in the patriarchal family, as depicted in this text, is to support and champion the father's dictatorial rights. The price of passively submitting to paternal authority, however, is high: both Bianca Maria and her mother pay with their lives.

In *Il delitto*, the dynamics of the mother-daughter relationship have changed, as has the presentation of the maternal figure. Serao emphasizes the similarities between mother and daughter, creating a sisterhood of suffering. Teresa's fate closely mirrors that of her mother, as both have been seduced and impregnated by unscrupulous noblemen. Her mother, Cecilia, although dead, seems to take on a more corporeal form as specifics of her life are introduced into the text. In *Il paese*, the mother was virtually unknown, overshadowed by her domineering husband and denied her own story. But whereas Bianca Maria's mother advises patient acquiescence rather than active rebellion, Cecilia does not want her daughter to suffer a fate similar to her own. She bequeaths to Teresa not a dying injunction, but a precious medallion holding the coded words that could save her daughter. Again, however, the outcome is bleak, for Teresa ignores her mother's guidance and repeats her destiny. The fact that Teresa dies in part because of her difficult pregnancy and childbirth speaks to the conflicted readings of motherhood in Serao's texts.

The character of the mother reaches its apogee in *La mano tagliata,* as Serao reconstructs the maternal figure, transforming her into a fundamental component of the text. She endows Maria Cabib with a history of her own, resurrecting her from the legions of long-dead and forgotten mothers of literary history. Serao also allows Maria her own amorous subplot, although she never attains the degree of subjectivity found in the protagonist of Sibilla Aleramo's 1906 novel *Una donna.* In this groundbreaking work, the heroine is allowed to be both maternal and sexual as she explores the social and cultural ramifications of being wife, mother, and lover. Serao does not demonstrate such a heightened awareness of the intersection of female roles, nor does she examine as closely the relationship between maternal and sexual attributes, a reflection perhaps of the author's own inherent conservatism. But *La mano tagliata* does anticipate the work of more consciously feminist writers who would later question the literary convention that denies mothers their sexuality.

Another important element of Serao's depiction of the maternal figure is the strong bond maintained between mother and daughter, a relationship that is doubly significant in Gothic texts, where the villains often turn out to be fathers and husbands.[52] Certainly the attachment between Maria and Rachele, even from afar, seems stronger than those between the women and their respective lovers. Casting Maria as the savior figure in *La mano tagliata* also reveals a powerful subversion of the traditional casting of romance or Gothic fiction.

In these texts dealing with mothers, Serao employs the same strategy found in her narratives depicting female friendships. By including the mother-daughter story, Serao shifts attention away from the privileged exclusivity of heterosexual couples in the novel. I would argue that this strategy is deliberate, part of Serao's effort to expand the definition and possibilities of literary plots. By doing so, she anticipates, in part, the work analyzed by Marianne Hirsch, who "reframe[s] these plot patterns in particular ways, discovering not only certain ideologies of maternity embedded within them, but also narrative patterns which call the more conventional constructions of the love plot into question."[53] The novel, which traditionally turns on male-female relationships, becomes, in the hands of both Hirsch and Serao, a forum in which to explore other bonds and examine long-ignored literary figures such as the mother and the daughter.

Moreover, Serao's Gothic texts subversively allow women to become actively involved in each other's destinies. Heroines do not turn toward their lovers, husbands, or fathers for support and the resolution of their stories but, rather toward the maternal figure. Serao moves, then, a step farther from her realist texts. In those works, friendships between women offered the support and affection not always found in their amorous relationships. In her Gothic tales, the friendships have strengthened into familial bonds. The mutual support expressed between friends becomes an even more significant transaction, turning literally on questions of life and death. In her works, Serao depicts a subterranean network of female bonding, hidden, perhaps from the eyes of those accustomed to seeing only male-female relationships. It is through these networks, however, that Serao's female characters learn to negotiate their own space within potentially threatening institutions such as the family and marriage.

Conclusion: A Literary Legacy

Matilde Serao's project of refashioning the conventions of various genres to articulate her own vision of female experiences largely confounded those evaluating her work according to long-entrenched literary standards. Rather than recognizing the complexity and richness of the author's multigenred approach, her work was instead appraised by contemporary critics through a series of dichotomies: "language-dialect; invention-mimesis; participation-detachment; literature-popular fiction."[1] Modern critics have added yet another contradiction to this catalog of antithetical divisions, one that emphasizes a more fundamental paradox in the author's ideological positions and her fictive and journalistic writings. Simply put, Serao's repeated entreaty in her writings that women devote themselves to the domestic sphere conflicts markedly with her own very public position in Italy's intellectual circles as a respected editor, reporter, and bestselling and critically acclaimed author. Certainly the example she herself set continually undermined her ardent statements against the participation of women in the professional and public domain. This contradiction must be taken up here, for it sheds light on Serao's literary production as a whole and also situates her more firmly in the spectrum of Italian female authors.

Through her journalistic activities, Serao was thoroughly conversant with the political, cultural, and social debates arising from the shifting currents of modernization in turn-of-the-century Italy. The sense of liberation that blossomed during this period of intense industrialization and continued consequences of the unification of the country was felt in particular by those groups traditionally marginalized from sites of authority. The "new woman" was born, a model of emancipated femalehood eager to take up the objectives of the nascent feminist movement. How did Serao respond to this evolving shift in ideological discourses concerning women? Despite, or perhaps because of, the social changes in Italy at the turn of the century, Serao's world view was essentially reactionary, especially as it concerned the position and condition of women. "I know, as many other women know," she wrote in one article, "that as the laws are written in modern society, there is no possible happiness for woman, in whatever condition she finds herself: neither in marriage, nor in free love, nor in illicit love." Serao goes on to bemoan how entrenched these laws are within the hegemonic social culture of Italy: "I know that nobody will change everything and that, therefore, it is not worth the pain of changing anything."[2]

This pessimistic conservatism is manifestly apparent in several of her journalism essays, which vehemently reject the political and social objectives of feminist groups. Convinced that women were inherently lacking in sophisticated analytic skills, for example, Serao opposed the notion of advanced education for young women as well as suffrage for women. And despite her own separation from her husband, she was utterly impassioned about the dangers implicit in proposed legislation to legalize divorce, asserting that the very social fabric of Italy would unravel with the dissolution of the sacred rite of marriage.[3]

These convictions reveal a woman patently unsympathetic to feminism's goals, although a private letter sent to a female friend and journalist indicates the author's ambivalence about the movement. In this letter, Serao writes that she is feminist "in her own way."[4] Neglecting, unfortunately, to define her own peculiar feminism, she instead goes on to explicate why women would ultimately reject the movement's objectives: "Dear Olga, feminism will never find anything that equals love for filling a woman's life; everything [else] will be of secondary importance."[5] Love, which for Serao meant not only the impassioned love between man and woman but also the bonds linking mother and child, was a woman's most sublime achievement and the ultimate purpose of her life.

An examination of Serao's fictive works further reveals the author's generally conservative perspective regarding women, although here she demonstrates a "politics of ambiguity" that prohibits a simplistic reading of her ideological convictions.[6] Certainly the dismal destinies of Serao's heroines personify her unshaken beliefs in the immutability of the world, and particularly of the role and position of women. Serao's female protagonist "has no power and can do nothing to change her condition because she is convinced that nothing can intervene to change a condition that is 'natural.'"[7] These female characters share a physical and spiritual entombment as they are enclosed within the domestic sphere, a condition Isabella Pezzini underscores when she notes, "The feminine universe [in Serao's works] is *closed:* the destiny of these women is always that of being 'buried alive.'"[8] The bleak future Serao plots for her heroines reflects the lack of social and professional opportunities for women in turn-of-the-century Italy, a situation that, despite her own anomalous example, cuts across social and economic lines.

Serao was hardly the only woman author creating female characters who were limited by literary as well as social expectations. Other nineteenth- and early-twentieth-century female writers, even those championing the tenets of feminism, failed to transcribe their own experiences and convictions on the written page. This inability to transmit female experiences reflects, perhaps, the anxiety inherent in infiltrating a literary establishment founded on male-authored precepts and maintaining one's tenuous position within it.[9] When female authors do free themselves from literary archetypes to create autonomous protagonists, these characters are often male rather than female. Serao herself wrote two novels featuring male protagonists: *La conquista di Roma*, which focuses on a southern Italian politician's experiences in Rome, and *Vita e avventure di Riccardo Joanna*, which features the tribulations of a struggling journalist. Rarely, however, did she depict adult female protagonists enjoying similarly productive lives in the public sphere.

Despite this fundamentally conservative orientation in her fictive works, Serao was unquestionably concerned with examining the experiences of her female protagonists as well as exploring the implications of those experiences in turn-of-the-century Italy. From this perspective, her general project of articulating, and occasionally condemning, the social conditions that give rise to the construction of restricted gender roles leads Gianni Infusino to call Serao "feminist in her way of conceiving woman, her engagement with society, her role as wife and mother."[10] Nancy Harrowitz, too, calls Serao's "a subtly feminist viewpoint after all, but tinged with bitterness and defeat."[11] Although I am reluctant to identify Serao by a label she so firmly repudiated, I recognize that despite the contradictions inherent in her writings, she significantly advanced the debate regarding the deleterious effects of cultural norms and expectations on women in both social and literary contexts. If her works were not more overtly innovative from an ideological standpoint, that was due in part to her awareness of Italy's history of relatively late (in comparison with other European nations) advancements in the political, economic, and cultural spheres, as well as the role social and religious discourses played in the construction of ideologies concerning women.

More meaningful than an examination of whether Serao observed the tenets of feminism in either her life or her writings, however, is the legacy of her work. Her position as one of the pioneers of the realist school locates her as an important font of inspiration for both male and female writers. Even more interesting are the ties linking Serao to subsequent generations of women authors, ties perhaps less apparent than those generated by her well-documented place in the *movimento verista*. The tradition of women who write is an important component of the feminist project to recuperate lost works, rehabilitate minor authors, and reposition women within the landscapes of national literatures. The modern critic must trace the "symbolic reference points" that link one woman author to another, argue the writers and theoreticians of the current Italian women's movement.[12] Female authors and scholars, often excluded from literary canons, must create a genealogy of writers in order to "provide a symbolic mediation between oneself and others, one's subjectivity and the world."[13] Many Italian women writing today turn back to nineteenth-century authors for thematic inspiration. These early female writers were the first to specifically and systematically address the marginalization of women in Italian society: "They denounced and underlined those mentalities that were full of stereotypes hostile to women . . . they represented the solitude of those who feel 'different.'" At the same time, these authors attempted the "de-edification of the traditional female role," an undertaking that today casts them as the precursors of the successive wave of more consciously feminist writers.[14]

Serao was part of this pioneering group of women authors giving voice to female experiences. Much work still must be done to uncover and assess the many connections between women writing today and their literary ancestors, but it is clear that certain thematic concerns are shared by the various generations of female authors. In Serao's case, for example, the incorporation of autobiographical elements in her fictive works, especially evident in the short stories "Telegrafi dello stato" and "Scuola normale feminile," is echoed later by three writers integral to the creation of a female genealogy: Sibilla Aleramo, Ada Negri, and Grazia Deledda. Like Serao, all three used the forum of the autobiographical narrative (*Una donna* 1906, *Stella mattutina* (Morning Star) 1921, and *Cosimo* (Cosimo) 1937, respectively), to challenge—some more radically than others—the social, cultural, legal, and political status of Italian women.[15]

Another theme central to Serao's depiction of women's experiences is that of female friendships, especially those fostered within an all-female space of work or school. The twentieth-century author Alba de Céspedes also structures many of her works around this theme. In the 1938 novel *Nessuna torna indietro* (There's No Turning Back), for example, this topic is placed in the foreground as de Céspedes depicts the relationships among girls who live in a religious boarding school. The *bildungsromanesque* quality of this text, with its obvious evocations of Serao's short stories in *Il romanzo della fanciulla,* is echoed in de Céspedes's 1949 novel *Dalla parte di lei* (On Her Side). In this work, the author traces the psychic development of the female protagonist, depicting, as does Serao, how gender-based social expectations lead to the limitation of both intellectual and emotional growth. This same theme permeates *Volevo i pantaloni* (Good Girls Don't Wear Trousers), a 1989 novel by Lara Cardella that delineates the tribulations of a young girl negotiating the passage between adolescence and adulthood in conservative southern Italy.[16]

The twin themes of female sexuality and identity, both of which are explored in Serao's romance and Gothic texts, form the basis of many works by late-twentieth-century women writers. Dacia Maraini's texts, for example, which articulate a strategy of liberation from sexual or social expectations, continue in a more radical manner Serao's investigation into these issues. An examination of family structure, particularly the mother-daughter relationship, has been a constant topos of feminist work, inspiring such novels as Francesca Sanvitale's *Madre e figlia* (Mother and Daughter) (1980) and Carla Cerati's *La cattiva figlia* (The Bad Daughter) (1990).[17] These later works were, of course, composed in a context significantly different from that of Serao, but I believe the seeds for these more innovative texts were planted in the earlier writings of those authors not yet able to repudiate the hegemonic social and literary ideologies governing turn-of-the-century Italy.

Serao's privileged position in the genealogy of female-authored Italian literature has been assured by her prolific production of both literary and journalistic endeavors, as well as by her genuine refashioning of traditional genre conventions. By reworking these established literary precepts, Serao restructured the traditional perspectives of canonical forms. She did so fully cognizant of the desires and dreams of her readers, most of whom, it must be noted, were female.

Despite the absence of the necessary archival resources that would specifically document the roles Serao's narratives played in the lives of her readers, a few general observations can be made. Many scholars have discussed the relationship between female author and female reader and have determined that it is based on a sense of mutuality. Santoro, for example, in her analysis of late-nineteenth-century female writers, describes this sense of shared experience: "[T]here is the pleasure of talking about one-self with someone who can understand, the reclaiming of one's own self, the search for identity, the joy of recounting one's own experience."[18] Umberto Eco, referring specifically to Serao and two of her popular cohorts, Carolina Invernizio and Liala, believes that these writers were successful in part because their texts mirrored the needs and desires of their readers.[19]

How did Serao's works achieve this bond between author and reader? Not only by depicting the life patterns so familiar to Italian women in that period, but also by incorporating more subversive elements into her texts. A contemporary reader pursuing the latest novel of Serao might not find a call for the complete overhaul of the familial or marital institutions. The astute reader, however, will be left with a clearer idea of how these institutions contribute to the social construction of gender and of gender roles. Equally important, these women-centered texts, with their emphasis on female concerns, create for the reader a sense of her own connection to a larger network of women. Here I would again evoke the metaphor of a fictive metropolis to describe the astonishing variety of women and of female experiences depicted in Serao's narratives and the sense of sisterhood that links the women together.

By focusing specifically on these multifaceted female experiences, Serao creates an historical document of her times, a chronicle originating in kitchens and sitting rooms rather than on the battlefields of official History.[20] Instead of participating in the historical and literary effacement of their life stories, modern women authors purposefully narrate their own history: "[T]he Italian women writers of the twentieth century, both in the novel as in the biography, are rejecting history with a capital H ... and are writing instead women's history, composed of tears and humiliations, then of silence, and finally of open rebellion."[21] Serao has helped to reclaim some of this neglected, ignored, and devalued history in her narratives. If she has not promulgated a revolutionary social system that restructures the entrenched rules governing the ideologies of gender and socioeconomic class, she has at least questioned the conventional mapping of female destiny. By questioning the traditional roles of women, Serao joined in the creation of a literary tradition used by future generations of Italian authors. If the contemporary proliferation of feminist-inspired and feminist-written works is a vast and intricate edifice, Serao helped to lay its foundation. Her narratives serve as a cornerstone upon which to build more revolutionary texts that incorporate the changing mores of the twentieth century. Serao has done this by revising literary genres so they express her vision of the rich panorama of female experiences, experiences that bind together her heroines in sorrow and joy, oppression and fulfillment.

Notes

INTRODUCTION

1. The metaphor of a fictional city of women originates with the medieval author Christine De Pizan, whose text *Cité des dames* describes an allegorical metropolis inhabited by exceptional and famous women. Although Serao focuses on ordinary and unknown women in the collection of newspaper articles contained in *Il ventre di Napoli* (Milan: Garzanti, 1962), both authors celebrate female experiences while examining women's roles in society.

2. Perhaps the only female figure missing from Serao's work is that of the prostitute. She told one interviewer that she had always regretted not writing a realist book about such a character, but that she was unable to "see behind the closed shutters" of such a life, and therefore was unable to create such a text. Quoted in Wanda De Nunzio Schilardi, *Matilde Serao Giornalista* (Lecce: Milella, 1986), 60.

3. Carol Lazzaro-Weis, *From Margins to Mainstream: Feminism and Fictional Modes in Italian Women's Writing, 1968–1990* (Philadelphia: University of Pennsylvania Press, 1993), 1.

4. Ralph Cohen, "History and Genre," *New Literary History* 17 (1986): 204.

5. "History and Genre," 214.

6. I rely in part on Nancy K. Miller's definition of female plots: "Female plot . . . is both what the culture has already inscribed for woman and its reinscription in the linear time of fiction. It is generally mapped by the heroine's engagement with the codes of the dominant ideology, her obligatory insertion within the institutions which in society and in novels name her—marriage, for example." See *Subject to Change: Reading Feminist Writing* (New York: Columbia University Press, 1988), 208.

7. Umberto Eco, introduction to *Carolina Invernizio, Matilde Serao, Liala* (Florence: La Nuova Italia, 1979), 9.

All translations are mine unless otherwise indicated.

8. These anthologies, which feature critical introductions and thorough bibliographies, include *La voce che è in lei: Antologia della narrativa femminile italiana tra '800 e '900* by Giuliana Morandini (Milan: Bompiani, 1980), which focuses on female authors writing in the late nineteenth and early twentieth centuries; *Narratrici italiane dell'Ottocento* by Anna Santoro (Naples: Federico & Ardia, 1987); and *Scrittrici italiane dal XIII al XX secolo. Testi e critica.* by Natalia Costa-Zalessow (Ravenna: Longo, 1982).

9. See in particular Lucienne Kroha, *The Women Writer in Late-Nineteenth-Century Italy: Gender and the Formation of Literary Identity* (New York: Mellen, 1992); Anna Santoro, *Narratrici italiane;* Paola Blelloch, *Quel Mondo dei Guanti e delle Stoffe . . . Profili di scrittrici italiane del '900* (Verona: Essedue, 1987); Vera Golini, "Critical Perspectives on Italian Women Writers at the Turn of the Cen-

tury," *Biblioteca di Quaderni d'italianistica* 4 (1988): 143–168; and Sharon Wood, *Italian Women's Writing 1860–1994*, Women in Context (London: Athlone, 1995).

10. Despite the ongoing discovery of lesser-known female authors, women apparently never infiltrated the ranks of writers in nineteenth-century Italy as they did in Europe and the United States. According to historian Michela De Giorgio, in 1879 only 4.1 percent of the 4,705 writers in Italy were women, and that figure includes authors with marginal talent. See *Le italiane dall'unità a oggi: Modelli culturali e comportamenti sociali* (Rome: Laterza, 1992), 377. However, as Santoro points out in her anthology, the act of writing must not be confused with that of publication. See *Narratrici italiane*, 7.

11. Patrizia Zambon has examined the significance of this lack of formal education among nineteenth-century Italian women authors. See "Leggere per scrivere. La formazione autodidattica delle scrittrici tra Otto e Novecento: Neera, Ada Negri, Grazia Deledda, Sibilla Aleramo," *Studi Novecenteschi* 16 (1989): 287–324.

12. De Giorgio, *Le italiane*, 388.

13. Antonia Arslan, "Ideologia e autorappresentazione. Donne intellettuali fra Ottocento e Novecento," in *Svelamento. Sibilla Aleramo: una biografia intellettuale*, ed. Annarita Buttafuoco and Marina Zancan (Milan: Feltrinelli, 1988), 164.

14. Elisabetta Rasy, *Le donne e la letteratura: Scrittrici eroine e ispiratrici nel mondo delle lettere* (Rome: Riuniti, 1984), 94.

Anna Santoro shares this position when she writes, "It is from her own experience, her own feelings and above all from her own impulses, from the physicality of her woman's body, from the horizon that her eye scans (the house, the family, the daily life), out of which comes forth the voice that narrates in the first place herself. . . . There exists, therefore, a project of narration that, all summed up, appears common in these female authors: if we ask which myths they wanted to touch, disprove, give credit to, attack, we realize that they all belong to the female experience." See "Narrativa di fine Ottocento: le scrittrici e il pubblico," *Italiana* IV (1992): 112–113.

15. Santoro, "Narrativa di fine Ottocento," 114.

16. *Quel Mondo dei Guanti*, 23.

17. "Ideologia e autorappresentazione," 168.

18. Luigi Capuana, *Letteratura Femminile*, ed. Giovanna Finocchiaro Chimirri (Catania: C.U.E.C.M., 1988), 20–21.

19. Regarding Serao, De Meis had this to say: "Serao . . . like all the other women [writers], only redid—with grace, with ability—that which was invented by the real creators of the novel form, Balzac, for example, or even Dumas. . . ." Quoted in Luigi Capuana, *Letteratura Femminile*, 20.

20. Enrico Nencioni, *Nuovi Saggi Critici di Letteratura Straniera e Altri Scritti* (Florence: Le Monnier, 1909), 312.

21. *Nuovi Saggi*, 356.

22. Federigo Verdinois, *Profili Letterari e Ricordi Giornalistici*, ed. Elena Craveri Croce (Florence: Le Monnier, 1949), 183–184.

23. Giuseppe A. Borgese, "Napoli e la Serao," *Corriere della Sera*, 28 July 1827, 3.

24. Pietro Pancrazi, *Scrittori italiani dal Carducci al D'Annunzio* (Bari: Laterza, 1937), 116.

25. Lola Bocchi, "Matilde Serao," *Almanacco della Donna Italiana* (Florence: Bemporad, 1928), 332.

26. The influence of Serao's sex on her work led occasionally to opposing critical interpretations. Benedetto Croce writes that Serao penetrates the "erotic feminine passionate nature, which only a woman can possess." See *Letteratura della nuova Italia*, vol. 3 (Bari: n.p., 1915), 36. However, Marie-Gracieuse Martin-Gistucci, in her monograph on Serao, believes the author's sex actually hinders a true understanding of her female characters. After analyzing the various types of heroines in Serao's work, she somewhat confusingly adds, "Perhaps because she was a woman, Matilde Serao did not understand the feminine problem." See *L'Oeuvre romanesque de Matilde Serao* (Grenoble: Presses Universitaires de Grenoble, 1973), 254.

27. Born in Greece of a Greek mother and an Italian father, Serao lived there only for the first few years of her life before the family moved to Naples. Except for a brief period in Rome, Serao spent the rest of her life in Naples.

28. Pietro Pancrazi, "La Serao Napoletana," *Nuova Antologia* 433 (1945): 101.

29. For a more detailed account of Serao's professional and personal life, see Anna Banti's biography, *Matilde Serao* (Turin: UTET, 1965).

30. Alessandro Scurani, "La Fortuna di Matilde Serao," *Letture. Rassegna critica del libro e dello spettacolo* 10 (1962): 647.

31. Letters to Gaetano Bonavenia. 22 March 1978; 23 June 1878. In "A furia di urti, di gomitate," *Nuova Antologia* 398 (1938):405.

32. R. Ceserani and E. Salibra, "Popular Literature in Nineteenth-Century Italy: *Letteratura amena*," *Canadian Review of Comparative Literature* 9 (1982): 368.

33. Serao often drew on her early professional experiences for her fictional work. In the realist novel *Vita e avventure di Riccardo Joanna* (Milan: Galli, 1887), the author describes the behind-the-scenes world of journalism in the nation's capital. Perhaps it is telling that Serao chose for this novel a male protagonist, one of the few in her works. Was she merely reflecting the scarcity of female journalists in late nineteenth-century Italy, or does this figure stand in for herself to some degree? Serao's use of autobiographical elements in her realist works, as well as her personal vision of this genre would suggest the latter interpretation.

34. *Matilde Serao*, 36.

35. Schilardi notes that toward her female readers, Serao directed "a message of moderation, of respectability, of conformity, even if sometimes this was clothed in an apparently revolutionary context." See *Matilde Serao*, 36.

36. Nancy Harrowitz, *Antisemitism, Misogyny and the Logic of Cultural Difference: Cesare Lombroso and Matilde Serao* (Lincoln: University of Nebraska Press, 1994), 98.

37. Serao's analysis of why the novel is the perfect format for the female writer reveals her essential conservatism, for she saw the novel as an arena in which the author can inspire "love of the family, of one's country, in summary, of everything that is part of the most elect, most pure, most ideal of life." See Schilardi, *Matilde Serao*, 153. Whether Serao actually followed her own dictate here is debatable, for surely many of her novels and short stories are interlaced with provocative themes. For example, her depiction of family dynamics, a topic addressed in chapter 3, seems designed to inculcate feelings of disrespect and rebellion toward the patriarchal family structure.

38. In her autobiography, Wharton describes a meeting with Serao, praising her "eager imagination" and adding that "culture and experience were fused in the glow of her powerful intelligence." See *A Backward Glance* (1933; reprint, New York: Scribner, 1964), 277.

39. For a more complete description of the correspondence between Serao and Mozzoni, see Piercarlo Masini, "Matilde Serao e Anna Maria Mozzoni: Una Polemica sull'Emancipazione Femminile," in *Eresie dell'Ottocento: Alle sorgenti laiche, umaniste e libertarie della democrazia italiana* (Milan: Editoriale Nuova, 1978), 275–285.

40. Wanda De Nunzio Schilardi, Dora Amato, and Judith Howard, in separate articles, have debated whether Serao's statements against the feminist movement should be given greater weight than her pioneering work as a female journalist and author. See Schilardi, "L'antifemminismo di Matilde Serao," in *La Parabola della Donna nella Letteratura Italiana dell'Ottocento*, ed. Gigliola De Donato (Bari: Adriatica Editrice, 1983), 277–305; Amato, "Femminismo e femminilità," in *Matilde Serao tra giornalismo e letteratura*, ed. Gianni Infusino (Naples: Guida, 1981), 105–109; and Howard, "The Feminine Vision of Matilde Serao," *Italian Quarterly* 18 (1975): 55–77.

41. I. T. Olken, "La virtù di Checchina: Anachronism and Resolution," *Romance Quarterly* 30 (1983): 48.

42. Harrowitz writes, "Her bitter and defeatist attitude shows Serao's ability to be brutally honest about what women in her time faced and what their possibilities were. Is this the statement of a woman who thought that men and women were treated equally? It is obviously not. It is certainly not the statement of a woman willing to fight for better conditions for women—but only, it would seem, because she feels it would be futile, so stacked are the odds against women." See *Antisemitism*, 102.

43. Nencioni's lengthy essay on Serao is a compilation of a series of articles completed as each of her works was published. Although he emphasized a stylistic approach, his insights are still interesting today. See *Nuovi Saggi*, 302–362. Croce wrote two long pieces on Serao, both focusing primarily on her realist narratives. He praises Serao's works, but he does imply that her literary skills are a crude amalgamation of the critical observation skills she learned as a journalist and her spontaneous emotions. With this evaluation, Croce joins other critics in promulgating the split between intellect and sentiment. See *Letteratura della nuova Italia*, 35–76, and "Note sulla Letteratura Italiana: Matilde Serao," *La Critica* 1 (1903): 321–351.

44. Anna Banti, *Matilde Serao*; Anthony Gisolfi, *The Essential Matilde Serao* (New York: Las Americas, 1968); Marie-Gracieuse Martin-Gistucci, *L'Oeuvre romanesque*; and Gianni Infusino, ed., *Matilde Serao tra giornalismo e letteratura* (Naples: Guida, 1981).

45. Susan Fraiman, *Unbecoming Women: British Women Writers and the Novel of Development* (New York: Columbia University Press, 1993), x.

46. Fredric Jameson, "Reification and Utopia in Mass Culture," *Social Text* 1 (1979): 133–134.

CHAPTER 1. REALIST REVISIONS

1. Although *verismo* has been recognized as a uniquely Italian interpretation of European realism, I will be using the terms "realism" and "*verismo*" inter-

changeably because of the similarities in the style and precepts of both movements. Serao herself, along with many critics, did not insist on maintaining linguistic distinctions when referring to the diverse national representations of this literary movement.

2. For a more thorough examination of the rise of *verismo* as a literary movement, see G. M. Carsaniga, *The Age of Realism*, ed. F. W. J. Hemmings (Middlesex, England: Pengiun, 1974); Vittorio Spinazzola, *Verismo e positivismo* (Milan: Garzanti, 1977); and Ferruccio Ulivi, *La letteratura verista* (Turin: ERI, 1972).

3. Anna Banti, "Matilde non sa scrivere," *Illustrazione italiana*, January 1949, 57.

4. Critics are unsure whether the short story "La virtù di Checchina" was first published in 1883 or 1884. Following Bruni's lead, in his preface to Serao's *Il romanzo della fanciulla* (Naples: Liguori, 1985), I will use the latter date. There is also some discrepancy about the publication date of the book itself. Again, I chose to observe Bruni's meticulously recreated chronology.

5. Michele Prisco, "Matilde Serao," *Terzo Programma* 3 (1963): 85.

6. *Letteratura della nuova Italia*, 36.

7. Francesco Bruno, *Letteratura meridionale* (Cosenza: Pellegrini, 1968), 223.
Carlo Madrignani also dismisses Serao's renderings of the tenets of realism as superficial and conventional, adding that her apparent "sentimentality" precludes a fundamental principle of *verismo*, that of the impersonality of the author. See *Ideologia e narrativa dopo l'Unificazione* (Rome: Giulio Savelli, 1974), 142.

8. In an 1894 interview with the journalist Ugo Ojetti, Serao defended her unpolished literary style, a criticism leveled against many Italian realist authors: "I believe that the vivacity of that uncertain language and of that broken style infuses my works with 'warmth,' and the warmth not only enlivens the characters but preserves them from the corruption of time. That's what I think. Will those other works (and there are few) written in a pure and icy language live on? We four (by that I mean Verga, [Federico] De Roberto, me and a little bit Capuana), accused of imprecision, have a public that follows us and reads us: why should we die?" See Ojetti, *Alla Scoperta dei Letterati*, ed. Pietro Pancrazi (Florence: Le Monnier, 1946), 276.

9. Luigi Capuana, *Studii sulla letteratura contemporanea*, ed. Paola Azzolini, Seconda Serie (Naples: Liguori, 1988), 72.

10. Quoted in Enrico Ghidetti, *Verga. Guida storico-critica* (Rome: Riuniti, 1979), 60.

11. Verga and Capuana were not the only proponents of *verismo;* Grazia Deledda incorporated realist tenets in her portraits of the lower economic classes found in her native Sardinia. Deledda is perhaps best known for her novels *Elias Portolu* (Elias Portolu) (1903) and *La madre* (The Mother) (1920), which focus on an analysis of fundamental human emotions set against a backdrop of Sardinian customs and traditions.

12. In a widely repeated criticism, the journalist and critic Edoardo Scarfoglio said, "Matilde doesn't know how to write." He made this comment in a review of Serao's novel *Fantasia* shortly before the two married. This criticism was not as harsh as it appears, however, for the entire quotation reads "Matilde doesn't know how to write. What can I do? I told her this before marrying her, I told

her after. She consoles herself: no one knows how to write in Italian. And here she's right." Quoted in Ugo Ojetti, *Cose viste,* vol. 4 (Milan: Treves, 1928), 148.

13. Serao, *Il romanzo della fanciulla,* 5–6. Subsequent references to this work are indicated parenthetically in the text.

14. Although strict adherents of realist doctrine encouraged authors to focus their attention on poor and humble protagonists, Serao refused to abide by such a stricture. In an 1878 letter, she wrote, "I mean by realism all of life, with its lofty poetry, with its modest prose, with its generous outbursts and its real misery. . . ." See Letters to Gaetano Bonavenia, 405. Although many of Serao's best realist works do emphasize problems faced by the lower classes, she often incorporated descriptions of other social classes in her narratives, thus expanding her realist panorama and giving the reader today a broader portrait of female experiences.

15. In nineteenth-century Italy, marriage was universally accepted as a normal and expected part of the life course, according to historian Michela De Giorgio, who adds that "there were no dissonant voices in the chorus lauding the beneficial effects of marriage." See *Le italiane,* 291. Priests, scientists, intellectuals, and writers all praised the institution of marriage, which, many agreed, was the only "vocation" open to women. "[M]atrimony for women was not a free choice, it was an obligatory passage, a condition of economic and social survival," she writes (*Le italiane,* 293).

16. Serao was not the only turn-of-the-century Italian woman writer to depict the disturbing repercussions of an unhappy marriage. In Neera's 1911 novel *Duello d'anime* (Dueling Souls), for example, the young heroine gradually loses her autonomy and self-identity as she suffers the abuse of her cruel and arrogant husband.

17. Anna Nozzoli, *Tabù e coscienza: La condizione femminile nella letteratura italiana del Novecento* (Florence: La Nuova Italia, 1978), 20.

18. For an analysis of female friendship and the role Isolina plays in this short story, see my "Checchina and Isolina: Female Friendship in Matilde Serao's 'La virtù di Checchina,'" *Romance Languages Annual* 3 (1991): 309–313. For an examination of the character of Isolina, see also I. T. Olken, who compares her to a female Svengali in "La virtù di Checchina," 45–59.

19. Anna Banti, Preface to *Il ventre di Napoli,* by Matilde Serao (Milan: Garzanti, 1962), x.

20. Carlo Madrignani, *Ideologia e narrativa,* 138.

21. Blelloch, *Quel Mondo dei Guanti,* 121.

22. Matilde Serao, "La virtù di Checchina," in *Il romanzo della fanciulla* (Naples: Liguori, 1985), 213. Subsequent references to this work are indicated parenthetically in the text.

23. If Isolina is the antithesis of Checchina, the elegant marquis becomes pointedly contrasted with the protagonist's boorish husband. The marquis is sensitive, courteous, and talks in well-modulated tones. Toto is crass and over-familiar, and he snores. A luxurious scent issues from the marquis's handkerchief, a far cry from the medicinal stench of carbolic acid that trails behind Toto. Serao's careful attention to differences among social classes is manifested by details such as these. In the opening section, Isolina wears Jockey Club perfume, while Checchina is surrounded by the less aromatic odor of cleaning solution.

24. Maryse Jeuland-Meynaud, *Immagini, linguaggio e modelli del corpo nell'opera narrativa di Matilde Serao* (Rome: Ateneo, 1986), 38.

Serao often used clothing as a metonymic representation of a character's social and economic status. In the novel *Storia di due anime* (The Story of Two Souls), for example, the reader can follow the fortunes of the female protagonist simply by observing her attire. As Gelsomina slowly sinks into a life of depravity and prostitution, she exchanges her simple black wool shawl for a flimsy straw hat and later for "a huge black hat, weighted with short black feathers. . . ." Vol. 1, *Serao*, ed. Pietro Pancrazi (1904; reprint, Milan: Garzanti, 1944), 760. The narrator calls the hat "the most obvious sign that a daughter of the common people had been corrupted, had become, wanted to become, bourgeois" (726).

25. Checchina may be remaking herself in Isolina's image, but she does not heed the lesson hidden by her friend's effusions: the financial and emotional cost that a woman pays for love. Isolina must deceive her husband, bribe her maid, and risk doing business with usurers in order to have the appropriate clothing and trinkets for her liaisons, which often end up being hurried and unsatisfying.

26. Sandra M. Gilbert and Susan Gubar, *The Madwoman in the Attic: The Woman Writer and the Nineteenth-Century Literary Imagination* (London: Yale University Press, 1979), 84.

27. *Immagini, linguaggio e modelli*, 121.

28. Jenijoy La Belle, *Herself Beheld: The Literature of the Looking Glass* (Ithaca: Cornell University Press, 1988), 24.

29. Carlo A. Madrignani, *Ideologia e narrativa*, 157.

30. I. T. Olken, "La virtù di Checchina," 58.

31. Not every contemporary critic was able to read this subtext. Raffa Garzia, in a monograph on Serao, complains that the story ends abruptly, and in fact demands to know what happens to Checchina after she returns home. See *Matilde Serao* (Rocca S. Casciano, Italy: Licinio Cappelli, 1916). Garzia is, in fact, incapable of reading beyond the ending. I borrow this phrase from Rachel Blau DuPlessis's work on narrative strategies, found in the text *Writing beyond the Ending: Narrative Strategies of Twentieth-Century Women Writers* (Bloomington: Indiana University Press, 1985). DuPlessis argues that the narratives for many nineteenth-century female protagonists ended in either death or marriage. This concept will be examined more fully in the following chapter.

32. Annis Pratt, *Archetypal Patterns in Women's Fiction* (Bloomington: Indiana University Press, 1981), 41.

33. This story apparently first appeared in the collection *Dal vero* (Milan: Baldini, Castoldi, 1905) which was first published in 1879. Selections from *Dal vero*, along with short stories from *Raccolta minima*, were published as *Pagina azzurra* in 1883. The book *La moglie di un grand'uomo* appeared in 1918 and contained this and other short stories. It is tempting to read this story as a reflection of Serao's unhappy union with the journalist Edoardo Scarfoglio, but it was evidently written before their 1885 marriage. Subsequent references to this short story are indicated parenthetically in the text.

34. This article first appeared 25 December 1906, in Serao's own newspaper, *Il Giorno*. It was reprinted in 1907 in the popular women's magazine *La Donna*, 3.

35. "Perchè le ragazze non si maritano?," 5. Subsequent references to this work are indicated parenthetically in the text.

Serao often used her newspaper columns to write about the sanctity of marriage and to denounce proposed legislation legalizing divorce. She, however, separated from her philandering husband and subsequently entered into a relationship with the lawyer Giuseppe Natale which lasted until his death in 1926, one year before her own. The couple had a child, Eleonora Natale, in 1905.

36. Matilde Serao, *Saper Vivere: Norme di buona creanza* (1900; reprint, Florence: Passigli, 1989), 242.

37. *Quel Mondo dei Guanti*, 35.

38. In his 1889 novel *Mastro-don Gesualdo*, Verga creates a strikingly similar scene, describing the inhabitants of a Sicilian village as they gather on their balconies to watch a religious procession. In both Verga's novel and Serao's short story the scene is used as a vehicle to present the various familial and amorous ties among the characters, as well as to analyze their social and economic connections.

39. Matilde Serao, "Non più," in *Il romanzo della fanciulla* (Naples: Liguori, 1985), 187. Subsequent references to this work are indicated parenthetically in the text.

40. *Le italiane*, 328–329.

41. This idealized vision of maternal sentiment found its way into Serao's prose. In the short story "Silvia," for example, a middle-aged woman finds emotional fulfillment through the pregnancy resulting from her late marriage. She feels "a singular joy" at the quickening of the child. See *Dal vero* (Milan: Baldini, Castoldi, 1905), 297. The protagonist's death in childbirth at the end of the story is validated as the definitive example of maternal sacrifice, although it also points to the very real physical dangers of childbirth in turn-of-the-century Italy.

42. Serao, Lettere di Matilde Serao a Olga Ossani Lodi (Febea), *Nuova Antologia* 448 (1950): 124.

43. *Immagini, linguaggio e modelli*, 81.

44. Interestingly, the introduction is dedicated to Paul Bourget, Serao's friend and a leading proponent of psychological and sentimental fiction. Bourget's influence on Serao, both thematically and stylistically, has been discussed by many critics and will be examined in greater detail in the following chapter.

45. Serao, *Suor Giovanna della Croce*, vol. 1, *Serao*, ed. Pietro Pancrazi (1901; reprint, Milan: Garzanti, 1944), 536. Subsequent references to this work are noted parenthetically in the text.

46. *Matilde Serao*, 243.

47. Dana A. Heller, *The Feminization of Quest-Romance: Radical Departures* (Austin: University of Texas Press, 1990), 19.

48. Serao's preoccupation with the importance of financial independence for women, a theme already noted in "La virtù di Checchina," is evident in this text as well. Her concern may have had some basis in her own experience. A 1904 letter, addressed to her editor in Rome, expresses her despair over the sum to be paid for two short books, "Two hundred lire per volume is rather little; a modest French journal would pay me 200 lire for an article. Italy is really an out-of-date country. And if we can't do it in journalism, how will we authors

eke out a living in literature?" See Edoardo A. Lèbano, "Una lettera inedita di Matilde Serao," *La Fusta* 1 (1976): 91–92.

49. *Immagini, linguaggio e modelli,* 131.

50. This story was republished in 1898 as a novella entitled "Storia di una monaca" (The Story of a Nun).

51. See Ursula Fanning, "Sentimental Subversion: Representations of Female Friendship in the Work of Matilde Serao," *Annali d'Italianistica* 7 (1989): 273–286.

52. Serao, "Per monaca," in *Il romanzo della fanciulla* (Naples: Liguori, 1985), 49. Subsequent references to this work are indicated parenthetically in the text.

53. *Il romanzo della fanciulla,* 4.

54. "Sentimental Subversion," 278.

55. One character, Anna Doria, declares that mothers, jealous of their young and vivacious daughters, impede their marriages and doom them to a life of spinsterhood. Ironically, it is Eva who jumps in to defend mothers.

56. "Sentimental Subversion," 284.

57. "Ideologia e autorappresentazione," 168.

58. Banti, *Matilde Serao,* 41.

59. For a more thorough examination of the traditional *Bildungsroman,* see Franco Moretti, *The Way of the World: The Bildungsroman in European Culture* (London: Verso, 1987) and Jerome H. Buckley, *Season of Youth: The Bildungsroman from Dickens to Golding* (Cambridge: Harvard University Press, 1974). Most critics examining the *Bildungsroman* have recognized the following elements as important in a character's successful self-realization: a relocation from country to city, direct experience with urban life, the search for a profession, self-education, and some sort of journey.

60. Ester Kleinbord Labovitz believes that a true female *Bildungsroman* did not arise until the twentieth century: "When cultural and social structures appeared to support women's struggle for independence, to go out into the world, engage in careers, in self-discovery and fulfillment, the heroine in fiction began to reflect these changes." See *The Myth of the Heroine: The Female Bildungsroman in the Twentieth Century* (New York: Lang, 1986), 6–7. I believe, however, that if the definition of the novel of development is broadened, earlier and illuminating texts written by prefeminist women can be included in a study of this subgenre.

61. I am thinking in particular of the work done by Eve Kornfeld and Susan Jackson, who believe that this subgenre "illuminates the social expectations of female life as well as the secret hopes and dreams which might not be revealed in another format." See "The Female *Bildungsroman* in Nineteenth-Century America: Parameters of a Vision," *Journal of American Culture* 10 (1987): 69. Perhaps even more significant for a genre-based study such as this is Marianne Hirsch's work that calls the *Bildungsroman* a direct descendent of the realist literary tradition. She traces this connection to that fact that the novel of development depicts "the progressive disillusionment of its protagonist in his *(sic)* encounters with the social reality." See "The Novel of Formation as Genre: Between Great Expectations and Lost Illusions," *Genre* 12 (1979): 301.

62. Perhaps the best example of an autobiographical *Bildungsroman* by an Italian woman writer is Sibilla Aleramo's *Una donna* (Turin: Sten, 1906). The text describes a young woman's adolescence, unhappy marriage, and eventual

decision to leave her husband and child. Fiora A. Bassanese points out that Aleramo attempted to create "a genderless novel of development" by incorporating both male and female models of maturation (147). See Bassanese, "*Una donna:* Autobiography as Exemplary Text," *Donna: Women in Italian Culture,* ed. Ada Testaferri. University of Toronto Studies 7 (Ottawa: Dovehouse Editions, 1989), 147. It would be interesting to read in Serao's own semiautobiographical works the seeds of future, more overtly personal and feminist works such as *Una donna.*

63. That the world of elementary school teaching in turn-of-the-century Italy was inhabited primarily by young women is made clear by the numbers enrolled in such institutes. In the 1883–1884 school year, 4,656 girls were registered as students, as opposed to 1,181 young men in comparable schools. Although women far outnumbered men in this field, their monthly stipend was about half that of their masculine colleagues, just one example of the gross disparity in working conditions between the sexes. See Annarita Buttafuoco, "Condizione delle donne e movimento di emancipazione femminile," in *L'Italia di Giolitti,* vol. 20, part 5 of *Storia della Società Italiana* (Milan: Teti, 1981), 152.

64. "Scuola normale feminile," in *Il romanzo della fanciulla* (Naples: Liguori 1985), 148. Subsequent references to the work are indicated parenthetically in the text.

65. *Le italiane,* 123.

66. With this text focusing on female students, Serao entered a hotly debated topic of nineteenth-century Italy—education for women. Although an 1859 law mandated two years' compulsory education for both boys and girls, it was not strictly enforced, and the illiteracy rate for women was significantly higher than that for men. In the 1880s, however, schools were officially opened to female students, and the number of girls attending school jumped dramatically.

67. Pratt, *Archetypal Patterns,* 29.

68. Isabella Diaz has apparently suffered a disfiguring illness. Her eyes glitter, her lips are stained by fever, her teeth ruined, and her eyelashes and brows completely absent. A poorly made wig perches uneasily on her head: "She was horrendous" (155).

69. Laura Gropallo, *Autori Italiani d'Oggi* (Turin: Nazionale, 1903), 186.

70. "Telegrafi dello stato," in *Il romanzo della fanciulla* (Naples: Liguori, 1985), 19. Subsequent references to the work are indicated parenthetically in the text.

71. Pratt, *Archetypal Patterns,* 14.

72. This article has been reprinted in Schilardi, *Matilde Serao,* 211–213.

73. "Nicoletta," in *La vita è così lunga* (Milan: Treves, 1918), 67. Subsequent references to this work are indicated parenthetically in the text.

74. "Il ventre di Napoli," (Milan: Garzanti, 1962), 126. Subsequent references to this work are indicated parenthetically in the text.

75. Serao's work anticipates Elvira Notari's popular silent films, which also used Naples as a background for her realist portrayals of humble protagonists. In fact, Notari, recognizing the similarity between her rendition of Neapolitan life and Serao's urban narratives, wanted to adapt the author's novels into films. Serao refused, claiming, according to one historian, that Notari's films were "lumpen." See Giuliana Bruno, *Streetwalking on a Ruined Map: Cultural Theory and the City Films of Elvira Notari* (Princeton: Princeton University Press, 1993), 242.

76. Darby Tench, "Gutting the Belly of Naples: Metaphor, Metonyny and the Auscultatory Imperative in Serao's City of *Pietà*," *Annali d'Italianistica* 7 (1989): 294.

77. Santoro, "Narrativa di fine Ottocento," 104.

Chapter 2. Romantic Interlude

1. I must note first the myriad of labels for works classified within this category, which falls under the general heading of "popular literature" or "*paraletteratura*." Texts such as domestic and sentimental novels, Gothic narratives, and detective and adventure tales have also been embraced by this broad category; modern-day critics examine soap operas, comic strips, and Harlequin romances as well. Even the term "romance novel" includes many variations. Two types of the romance that will not be examined in this chapter are the sentimental novel, which generally focuses on a poor but virtuous heroine who succeeds in making a good marriage, and the mass-produced romance, or "*romanzo rosa.*" This second type also features a male-female relationship and a happy ending, but because of its formulaic structure, it is generally considered the least literary of these various narrative formats. The Gothic text will be examined in the following chapter.

2. For an overview of popular literature in Italy during the 1800s, see Ceserani and Salibra, "Popular Literature."

3. Many critics have approached the study of popular literature through an analysis of its characteristics or its chronology. Gramsci, for example, classified the various manifestations of popular literature into seven types, ranging from the ideological novels of Hugo, to the historical narratives of Dumas, to Verne's adventure tales. Serao's works fall under his definition of the "*romanzo sentimentale*," which he describes as "not political in a strict sense, but in which is expressed what could be called 'a sentimental democracy.'" See *Letteratura e vita nazionale* (Turin: Eiunaudi, 1966), 110. Umberto Eco, in his extensive writings on popular literature and culture, has focused primarily on the "*romanzo popolare*," or mass-marketed novel. Eco traces three stages in its evolution, beginning with the "*periodo romantico-eroico*" in the 1830s, characterized by the texts of Sue and Balzac, and ending with the "*neo-eroico*" period of the early 1900s, as seen in the works of Lupin and Fantomas. The works examined in this study represent the middle stage, or "*periodo borghese*," which gained popularity in the 1890s and which often featured a "man of the people" as protagonist rather than a larger-than-life hero. See *Il Superuomo di Massa* (Milan: Bompiani, 1990). More productive for this study is Antonia Arslan's approach, which relies on a broader, more inclusive definition. She calls popular literature both didactic and entertaining; above all, it is a "literature that wants to be read." "The love of reading" becomes the text's most compelling characteristic. See *Dame, Droga e Galline. Romanzo popolare e romanzo di consumo tra Ottocento e Novecento* (Milano: Unicopli, 1986), 14–15.

4. *Letteratura e vita nazionale*, 121. Giuliano Manacorda has briefly examined Serao's romance texts in light of Gramscian theory of popular literature. See "L'opera di Matilde Serao entro

l'ipotesi gramsciana di una letteratura nazional-popolare," in *Matilde Serao tra giornalismo e letteratura*, ed. Gianni Infusino (Naples: Guida, 1981), 15–27.

5. Clark, *Sentimental Modernism: Women Writers and the Revolution of the Word* (Bloomington: Indiana University Press, 1991), 2.

6. *Sentimental Modernism*, 20–21.

7. Jameson, *The Political Unconscious: Narrative as a Socially Symbolic Act* (Ithaca: Cornell University Press, 1981), 104.

8. Rasy, *Le donne*, 97.

9. Tania Modleski, *Loving with a Vengeance: Mass-Produced Fantasies for Women* (New York: Routledge, 1982), 25.

10. Diane Elam, *Romancing the Postmodern* (New York: Routledge, 1992), 76.

11. *Romancing the Postmodern*, 102.

12. Joseph Spencer Kennard, writing in 1905, called Serao's romance novels immoral and corrupting. He singled out *Addio, amore!* as especially profane: "The novel is immoral not only because an unhealthy gloss of sentimentality gilds the most revolting vice, but also because its love scenes contain that spicy flavor of licentiousness that is a real poison for youth." See *Romanzi e Romanzieri Italiani*, vol. 2 (Florence: G. Barbèra, 1905), 46.

Maria Luisa Astaldi, writing during the years of fascism, also reproaches Serao for presenting scandalous material. She specifically criticizes the image of women in the author's romance novels: "Pale, unhealthy women, but no longer like those resigned, gentle women of romantic myths; women all fits, impulses and whims, who, sheltering themselves behind the banner of passion—which, according to them, bestows all the rights—and releasing their worst attribute." See *Nascita e vicende del romanzo italiano* (Milan: Treves, 1939), 104. Serao's depiction of her romantic heroines undermines fascist ideology that calls for morally and physically sound guardians of the family.

13. *The Essential Matilde Serao*, 128.

14. For a general overview of Liala and Carolina Invernizio, see *Carolina Invernizio, Matilde Serao, Liala*, Umberto Eco, et al. For an examination of the *romanzo rosa*, see Maria Pia Pozzato, *Il romanzo rosa* (Milan: Europei, 1982) and Anna Banti, "Storia e Ragioni del 'Romanzo Rosa,'" *Paragone* (February 1953): 28–34.

15. Daniela Curti, "Il Linguaggio del Racconto Rosa: Gli Anni 20 ad Oggi," in *Lingua Letteraria e Lingua dei Media nell'Italiano Contemporaneo* (Florence: Le Monnier, 1987), 159.

16. DuPlessis, *Writing Beyond the Ending*, 5.

17. "Paolo Spada," in *Fior di passione* (Milan: Baldini, Castoldi, 1899), 39. Subsequent references to this work are indicated parenthetically in the text.

18. Schilardi, *Matilde Serao*, 32.

19. Gilbert and Gubar, *The Madwoman in the Attic*, 316.

20. Matilde Serao, *Tre donne* (Rome: Voghera, 1905) 44. Subsequent references to this work are indicated parenthetically in the text.

21. Serao's romance narratives often feature foreign names and phrases, creating a certain cachet and emphasizing the upper-class environs.

22. DuPlessis, *Writing Beyond the Ending*, 16.

23. Joseph Spencer Kennard, for example, has written that "love is for Serao the sole master-passion, the only fount of joy and sorrow." See "Woman in the Italian Novel," *North American Review* 188 (1908): 589. But he has neglected to

investigate the ramifications of this emotion, particularly on the author's female characters.

24. "La grande fiamma," *Nuova Antologia* 103 (1889):103. Subsequent references to this work are indicated parenthetically in the text.

25. DuPlessis, *Writing Beyond the Ending*, x.

26. This idea of an *a priori* construction of selfhood is in itself troubling, as Judith Butler points out in her provocative text *Gender Trouble: Feminism and the Subversion of Identity* (New York: Routledge, 1990). The intersection of normative and performative models of behavior is clearly an important issue in both feminist studies and literary criticism and merits further discussion. For the purposes of this study, however, the focus will instead be on the specific textual evidence of each heroine's socioeconomic world, rather than inferring cultural conditions that may or may not give rise to certain gendered roles.

27. In this text, Serao appears to emulate the structure of the traditional "sentimental novel," which typically turns on the "fall" of a poor but virtuous heroine. The trope of a heroine's seduction as a narrative framework is a longstanding literary tradition. Nancy K. Miller's examination of eighteenth-century works, for example, finds the narratives are often dependent on the "uses and abuses" of a heroine's chastity. See *The Heroine's Text: Readings in the French and English Novel, 1722–1782* (New York: Columbia University Press, 1980), 4.

28. "[S]he was so poor because she did not want to have a protector." *La ballerina*, vol. 1, *Serao*, ed. Pietro Pancrazi (1899; reprint, Milan: Garzanti, 1944), 31. Subsequent references to the work are indicated parenthetically in the text.

29. The only exception to this comes in the form of Gaetanella, a young girl who dresses Carmela's hair before performances. But despite a bond of affection between the two humble young women, Carmela ignores Gaetanella's oblique warnings about the fate of those who ruin themselves for men.

30. Although I have not addressed Serao's works from a structural viewpoint, this text offers an excellent refutation of the frequent criticism leveled against the author for allegedly weak organizational skills. Instead, this novel is a model of meticulous planning. The second and third sections of the text end with the heroine overhearing Ferdinando remarking, "What a fool!" (the first time occurs when he learns she is a virgin; the second when he learns to whom she has relinquished her virtue). The opening section of the novel describes the resting place of Amina Boschetti, while the final section portrays Ferdinando's place of death.

31. Dainty appetites have traditionally been linked with chaste heroines, as Helena Michie has discovered in her study of fictional depictions of eating. See *The Flesh Made Word: Female Figures and Women's Bodies* (Oxford: Oxford University Press, 1987), 16.

32. It is unclear just why Ferdinando commits suicide. The dancers speculate that he was either grief-stricken over an unhappy relationship with a married woman or troubled by financial woes.

33. "Women in the Italian Novel," 590.

34. "O Giovannino o la morte," in *L'Occhio di Napoli* (Milan: Garzanti, 1962), 242. Subsequent references to the work are indicated parenthetically in the text.

35. A 1942 film titled "Via delle Cinque Lune" (Five Moon Street), directed by Luigi Chiarini and loosely based on this short story, significantly changes the

focus of the text. The film, considerably less nuanced than the short story, maintains the original conflict between the two women but casts the male protagonist as a basically sympathetic character who becomes caught in the snare of the conniving stepmother. An even more dramatic change involves the death of Chiarini, here renamed Inez. In the film the death is ambiguously depicted, suggesting either a suicide or an accident. The rewriting of the original ending causes the focus to shift away from the heroine's deliberate decision to kill herself. See *Via delle Cinque Lune*, dir. Luigi Chiarini, Centro Sperimentale di Cinematografia, 1942.

36. Marianne Hirsch, "Spiritual *Bildung:* The Beautiful Soul as Paradigm," in *The Voyage In: Fictions of Female Development*, ed. Elizabeth Abel, Marianne Hirsch, and Elizabeth Langland (Hanover: University Press of New England, 1983), 44.

37. Matilde Serao, "Livia Spera," in *La vita è così lunga* (Milan: Treves, 1918), 53. Subsequent references to this work are indicated parenthetically in the text.

38. Michela De Giorgio, "The Catholic Model," in *A History of Women in the West: Emerging Feminism from Revolution to World War*, ed. Geneviève Fraisse and Michelle Perrot; trans. Joan Bond Sax (Cambridge: Harvard University Press, 1993), 179.

39. Indeed, Isabella Pezzini remarks that Serao's heroines "are often presented to us as they are reading, as if they were learning from novels, and especially from prohibited ones." See "Matilde Serao," in *Carolina Invernizio, Matilde Serao, Liala* (Florence: La Nuova Italia, 1979), 73.

40. Bourget's literary styles loosely duplicate the various genres employed by Serao during her career. His first works followed the naturalist school, his later works tended to be more psychological, and his final texts dealt primarily with religious themes. For biographical information, see Armand E. Singer, *Paul Bourget* (Boston: Hall, 1976). For an examination of the relationship between Bourget and Serao, see Marie-Gracieuse Martin-Gistucci, "Une Amitié 'Paradoxale' de Paul Bourget," in *Paul Bourget et L'Italie*, ed. Marie-Gracieuse Martin-Gistucci (Geneva: Slatkine, 1985).

41. Bourget's wife Minnie translated Serao's most ambitious novel, *Il paese di cuccagna*, into French in 1898. Bourget wrote the preface. Also that year, Bourget dedicated the novel *La duchesse bleue* to Serao, comparing her to Zola and Maupassant. Three years later, Serao returned the favor, dedicating *Suor Giovanna della Croce* to her friend.

42. It is interesting to note the careful, and I would argue deliberate, use of vocal expression in this short story and the preceding two texts. As *La ballerina* draws to a close, Carmela prays aloud over the body of her beloved. The resolution of "O Giovannino o la morte" is marked by the piercing scream of Chiarina as she discovers her fiancé's duplicity. In "Livia Spera," however, the heroine's voice is not heard at all; she is silenced, yet her actions, particularly this cryptic smile, speak to a strength of character and a degree of self-control not exhibited by the other two female protagonists.

43. Livia embodies the definition of "woman" that Judith Butler includes in her analysis of identity: "[W]oman itself is a term in process, a becoming, a constructing that cannot rightfully be said to originate or to end." See *Gender*

Trouble, 33. The open-ended resolution of "Livia Spera," and the very ambiguity surrounding the title character point to the heroine's fluidity.

44. As Diane Elam has already noted, the romance narrative's freedom from the strictures and traditions governing canonical texts allows it to more openly express female experiences: "[R]omance seems to be the terrain upon which female desire can work, outside the testamentary realism that enacts male desire as law." In other words, the very nature of the romance text can generate a more perceptive analysis of female desire. See *Romancing the Postmodern,* 127.

45. See Mario Praz's excellent study *La carne, la morte e il diavolo nella letteratura romantica* (Florence: Sansoni, 1976) for a more thorough investigation of the various manifestations of the *femme fatale.*

46. For more on the relationship between social ideology and the rise of the *femme fatale* in literature, see Annamaria Cavalli Pasini's illuminating text *La Scienza del Romanzo: Romanzo e cultura scientifica tra Otto e Novecento* (Bologna: Pàtron, 1982).

47. Serao conflates the image of the *femme fatale* with that of Rome itself in the 1885 novel *La conquista di Roma,* vol. 2, *Serao,* ed. Pietro Pancrazi (Milan: Garzanti, 1944). Francesco Sangiorgio, a humble deputy from the south, is captivated by his stay in the city, which appears to him "like a feminine apparition" (282) and "a woman beloved" (286). Serao tracks Sangiorgio's meteoric rise and equally remarkable fall against the metaphoric images of Rome as a seductive, and ultimately destructive, woman. In this novel, Serao's fictive city of women becomes the city *as* woman.

48. As Sandra Gilbert and Susan Gubar write, "[A] woman writer must examine, assimilate, and transcend the extreme images of 'angel' and 'monster' which male authors have generated for her." See *The Madwoman in the Attic,* 17.

49. Nina Auerbach, for example, rehabilitates the *femme fatale,* which she refers to as the "demon," from its traditionally negative connotations. She also recognizes the innate connections among the primary archetypes of female characters, including with the "angel in the house" and the "demon" two others, the "old maid" and the "fallen woman": "Discussing each type separately falsifies the fluid boundaries among them, for together they place women at the junction between the social and the spiritual, the humanly perishable and the transcendently potent." See *Woman and the Demon: The Life of a Victorian Myth* (Cambridge, Harvard University Press, 1982), 63–64.

50. Matilde Serao, *Cuore infermo* (1881; reprint, Rome: Lucarini, 1988), 5–6. Subsequent references to this work are indicated parenthetically in the text.

51. Ursula Fanning, in her excellent and provocative article "Angel vs. Monster," reads this text as an illustration of the "female double," a device some nineteenth-century women authors used to address the many facets of female characters. She goes on to trace a similar thematic and stylistic approach in the novels *Fantasia* and *Addio, amore!.* See "Angel vs. Monster: Serao's Use of the Female Double," *The Italianist* 7 (1987): 63–88.

52. "Angel vs. Monster," 70.

53. Using Marcello as an intermediary, Lalla even asks to visit the family chapel, a symbol of Beatrice's virtue and social standing. Beatrice refuses.

54. *Antisemitism,* 87.

55. Fanning, "Angel vs. Monster," 71.

56. *Nuovi Saggi*, 319.

57. In his review of the novel, Serao's future husband, the journalist Edoardo Scarfoglio, harshly criticized what he claimed were mediocre linguistic skills, unrealistic characters, and a weak structure. See the essay in *Il Libro di Don Chisciotte* (Florence: A. Quattrini, 1911). Other critics were more discerning. Croce praised the text as being "perfectly balanced" ("Note sulla Letteratura Italiana" 344), whereas Enrico Nencioni, despite his reservations about the work's alleged immorality, called it "the most original and the best structured among the Italian novels published in these last years" (*Nuovi Saggi*, 333).

58. Matilde Serao, *Fantasia*, vol. 2, *Serao*, ed. Pietro Pancrazi (1883; reprint, Milan: Garzanti, 1944), 29–30. Subsequent references to the work are indicated parenthetically in the text.

59. Diane Price Herndl, *Invalid Women: Figuring Feminine Illness in American Fiction and Culture, 1840–1940* (Chapel Hill: University of North Carolina Press, 1993), 114.

60. This scene at the agricultural exhibition seems inspired by the fair scene in Gustave Flaubert's 1857 novel *Madame Bovary*. For a more complete comparison of the two texts, see Lucienne Kroha, "Matilde Serao's *Fantasia:* An Author in Search of a Character," Italianist 7 (1987): 45–62.

61. Rather, it is Andrea who is cast as the aggressor. Serao paints the scene in hunting metaphors, with Andrea telling Lucia that he kills rabbits not for the meat but "because it pleases me" (168).

62. In this novel, as in *La ballerina*, Serao displaces the expression of sexuality onto a depiction of appetite. As Lucia and Andrea become more engrossed in their affair, the sexual metaphors become more striking. At dinner one day, Lucia offers Andrea a pear from which she has already taken a healthy bite. He takes it, matching his teeth to the marks hers have left in a symbol of their physical union (206). Tellingly, Andrea's once hearty appetite changes dramatically under the influence of Lucia. No longer able to stomach heavy meals, he takes to Lucia's strange diet of watered wine, delicacies, and sweets.

63. Helena Michie, in her study of nineteenth-century literature, explains the connection between needlework and sexuality: "While on the surface it is a safe, dainty, and appropriately feminine way of filling up time and hope chests, sewing is also a way of repressing and, therefore, implicitly admitting unlawful and dangerous sexual needs." See *The Flesh Made Word*, 41. A scene from *Fantasia* illustrates her point. While the young women of the boarding school embroider, they discuss in hushed tones forbidden novels, such as the works of Zola and Dumas' *La Dame aux Camélias*.

64. "Lettere di Matilde Serao a Olga Ossani Lodi (Febea)," 123.

65. Fanning, "Angel vs. Monster," 82.

66. Serao, *Addio, amore!* (1890; reprint, Rome: Edizioni delle donne, 1977), 15. Subsequent references to the work are indicated parenthetically in the text.

67. In her study of Serao, Harrowitz examines the connection between the various physical manifestations of Anna's passion and its religious overtones, especially those concerning the imagery of blood. See the discussion in *Antisemitism*.

68. Serao continues the story of Cesare and Laura in the 1893 sequel, *Castigo*. In this narrative, Cesare has married Laura despite his realization that he loved—

and continues to love—his first wife. The following chapter includes a more complete discussion of this work.

69. Deanna Shemek postulates that the final epitaph, combined with Anna Acquaviva's surname, "takes on the even broader significance of life itself implied in the character's name." See "Prisoners of Passion: Women and Desire in Matilde Serao's *Romanzi d'Amore*," *Italiana* 3 (1988): 246.

70. *La Scienze del Romanzo*, 218.

While Cavalli Pasini's study rests in part on socioscientific beliefs such as Darwinism and positivism, anthropologist Sherry Ortner bases her analysis of the dichotomy between instinct and intellect on observations of various cultural systems. Ortner's terminology differs from that of Cavalli Pasini, but her thesis is strikingly similar. Women, Ortner writes, are often seen as being more closely affiliated with nature because of their physiological and social roles. Men, on the other hand, traditionally denied an active role in the reproductive process, transfer their creative energies to the production of culture. Over time, the male role gains status, while the female role, and women in general, become devalued. "[T]hat sense of distinctiveness and superiority rests precisely on the ability to transform—to 'socialize' and 'culturalize'—nature," Ortner asserts. See "Is Female to Male as Nature Is to Culture?," in Woman, Culture and Society, ed. Michelle Z. Rosaldo (Stanford: Stanford University Press, 1974), 73. For the author's revisionary comments on this controversial essay, see "So, *Is* Female to Male as Nature Is to Culture?," in *Making Gender: The Politics and Erotics of Culture* (Boston: Beacon Press, 1996), 173–180.

71. Elisabetta Rasy, *La lingua della nutrice: Percorsi e tracce dell'espressione femminile* (Rome: Edizioni delle donne, 1978), 82.

72. "Matilde Serao," 74.

73. Massimo Romano, *Mitologia Romantica e Letteratura Popolare: Struttura e sociologia del romanzo d'appendice* (Ravenna: Longo, 1977), 7.

Rachel DuPlessis reiterates this position, writing, "Any fiction expresses ideology; for example, romance plots of various kinds and the fate of female characters express attitudes at least toward family, sexuality, and gender" (*Writing Beyond the Ending*, x).

74. Although we lack the necessary documentation regarding Serao's public, it is tempting to examine her works in light of the rise of reader-response criticism. Janice Radway calls romance fiction "compensatory literature," allowing female readers to live vicariously through the adventures of the heroines: "It supplies [the female readers] with an important release that is proscribed in daily life because the social role with which they identity themselves leaves little room for guiltless, self-interested pursuit of individual pleasure." See *Reading the Romance: Women, Patriarchy, and Popular Literature* (Chapel Hill: University of North Carolina Press, 1984), 95–96. Perhaps Serao's readers in turn-of-the-century Italy found provocative subtexts in her romance narratives. For further analysis on how the very act of romance reading is subversive, see Diane Elam, *Romancing the Postmodern*.

75. "Prisoners of Passion," 252.

CHAPTER 3. FAMILY GOTHIC

1. Robert D. Hume, "Gothic Versus Romantic: A Revaluation of the Gothic Novel," *PMLA* 84 (1969): 288.

2. Eve Kosofsky Sedgwick, *The Coherence of Gothic Conventions* (New York: Metheun, 1980), 9–10.

3. For an interesting discussion of twentieth-century Gothics, see Elizabeth MacAndrew, *The Gothic Tradition in Fiction* (New York: Columbia University Press, 1979). Feminist critics interested in popular literature have also explored the modern Gothic as a vehicle for escapist fantasy. Many critics working in this area offer interesting analyses of the construction of female identity within the thematic structure of the genre. See in particular Kay J. Mussell, "'But Why Do They Read Those Things': The Female Audience and the Gothic Novel," in *The Female Gothic*, ed. Juliann E. Fleenor (London: Eden Press, 1983), 57–68, and Modleski, *Loving With a Vengeance*.

4. For a more complete analysis of the role of gender in the creation of Gothic texts, see Ellen Moers, *Literary Women* (New York: Oxford University Press, 1976); Eugenia C. DeLamotte, *Perils of the Night: A Feminist Study of Nineteenth-Century Gothic* (New York: Oxford University Press, 1990); Kari J. Winter, *Subjects of Slavery, Agents of Change: Women and Power in Gothic Novels and Slave Narratives, 1790–1865* (Athens: University of Georgia Press, 1992); and the collection of essays found in Fleenor, *The Female Gothic*.

5. Leonard Wolf, "Gothic Novels," Review of *Gothic Novels*, ed. Devendra Varma, *New York Times*, 14 January 1973, Book Review section: 2.

6. *Subjects of Slavery*, 21.

7. Introduction, *The Female Gothic*, 24.

Fleenor has devised perhaps the most thorough definition of the Female Gothic. In full, it reads: "[The Gothic] is essentially formless, except as a quest; it uses the traditional spatial symbolism of the ruined castle or an enclosed room to symbolize both the culture and the heroine; as a psychological form, it provokes various feelings of terror, anger, awe, and sometimes self-fear and self-disgust directed toward the female role, female sexuality, female physiology, and procreation; and it frequently uses a narrative form which questions the validity of the narration itself. It reflects a patriarchal paradigm that women are motherless yet fathered and that women are defective because they are not males" (15).

8. Romano, *Mitologia*, 30.

9. *The Political Unconscious*, 144.

10. Lawrence Venuti, introduction to *Fantastic Tales*, by Ugo Igino Tarchetti, trans. and ed. Lawrence Venuti (San Francisco: Mercury House, 1992), 9.

11. Gilberto Finzi, preface to *Racconti neri della scapigliatura* (Milan: Mondadori, 1980), 5.

12. Matilde Serao, "Un inventore," in *Fior di passione* (Milan: Baldini, Castoldi, 1899), 228. Subsequent references to the work are indicated parenthetically in the text.

13. William Patrick Day, *In the Circles of Fear and Desire: A Study of Gothic Fantasy* (Chicago: University of Chicago Press, 1985), 17.

14. Mary Wollstonecraft Shelley, *Frankenstein, or, the Modern Prometheus* (Washington: Orchises, 1988), 32.

15. I have used the title of the story as it appeared in the 1899 edition of *Fior di passione* (Milan: Baldini, Castoldi, 1899). Several bibliographies of Serao's work, however, refer to the story as "La donna dall'abito nero e dal ramo di corallo rosso." References to the work are indicated parenthetically in the text.

16. "Angel vs. Monster," 80.

17. See Elaine Showalter's illuminating study of the history of the medical establishment's treatment of female madness in *The Female Malady: Women, Madness, and English Culture, 1830–1980* (Middlesex, England: Penguin, 1985).

18. Sedgwick, *The Coherence of Gothic Conventions*, 143.

19. Matilde Serao, *Castigo* (1893; reprint, Milan: Garzanti, 1977), 26. Subsequent references to this work are indicated parenthetically in the text.

20. *Antisemitism*, 96.

21. DeLamotte, *Perils of the Night*, 166.

22. *Antisemitism*, 97.

23. Eve Kosofsky Sedgwick maintains that even the name of the Gothic heroine reflects her condition as both inexperienced and unspoiled: "The women's names suggest the blank, the white, the innocent, and the pristine . . ." (*The Coherence of Gothic Conventions*, 155).

24. Marianne Hirsch, *The Mother/Daughter Plot: Narrative, Psychoanalysis, Feminism* (Bloomington: Indiana University Press, 1989), 57.

25. Day, *In the Circles*, 76.

26. Massimo Romano writes that the Gothic castle is the site of the unknown, the unimaginable, and the irrational: "[I]t is the realm of the confusion of sentiments and of the contradictions of instincts, the inferno where one escapes the harmonious and reassuring order of reason" (*Mitologia*, 18).

27. Matilde Serao, *Il paese di cuccagna* (1891; reprint, Milan: Garzanti, 1981), 151. Subsequent references to this work are indicated parenthetically in the text.

28. Simone de Beauvoir clarifies this gender-based role, writing that a mother is typically "made guardian of morals; servant of man, servant of the powers that be, she will tenderly guide her children along appointed ways." See *The Second Sex*, trans. and ed. H. M. Parshley (New York: Random, 1989), 173. This citation examines how the mother is effectively erased from this transmission as patriarchal ideology passes through her to her children.

29. Dr. Antonio Amati acts as a counterpoint to Bianca Maria's father. Not only does Amati love and attempt to protect the young girl, he embodies the attributes of the quintessential man of science, a late nineteenth-century preoccupation complementing that of the Gothic emphasis on the supernatural. Serao uses Amati as a spokesman for contemporary views on positivism, whereas Bianca Maria's father, with his fervent belief in mysticism, represents the world of the occult. Significantly, Amati fails miserably in his attempts to save Bianca Maria from physical and psychic destruction. The author, then, refashions the romantic Gothic narrative to challenge positivism's place in cultural hegemony.

30. Serao frequently alluded to French and British authors in her works, with particular emphasis on Shakespeare. In *Castigo*, for example, she refers to *The Winter's Tale* and *Hamlet*. Her allusions to Shakespearan texts are particularly intriguing in *Il paese*, for they evoke memories of Serao's own mother. According to Anna Banti's biography, Serao remained unlettered until the age of nine. Her first encounter with books came during a long illness and convalescence of her mother's, who used the family volume of Shakespeare to teach her daughter the fundamentals of reading and writing.

31. Claire Kahane, in her work on the Gothic, finds that the genre's focus is specifically on the mother-daughter relationship: "[W]hat I see repeatedly

locked into the forbidden center of the Gothic . . . is the spectral presence of a dead-undead mother, archaic and all-encompassing, a ghost signifying the problematics of female identity which the heroine must confront." See "Gothic Mirrors and Feminine Identity," *Centennial Review* 24 (1980): 47–48. Her theory ties in with that of Hirsch on the narrative and thematic importance of the absent mother.

32. This novel was one of the few narratives Serao published under a pseudonym, choosing a male moniker: Francesco Sangiorgio. The preface to the novel, however, was signed by Serao. The novel was reissued in 1916 under the title *Temi il leone* (Fear the Lion), and then republished again with its original title. (Francesco Sangiorgio is the name of the protagonist in the 1885 novel *La conquista di Roma.*)

33. Female protagonists within the Gothic framework are closely related to their cousins in romance texts. Syndy McMillen Conger emphasizes the inherent purity of the typical Gothic heroine: "Physically slight, emotionally passive, and intellectually ill-trained—wherein lies such a heroine's stature? Primarily in her moral impeccability." Contrasting with this exaggerated version of the "angel in the house" is a figure with many of the same attributes of the *femme fatale:* "She has the independence of spirit, the emotional vibrancy, the ingenuity, and the moral fallibility the heroine lacks, but she pays the price for these strengths. She is their victim." See "The Reconstruction of the Gothic Feminine Ideal in Emily Brontë's *Wuthering Heights,*" in *The Female Gothic,* ed. Juliann E. Fleenor, 95.

34. Matilde Serao, *Il delitto di via Chiatamone,* 2 vols. (1908; reprint, Florence: Salani, 1979), 1:5. Subsequent references to this work are indicated parenthetically in the text.

The specificity in this reference lends a realistic tenor to a narrative that becomes increasingly fantastic. Serao is rarely this specific, referring often to seasonal events, but seldom to precise years or dates.

35. The traditional taxonomy of literary heroines is succinctly explained by San Luciano: "The women born and existing for love are women of love and should not pretend to enter into the phalanx of women born and existing for family and virtue" (1:89). Using San Luciano as a mouthpiece, Serao sums up the conventions with which female authors worked in turn-of-the-century Italy.

36. As in many Gothic narratives, the story line in *Il delitto* is remarkably convoluted, resting on confused family ties, disguises, inheritances, and potentially incestuous relations. These elements, along with the use of prophetic dreams, portentous meteorological events, and a general atmosphere of persecution and terror, create the structure and tenor of an archetypal Gothic text. For an analysis of the genealogical mystery lying at the heart of this novel, see Nancy Harrowitz, "Medicine and the Orphan's Body," *Stanford Italian Review* 9 (1990): 53–66.

37. Fanning, "Serao's Gothic Revisions: Old Tales Through New Eyes," *The Italianist* 12 (1992): 36.

38. Gennarino, like San Luciano, has bought into the valuation of women based on the expression of their sexuality. Even though he continues to love Teresa, he no longer respects her after discovering that she has succumbed to San Luciano's advances. He could never marry her, Gennarino tells Anthonia,

because "She has sinned." He defends himself, in a terse recapitulation of prevailing ideology, by saying, "Honor is honor" (1:316).

39. The use of the medallion recalls a similar device in Ann Radcliffe's *The Italian, or the Confessional of the Black Penitents: A Romance* (New York: Oxford University Press, 1968). In that novel, the heroine, who wears a miniature medallion of her father, is saved from an attempt on her life when her father recognizes his long-lost daughter. The medallion in both texts serves as a metonymic device to disclose family ties.

40. As Marianne Hirsch points out in *The Mother/Daughter Plot*, "[T]hat absence, the silence of mothers about their own fate and the details of their lives, insures that those lives, those stories would be repeated by their daughters" (67).

41. Serao also distances Teresa from the conventional Romance tenet that links the maternal role with a spiritual or emotional epiphany. Neera, for example, in her 1890 novel *L'indomani* (The Next Day), depicts a woman psychically transformed and revitalized upon becoming pregnant.

42. This gloomy old house, full of empty rooms and endless staircases, becomes the forbidding castle of Gothic fiction. The detachment Teresa feels from the maternal role is emphasized by her physical and emotional isolation, for she is left alone for days on end in this country house as San Luciano amuses himself in Naples. Later, the house becomes not the scene of domestic bliss, but the setting for both a wrenching childbirth and a mockery of the marriage rite.

43. Just as Serao revises the depiction of the maternal figure, the image of the *femme fatale* in this text proves to be innovative too. The author manipulates the complementary themes of commerce and sexuality, revealing an economy of female sexuality. When Anthonia, in an attempt to entrap San Luciano, bargains with him over how much her sexual favors are worth, she is both revealing and damning the commodification of sexual activity. Anthonia empowers herself through this very act of self-objectification, appropriating and then manipulating the role of courtesan.

44. Fanning, "Serao's Gothic," 40.

45. For a more detailed analysis of the relationship between the Gothic and the detective narrative, see William Patrick Day, *In the Circles of Fear.*

46. Matilde Serao, *La mano tagliata* (1912; reprint, Florence: Salani, 1936), 393. Subsequent references to this work are indicated parenthetically in the text.

47. Henner, called *Il Maestro* by his followers, is the leader of a loosely connected community of Jews from across the continent. His religious and political activities are actually quite benevolent, although they are presented as both mysterious and conspiratorial.

48. Helena Michie, in her study of Victorian literature, has found that the hands "form a synecdochal chain where the heart represented by the hand is in itself a synecdoche for more obviously sexual parts of the body that enter into a heroine's decision about whom to marry." Obtaining a woman's hand in marriage, she adds, "is an entrance into the female body" (*The Flesh Made Word*, 98).

49. Deanna Shemek reads the severed hand as "an implicit critique of the poetic *bella mano* and of the Petrarchan lyric tradition in general. The lyric canon conventionally elides woman's bodily presence and features a catalogue of abstracted, idealized parts of the female body." Shemek also examines the

truncated body part as a form of "female castration." See "Prisoners of Passion, 249.

50. Nancy Harrowitz, in her article "Matilde Serao's *La mano tagliata:* Figuring the Material in Mystery," *Stanford Italian Review* 7 (1987): 191–204, investigates the possibility of the hand as a mediating object between two opposing racial and religious groups. In her book *Antisemitism,* Harrowitz expands her interesting examination of the religious aspect of this text, discussing the generally negative portrayal of the male Jewish characters (Henner and Mosè), compared to the positive portraits of female Christianity (Maria and Rachele). Although not denying the underlying antisemitism of the work, Harrowitz posits the theory that this is a deliberate move on the author's part to rescue her heroines from a male-dominated world: "For Serao, the figure of the Jew is predominantly male, as she converts her female Jewish characters in order to save them both from patriarchy and from marginality" (137).

It is also interesting, in light of the Gothic's traditionally negative depiction of the Catholic Church, to see the conventions turned in Serao's text. The religious makeup of Italy, of course, would preclude the sort of virulent attacks on Catholicism found in Ann Radcliffe's *The Italian* and Matthew Lewis, *The Monk: A Romance,* ed. Howard Anderson (London: Oxford University Press, 1973).

51. Shemak, "Prisoners of Passion," 251.

52. As Kari Winter writes, "Pained by the disempowerment of women in the patriarchal family yet still yearning for fulfillment within a human society, female writers of Gothic fiction recognized the importance of solidarity among women." See *Subjects of Slavery,* 106.

53. *The Mother/Daughter Plot,* 9.

CONCLUSION

1. Antonio Palermo, *Da Mastriani a Viviani: Per una storia della letteratura a Napoli fra Otto e Novecento* (Naples: Liguori, 1972), 60.

2. Schilardi, *Matilde Serao,* 222.

3. Articles dealing with these issues and others regarding women can be found in Schilardi, *Matilde Serao.*

4. The letter, sent to Olga Ossani Lodi, was published in *Il Giorno* on 6 September 1905 and reprinted in Amato's article "Femminismo e femminilità."

5. Amato, "Femminismo e femminilità, 106.

6. Harrowitz, "Double Marginality: Matilde Serao and the Politics of Ambiguity," in *Italian Women Writers from the Renaissance to the Present. Revising the Canon,* ed. Maria Ornella Marotti (University Park: The Pennsylvania State University Press, 1996), 92.

7. Schilardi, "L'antifemminismo di Matilde Serao," 281.

8. "Matilde Serao," 75.

9. As Carolyn G. Heilbrun notes, "With remarkably few exceptions, women writers do not imagine women characters with even the autonomy they themselves have achieved." See *Reinventing Womanhood* (New York: Norton, 1979), 71.

10. Gianni Infusino, "Aristocrazia e popolo. (Le donne negli scritti di Matilde Serao,)" in *Matilde Serao tra giornalismo e letteratura,* ed. Gianni Infusino (Naples: Guida, 1981), 72.

11. "Double Marginality," 92.

Tellingly, in her discussion of Serao's depiction of female characters, Harrowitz uses the same dualistic divisions that Serao and many other authors employed in their fictive works: "She is both the threatening monsteress who questions the status of women . . . and the would-be angel of domesticity . . ." ("Double Marginality," 92). By using this terminology, Harrowitz points to how entrenched these categorizations of femaleness are in critical as well as literary discourses.

12. Milan Women's Bookstore Collective, *Sexual Difference: A Theory of Socio-Symbolic Practice* (Bloomington: Indiana University Press, 1990), 27.

13. Milan Women's Bookstore Collective, *Sexual Difference*, 2.

14. Santoro, "Narrativa di fine Ottocento," 114.

15. Aleramo, *Una donna;* Ada Negri, *Stella mattutina: Tutte le opere di Ada Negri,* 2 vols. (Milan: Mondadori, 1966); and Grazia Deledda, *Cosima. Romanzi e novelle,* ed. Natalino Sapegno (Milan: Mondadori, 1971).

16. Alba De Céspedes, *Nessuna torna indietro* (Milan: Mondadori, 1938); *Dalla parte di lei* (Milan: Mondadori, 1949); and Lara Cardella, *Volevo i pantaloni* (Milan: Mondadori, 1989).

17. Francesca Sanvitale, *Madre e figlia* (Turin: Einaudi, 1980); Carla Cerati, *La cattiva figlia* (Piacenza: Frassinelli, 1990).

18. "Narrativa," 119.

19. Introduction, *Carolina Invernizio,* 25.

20. Feminist historian Gerda Lerner, discussing this idea of gendered representations of history, has coined the expression "dialectic of women's history" to refer to "[t]he tension between women's actual historical experience and their exclusion from interpreting that experience." See *The Creation of Patriarchy* (New York: Oxford University Press, 1986), 5.

21. Blelloch, *Quel Mondo dei Guanti,* 58.

Bibliography

Aleramo, Sibilla. *Una donna*. Turin: Sten, 1906.

Amato, Dora. "Femminismo e femminilità." In *Matilde Serao tra giornalismo e letteratura*. Edited by Gianni Infusino, 103–109. Naples: Guida, 1981.

Arslan, Antonia. "Ideologia e autorappresentazione. Donne intellettuali fra Ottocento e Novecento." In *Svelamento. Sibilla Aleramo: una biografia intellettuale*. Edited by Annarita Buttafuoco and Marina Zancan, 164–177. Milan: Feltrinelli, 1988.

———, ed. *Dame, Droga e Galline. Romanzo popolare e romanzo di consumo tra Ottocento e Novecento*. Milan: Unicopli, 1986.

Astaldi, Maria Luisa. *Nascita e vicende del romanzo italiano*. Milan: Treves, 1939.

Auerbach, Nina. *Woman and the Demon: The Life of a Victorian Myth*. Cambridge: Harvard University Press, 1982.

Banti, Anna. "Matilde non sa scrivere." *Illustrazione italiana*, 9 January 1949, 57.

———. Introduction to *L'Occhio di Napoli*, by Matilde Serao, v–xii. Milan: Garzanti, 1962.

———. *Matilde Serao*. Turin: UTET, 1965.

———. "Storia e Ragioni del 'Romanzo Rosa,'" *Paragone*, February 1953, 28–34.

Bassanese, Fiora A. "*Una donna*: Autobiography as Exemplary Text." In *Donna: Women in Italian Culture*. Edited by Ada Testaferri, 131–152. University of Toronto Italian Studies 7. Ottawa: Dovehouse Editions, 1989.

Beauvoir, Simone de. *The Second Sex*. Translated and edited by H. M. Parshley. New York: Random, 1989.

La Belle, Jenijoy. *Herself Beheld: The Literature of the Looking Glass*. Ithaca: Cornell University Press, 1988.

Blelloch, Paola. *Quel Mondo dei Guanti e delle Stoffe. . . . Profili di scrittrici italiane del '900*. Verona: Essedue, 1987.

Bocchi, Lola. "Matilde Serao." *Almanacco della Donna Italiana*, 331–337. Florence: Bemporad, 1928.

Borgese, Giuseppe A. "Napoli e la Serao," *Corriere della Sera*, 28 July 1927, 3.

Bruno, Francesco. *Letteratura meridionale*. Cosenza: Pellegrini, 1968.

Bruno, Giuliana. *Streetwalking on a Ruined Map: Cultural Theory and the City Films of Elvira Notari*. Princeton: Princeton University Press, 1993.

Buckley, Jerome H. *Season of Youth: The Bildungsroman from Dickens to Golding*. Cambridge: Harvard University Press, 1974. x

Butler, Judith. *Gender Trouble: Feminism and the Subversion of Identity*. New York: Routledge, 1990.

Buttafuoco, Annarita. "Condizione delle donne e movimento di emancipazione femminile." In *L'Italia di Giolitti*, Vol. 20, Part 5 of *Storia della Società Italiana*, 145–185. Milan: Teti, 1981.

Capuana, Luigi. *Letteratura Femminile*. Edited and introduction by Giovanna Finocchiaro Chimirri. Catania: C.U.E.C.M., 1988.

————. *Studii sulla letteratura contemporanea*. Seconda Serie. Edited by Paola Azzolini, vii–xlvii, 69–84. Naples: Liguori, 1988.

Carsaniga, G. M. *The Age of Realism*. Edited by F. W. J. Hemmings. Middlesex, England: Penguin, 1974.

Cardella, Lara. *Volevo i pantaloni*. Milan: Mondadori, 1989.

Cavalli Pasini, Annamaria. *La Scienza del Romanzo: Romanzo e cultura scientifica tra Otto e Novecento*, 205–257. Bologna: Pàtron, 1982.

Cerati, Carla. *La cattiva figlia*. Piacenza: Frassinelli, 1990.

Ceserani, R. and Salibra, E. "Popular Literature in Nineteenth-Century Italy: *Letteratura amena*." *Canadian Review of Comparative Literature* 9 (1982): 361–382.

Clark, Suzanne. *Sentimental Modernism: Women Writers and the Revolution of the Word*. Bloomington: Indiana University Press, 1991.

Cohen, Ralph. "History and Genre." *New Literary History* 17 (1986): 203–218.

Conger, Syndy McMillen. "The Reconstruction of the Gothic Feminine Ideal in Emily Brontë's *Wuthering Heights*." In *The Female Gothic*, edited and introduction by Juliann E. Fleenor, 91–106. London: Eden Press, 1983.

Costa-Zalessow, Natalia. *Scrittrici italiane dal XIII al XX secolo. Testi e critica*. Ravenna: Longo, 1982.

Croce, Benedetto. *Letteratura della nuova Italia*. Vol. 3, 35–76. Bari: N.p., 1915.

————. "Note sulla Letteratura Italiana: Matilde Serao." *La Critica* 1 (1903): 321–351.

Curti, Daniela. "Il Linguaggio del Racconto Rosa: Gli Anni 20 ad Oggi." In *Lingua Letteraria e Lingua dei Media nell'Italiano Contemporaneo*, 156–173. Florence: Le Monnier, 1987.

D'Annunzio, Gabriele. *Trionfo della morte*. 1894. Reprint, Milan: Mondadori, 1940.

Day, William Patrick. *In the Circles of Fear and Desire: A Study of Gothic Fantasy*. Chicago: University of Chicago Press, 1985.

De Céspedes, Alba. *Nessuna torna indietro*. Milan: Mondadori, 1938.

————. *Dalla parte di lei*. Milan: Mondadori, 1949.

De Giorgio, Michela. "The Catholic Model." Translated by Joan Bond Sax. In *A History of Women in the West: Emerging Feminism from Revolution to World War*. Edited by Geneviève Fraisse and Michelle Perrot, 166–197. Cambridge: Harvard University Press, 1993.

————. *Le italiane dall'unità a oggi: Modelli culturali e comportamenti sociali*. Rome: Laterza, 1992.

DeLamotte, Eugenia C. *Perils of the Night: A Feminist Study of Nineteenth-Century Gothic*. New York: Oxford University Press, 1990.

Deledda, Grazia. *Cosima. Romanzi e novelle*. Edited by Natalino Sapegno. Milan: Mondadori, 1971.

DuPlessis, Rachel B. *Writing Beyond the Ending: Narrative Strategies of Twentieth-Century Women Writers.* Bloomington: Indiana University Press, 1985.

Eco, Umberto. *Il Superuomo di Massa.* Milan: Bompiani, 1990.

———. Introduction to *Carolina Invernizio, Matilde Serao, Liala,* 3–27. Florence: La Nuova Italia, 1979.

Elam, Diane. *Romancing the Postmodern.* New York: Routledge, 1992.

Fanning, Ursula. "Angel vs. Monster: Serao's Use of the Female Double." *The Italianist* 7 (1987): 63–88.

———. "Sentimental Subversion: Representations of Female Friendship in the Work of Matilde Serao." *Annali d'Italianistica* 7 (1989): 273–286.

———. "Serao's Gothic Revisions: Old Tales Through New Eyes." *The Italianist* 12 (1992): 32–41.

Finzi, Gilberto. Preface to *Racconti neri della scapigliatura,* 5–15. Milan: Mondadori, 1980.

Fleenor, Juliann E. Edited by and introduction to *The Female Gothic,* 3–28. London: Eden Press, 1983.

Fraiman, Susan. *Unbecoming Women: British Women Writers and the Novel of Development.* New York: Columbia University Press, 1993.

Garzia, Raffa. *Matilde Serao.* Rocca S. Casciano, Italy: Licinio Cappelli, 1916.

Ghidetti, Enrico. *Verga. Guida storico-critica,* 59–60. Rome: Riuniti, 1979.

Gilbert, Sandra M., and Susan Gubar. *The Madwoman in the Attic: The Woman Writer and the Nineteenth-Century Literary Imagination.* London: Yale University Press, 1979.

Gilman, Charlotte Perkins. *The Yellow Wallpaper.* Old Westbury: The Feminist Press, 1973.

Gisolfi, Anthony M. *The Essential Matilde Serao.* New York: Las Americas, 1968.

Golini, Vera. "Critical Perspectives on Italian Women Writers at the Turn of the Century." *Biblioteca di Quaderni d'italianistica* 4 (1988): 143–168.

Gramsci, Antonio. *Letteratura e vita nazionale,* 103–140. Turin: Einaudi, 1966.

Gropallo, Laura. *Autori Italiani d'Oggi,* 175–269. Turin: Nazionale, 1903.

Harrowitz, Nancy. *Antisemitism, Misogyny and the Logic of Cultural Difference: Cesare Lombroso and Matilde Serao.* Lincoln: University of Nebraska Press, 1994.

———. "Double Marginality: Matilde Serao and the Politics of Ambiguity." In *Italian Women Writers from the Renaissance to the Present. Revising the Canon,* edited by Maria Ornella Marotti, 85–94. University Park: The Pennsylvania State University Press, 1996.

———. "Matilde Serao's *La mano tagliata:* Figuring the Material in Mystery." *Stanford Italian Review* 7 (1987): 191–204.

———. "Medicine and the Orphan's Body." *Stanford Italian Review* 9 (1990): 53–66.

Heilbrun, Carolyn G. *Reinventing Womanhood.* New York: Norton, 1979.

Heller, Dana A. *The Feminization of Quest-Romance: Radical Departures,* 1–39, 119–123. Austin: University of Texas Press, 1990.

Herndl, Diane Price. *Invalid Women: Figuring Feminine Illness in American Fiction and Culture, 1840–1940.* Chapel Hill: University of North Carolina Press, 1993.

Hirsch, Marianne. *The Mother/Daughter Plot: Narrative, Psychoanalysis, Feminism.* Bloomington: Indiana University Press, 1989.

———. "The Novel of Formation as Genre: Between Great Expectations and Lost Illusions." *Genre* 12 (1979): 293–311.

———. "Spiritual *Bildung:* The Beautiful Soul as Paradigm." In *The Voyage In: Fictions of Female Development,* edited by Elizabeth Abel, Marianne Hirsch, and Elizabeth Langland, 23–48. Hanover: University Press of New England, 1983.

Hoffmann, E. T. A. "The Sand-Man." In *The Best Tales of Hoffmann,* edited by E. F. Bleiler, 183–214. New York: Dover, 1967.

Howard, Judith J. "The Feminine Vision of Matilde Serao." *Italian Quarterly* 18 (1975): 55–77.

Hume, Robert D. "Gothic Versus Romantic: A Revaluation of the Gothic Novel." *PMLA* 84 (1969): 282–290.

Infusino, Gianni. "Aristocrazia e popolo. (Le donne negli scritti di Matilde Serao.)" In *Matilde Serao tra giornalismo e letteratura,* edited by Gianni Infusino, 61–72. Naples: Guida, 1981.

———. ed. *Matilde Serao tra giornalismo e letteratura.* Naples:Guida, 1981.

Jameson, Fredric. *The Political Unconscious: Narrative as a Socially Symbolic Act.* Ithaca: Cornell University Press, 1981.

———. "Reification and Utopia in Mass Culture." *Social Text* 1 (1979): 130–148.

Jeuland-Meynaud, Maryse. *Immagini, linguaggio e modelli del corpo nell'opera narrativa di Matilde Serao.* Rome: Ateneo, 1986.

Kahane, Claire. "Gothic Mirrors and Feminine Identity." *Centennial Review* 24 (1980): 43–64.

Kennard, Joseph Spencer. *Romanzi e Romanzieri Italiani,* 33–70. Vol. 2. Florence: G. Barbèra, 1905.

———. "Woman in the Italian Novel." *North American Review* 188 (1908): 584–597.

Kornfeld, Eve, and Susan Jackson. "The Female *Bildungsroman* in Nineteenth-Century America: Parameters of a Vision." *Journal of American Culture* 10 (1987): 69–75.

Kroha, Lucienne. "Matilde Serao's *Fantasia:* An Author in Search of a Character." *Italianist* 7 (1987): 45–62.

———. *The Woman Writer in Late-Nineteenth-Century Italy: Gender and the Formation of Literary Identity.* New York: Mellen, 1992.

Labovitz, Ester Kleinbord. *The Myth of the Heroine: The Female Bildungsroman in the Twentieth Century. Dorothy Richardson, Simone de Beauvoir, Doris Lessing, Christa Wolf.* New York: Lang, 1986.

Lazzaro-Weis, Carol. *From Margins to Mainstream: Feminism and Fictional Modes in Italian Women's Writing, 1968–1990.* Philadelphia: University of Pennsylvania Press, 1993.

Lèbano, Edoardo A. "Una lettera inedita di Matilde Serao." *La Fusta* 1 (1976): 91–93.

Lerner, Gerda. *The Creation of Patriarchy*. New York: Oxford University Press, 1986.

Lewis, Matthew. *The Monk: A Romance*. Edited by Howard Anderson. London: Oxford University Press, 1973.

MacAndrew, Elizabeth. *The Gothic Tradition in Fiction*. New York: Columbia University Press, 1979.

Madrignani, Carlo A. *Ideologia e narrativa dopo l'Unificazione*. Rome: Giulio Savelli, 1974.

Manacorda, Giuliano. "L'opera di Matilde Serao entro l'ipotesi gramsciana di una letteratura nazional-popolare." In *Matilde Serao tra giornalismo e letteratura*. Edited by Gianni Infusino, 15–27. Naples: Guida, 1981.

Martin-Gistucci, Marie-Gracieuse. "Une Amitié 'Paradoxale' de Paul Bourget." In *Paul Bourget et L'Italie*, edited by Marie-Gracieuse Martin-Gistucci, 95–107. Geneva: Slatkine, 1985.

———. *L'Oeuvre romanesque de Matilde Serao*. Grenoble: Presses Universitaires de Grenoble, 1973.

Masini, Piercarlo. "Matilde Serao e Anna Maria Mozzoni: Una Polemica sull'Emancipazione Femminile." In *Eresie dell'Ottocento: Alle sorgenti laiche, umaniste e libertarie della democrazia italiana*, 275–285. Milan: Editoriale Nuova, 1978.

Michie, Helena. *The Flesh Made Word: Female Figures and Women's Bodies*. Oxford: Oxford University Press, 1987.

Milan Women's Bookstore Collective. *Sexual Difference: A Theory of Socio-Symbolic Practice*. Bloomington: Indiana University Press, 1990.

Miller, Nancy K. *The Heroine's Text: Readings in the French and English Novel, 1722–1782*. New York: Columbia University Press, 1980.

———. *Subject to Change: Reading Feminist Writing*. New York: Columbia University Press, 1988.

Modleski, Tania. *Loving with a Vengeance: Mass-Produced Fantasies for Women*. New York: Routledge, 1982.

Moers, Ellen. *Literary Women*. New York: Oxford University Press, 1976.

Morandini, Giuliana. *La voce che è in lei: Antologia della narrativa femminile italiana tra '800 e '900*. Milan: Bompiani, 1980.

Moretti, Franco. *The Way of the World: The Bildungsroman in European Culture*. London: Verso, 1987.

Mussell, Kay J. "'But Why Do They Read Those Things': The Female Audience and the Gothic Novel." In *The Female Gothic*. Edited and introduction by Juliann E. Fleenor, 57–68. London: Eden Press, 1983.

Negri, Ada. *Stella mattutina: Tutte le opere di Ada Negri*, 2 Vols. Milan: Mondadori, 1966.

Nencioni, Enrico. *Nuovi Saggi Critici di Letteratura Straniera e Altri Scritti*, 302–362. Florence: Le Monnier, 1909.

Nozzoli, Anna. *Tabù e coscienza: La condizione femminile nella letteratura italiana del Novecento*. Florence: La Nuova Italia, 1978.

Ojetti, Ugo. *Cose viste*. Vol. 4, 142–151. Milan: Treves, 1928.

———. *Alla Scoperta dei Letterati.* Edited by Pietro Pancrazi. Florence: Le Monnier, 1946.

Olken, I. T. "La virtù di Checchina: Anachronism and Resolution." *Romance Quarterly* 30 (1983): 45–59.

Ortner, Sherry B. "Is Female to Male as Nature Is to Culture?" In *Woman, Culture and Society.* Edited by Michelle Z. Rosaldo, 67–87. Stanford: Stanford University Press, 1974.

———. "So, *Is* Female to Male as Nature is to Culture?" In *Making Gender: The Politics and Erotics of Culture,* 173–180. Boston: Beacon Press, 1996.

Palermo, Antonio. *Da Mastriani a Viviani: Per una storia della letteratura a Napoli fra Otto e Novecento.* Naples: Liguori, 1972.

Pancrazi, Pietro. *Scrittori italiani dal Carducci al D'Annunzio.* Bari: Laterza, 1937.

———. "La Serao Napoletana." *Nuova Antologia* 433 (1945): 97–111.

Pezzini, Isabella. "Matilde Serao." In *Carolina Invernizio, Matilde Serao, Liala,* 61–94. Florence: La Nuova Italia, 1979.

Pozzato, Maria Pia. *Il romanzo rosa.* Milan: Europei, 1982.

Pratt, Annis. *Archetypal Patterns in Women's Fiction.* Bloomington: Indiana University Press, 1981.

Praz, Mario. *La carne, la morte e il diavolo nella letteratura romantica.* Florence: Sansoni, 1976.

Prisco, Michele. "Matilde Serao." *Terzo Programma* 3 (1963): 57–95.

Radcliffe, Ann. *The Italian, or the Confessional of the Black Penitents: A Romance.* New York: Oxford University Press, 1968.

Radway, Janice A. *Reading the Romance: Women, Patriarchy, and Popular Literature.* Chapel Hill: University of North Carolina Press, 1984.

Rasy, Elisabetta. *Le donne e la letteratura. Scrittrici eroine e ispiratrici nel mondo delle lettere.* Rome: Riuniti, 1984.

———. *La lingua della nutrice: Percorsi e tracce dell'espressione femminile.* Rome: Edizioni delle donne, 1978.

Romano, Massimo. *Mitologia Romantica e Letteratura Popolare: Struttura e sociologia del romanzo d'appendice.* Ravenna: Longo, 1977.

Salsini, Laura A. "Checchina and Isolina: Female Friendship in Matilde Serao's 'La virtù di Checchina.'" *Romance Languages Annual* 3 (1991): 309–313.

Santoro, Anna. "Narrativa di fine Ottocento: le scrittrici e il pubblico." *Italiana* IV (1992): 103–126.

———. *Narratrici italiane dell'Ottocento.* Naples: Federico & Ardia, 1987.

Sanvitale, Francesca. *Madre e figlia.* Turin: Einaudi, 1980.

Scarfoglio, Edoardo. *Il Libro di Don Chisciotte.* Florence: A. Quattrini, 1911.

Schilardi, Wanda De Nunzio. "L'antifemminismo di Matilde Serao." In *La Parabola della Donna nella Letteratura Italiana dell'Ottocento,* edited by Gigliola De Donato, 277–305. Bari: Adriatica Editrice, 1983.

———. *Matilde Serao Giornalista.* Lecce: Milella, 1986.

Scurani, Alessandro. "La Fortuna di Matilde Serao." *Letture. Rassegna critica del libro e dello spettacolo* 10 (1962): 643–658.

Sedgwick, Eve Kosofsky. *The Coherence of Gothic Conventions.* New York: Metheun, 1980.

Serao, Matilde. *Addio, amore!.* 1890. Reprint, Rome: Edizioni delle donne, 1977.

————. *La ballerina.* 1899. Vol. 1 of *Serao.* Edited by Pietro Pancrazi. Reprint, Milan: Garzanti, 1944.

————. *Castigo.* 1893. Reprint, Milan: Garzanti, 1977.

————. *La conquista di Roma.* 1885. Vol. 2 of *Serao.* Edited by Pietro Pancrazi. Reprint, Milan: Garzanti, 1944.

————. *Cuore infermo.* 1881. Reprint, Rome: Lucarini, 1988.

————. *Il delitto di via Chiatamone.* 1908. 2 vols. Reprint, Florence: Salani, 1979.

————. "La donna dell'abito nero e del ramo di corallo rosso. In *Fior di passione,* 105–116. Milan: Baldini, Castoldi, 1899.

————. *Fantasia.* 1883. Vol. 2 of *Serao.* Edited by Pietro Pancrazi. Reprint, Milan: Garzanti, 1944.

————. "O Giovannino o la morte." In *L'occhio di Napoli,* 231–272. Milan: Garzanti, 1962.

————. "La grande fiamma." *Nuova Antologia* 103 (1889): 102–116, 325–346.

————. "Un inventore." In *Fiori di passione,* 225–239. Milan: Baldini, Castoldi, 1899.

————. "Lettere di Matilde Serao a Olga Ossani Lodi (Febea)." *Nuova Antologia* 448 (1950): 113–132.

————. Letters to Gaetano Bonavenia. 22 March 1878; 23 June 1878. In "A furia di urti, di gomitate." *Nuova Antologia* 398 (1938): 402–412.

————. "Livia Speri." In *La vita è così lunga,* 45–54. Milan: Treves, 1918.

————. *La mano tagliata.* 1912. Reprint, Florence: Salani, 1936.

————. "La moglie di un grand'uomo." In *Dal vero,* 59–66. Milan: Baldini, Castoldi, 1905.

————. "Nicoletta." In *La vita è così lunga,* 67–74. Milan: Treves, 1918.

————. "Paolo Spada." In *Fior di passione,* 31–43. Milan: Baldini, Castoldi 1899.

————. *Il paese di cuccagna.* 1891. Reprint, Milan: Garzanti, 1981.

————. "Perchè le ragazze non si maritano?" *La Donna* 3 (1907): 5.

————. *Il romanzo della fanciulla.* 1885. Reprint, with a preface by Francesco Bruni, Naples: Liguori, 1985.

————. *Saper Vivere: Norme di buona creanza.* 1900. Reprint, Florence: Passigli, 1989.

————. "Silvia." In *Dal vero,* 285–306. Milan: Baldini, Castoldi, 1905.

————. *Storia di due anime.* 1904. Vol. 1 of *Serao.* Edited by Pietro Pancrazi. Reprint, Milan: Garzanti, 1944.

————. *Suor Giovanna della Croce.* 1901. Vol. 1 of *Serao,* edited by Pietro Pancrazi. Reprint, Milan: Garzanti, 1944.

————. *Tre donne.* Rome: Voghera, 1905.

————. "Il ventre di Napoli." In *L'occhio di Napoli,* preface by Anna Banti, 124–169. Milan: Garzanti, 1962.

―――. "La virtù di Checchina." In *Il romanzo della fanciulla*, preface by Francesco Burni. Napoli: Liguori, 1985.

―――. *Vita e avventure di Riccardo Joanna*. Milan: Galli, 1887.

Shelley, Mary Wollstonecraft. *Frankenstein, or, the Modern Prometheus*. Washington: Orchises, 1988.

Shemek, Deanna. "Prisoners of Passion: Women and Desire in Matilde Serao's *Romanzi d'Amore*." *Italiana* 3 (1988): 243–254.

Showalter, Elaine. *The Female Malady: Women, Madness, and English Culture, 1830–1980*. Middlesex, England: Penguin, 1985.

Singer, Armand E. *Paul Bourget*. Boston: Hall, 1976.

Spinazzola, Vittorio. *Verismo e positivismo*. Milan: Garzanti, 1977.

Tarchetti, Igino Ugo. *Fosca*. 1869. Reprint, Milan: Mondadori, 1981.

Tench, Darby. "Gutting the Belly of Naples: Metaphor, Metonymy and the Auscultatory Imperative in Serao's City of *Pietà*." *Annali d'Italianistica* 7 (1989): 287–299.

Ulivi, Ferruccio. *La letteratura verista*. Turin: ERI, 1972.

Venuti, Lawrence. Introduction to *Fantastic Tales*, by Igino Ugo Tarchetti. Edited and translated by Lawrence Venuti, 1–19. San Francisco: Mercury House, 1992.

Verdinois, Federigo. *Profili Letterari e Ricordi Giornalistici*. Edited by Elena Craveri Croce, 177–189. Florence: Le Monnier, 1949.

Via delle Cinque Lune. Directed by Luigi Chiarini. Centro Sperimentale di Cinematografia, 1942.

Wharton, Edith. *A Backward Glance*. 1933. Reprint, New York: Scribner, 1964.

Winter, Kari J. *Subjects of Slavery, Agents of Change: Women and Power in Gothic Novels and Slave Narratives, 1790–1865*. Athens: University of Georgia Press, 1992.

Wolf, Leonard. "Gothic Novels." Review of *Gothic Novels*. Edited by Devendra Varma. *New York Times*. 14 January 1973, Book Review section: 2, 28.

Wood, Sharon. *Italian Women's Writing 1860–1994*. Women in Context. London: Athlone, 1995.

Zambon, Patrizia. "Leggere per scrivere. La formazione autodidattica delle scrittrici tra Otto e Novecento: Neera, Ada Negri, Grazia Deledda, Sibilla Aleramo." *Studi Novecenteschi* 16 (1989): 287–324.

Index